AF352740

The Digitized Campus

The Digitized Campus

Artificial Intelligence and Big Data in Higher Education

Edited by Frank Fernandez, Neal H. Hutchens,
Rachel Dean Divaker, Vanessa Miller,
and Brandi Hephner LaBanc

Cover credit: Shutterstock
Published by State University of New York Press, Albany
© 2026 State University of New York
All rights reserved
Printed in the United States of America

No part of this book may be used or reproduced in any manner whatsoever without written permission. No part of this book may be stored in a retrieval system or transmitted in any form or by any means including electronic, electrostatic, magnetic tape, mechanical, photocopying, recording, or otherwise without the prior permission in writing of the publisher.

Links to third-party websites are provided as a convenience and for informational purposes only. They do not constitute an endorsement or an approval of any of the products, services, or opinions of the organization, companies, or individuals. SUNY Press bears no responsibility for the accuracy, legality, or content of a URL, the external website, or for that of subsequent websites.

EU GPSR Authorised Representative:
Logos Europe, 9 rue Nicolas Poussin, 17000, La Rochelle, France
contact@logoseurope.eu

For information, contact State University of New York Press, Albany, NY
www.sunypress.edu

Library of Congress Cataloging-in-Publication Data

Names: Fernandez, Frank, editor | Hutchens, Neal H., editor | Divaker, Rachel Dean, editor | Miller, Vanessa, editor | LaBanc, Brandi Hephner, editor
Title: The digitized campus : artificial intelligence and big data in higher education / edited by Frank Fernandez, Neal H. Hutchens, Rachel Dean Divaker, Vanessa Miller, and Brandi Hephner LaBanc.
Description: Albany : State University of New York Press, [2026] | Includes bibliographical references and index.
Identifiers: LCCN 2025051318 | ISBN 9798855807684 (hardcover) | ISBN 9798855807707 (epub) | ISBN 9798855807714 (pdf)
Subjects: LCSH: Artificial intelligence—Educational applications | Educational technology | Education, Higher | Universities and colleges—Administration—Data processing
Classification: LCC LB1028.43 .D556 2026
LC record available at https://lccn.loc.gov/2025051318

Contents

1

The Rise of Artificial Intelligence and Big Data in Higher Education

Rachel Dean Divaker and Frank Fernandez

Artificial intelligence (AI) and "big data" are transforming the landscape of higher education, sparking excitement, speculation, and concern among administrators and faculty (D'Agostino, 2023; Dennis, 2018). For years, campuses rushed to embrace social media platforms, like TikTok, to recruit applicants and connect with students (Rowan-Kenyon et al., 2018; Rowan-Kenyon & Martínez Alemán, 2016). Then, beginning in 2023, public universities across the U.S. began urging students to delete their TikTok accounts over suspicion of security threats regarding users' personal information (Tolentino, 2023). Some colleges and universities went so far as to ban students from using TikTok while connected to campus Wi-Fi networks out of fear that the platform is continually collecting and storing sensitive user data to share with the Chinese government (Cho, 2023).

While some have pushed back against this claim, saying that TikTok's data collection is no different than the data collected by its peer competitors (Mueller & Farhat, 2023; Tidy, 2024), this one example raises important considerations about the impact of technological advancements on data collection and the future of higher education. How did campuses go from embracing and encouraging the use of a digital tool like TikTok to asking students to abandon it? Given the uncertainties around technology surveillance and regulation, this example shows that campuses must continuously scan the landscape for the emergence of new technologies. After assessing risks and choosing whether to adopt new platforms, higher education leaders must regularly assess ongoing risks and benefits to stay informed on best practices for data governance. Beyond simply calculating financial costs, they must consider multiple legal obligations, like protecting student data (Hutchens & Hulbert, 2016) and claiming university-created intellectual property, whether through research (Fernandez & Hutchens, 2023) or online instruction (Rooksby, 2020).

Higher education is not simply reacting to technological change — it shapes it. Since at least the mid-20th century, university researchers connected industry experts and private philanthropy to bring AI into academia. As early as 1956, Dartmouth College hosted summer workshops on the topic with funding from the Rockefeller Foundation (Nilsson, 2009). By the early 21st century, learning

1

management systems and online courses — not to mention dozens of other online platforms — were ubiquitous tools for running colleges and universities that produce unprecedented amounts of data (Lane & Finsel, 2014).

AI and big data are no longer confined to data and computer science fields but are rapidly gaining momentum in other industries like healthcare, finance, e-commerce, travel, and transportation (Gurtu, 2021). Like in other sectors, higher education providers must keep pace with how other industries are using AI and big data to bring down costs and improve campus administration (Webber & Zheng, 2020). In addition to their academic and administrative uses across college campuses, institutions can also use AI to support sustainability initiatives across campuses. For example, "green algorithms" use the power of AI to support sustainability goals to reduce energy consumption across campus buildings to create more resilient college campuses (Nieto-Rodriguez & Vargas, 2023). As AI continues to advance, we will likely see traditionally separate fields like sustainability and higher education increasingly converge to create new opportunities for innovation and meaningful impact.

The purpose of this volume is to better understand these powerful resources and consider the legal responsibilities that bind colleges and universities when they use them, the potential uses of AI and big data in higher education, and principles for how colleges and universities *should* use AI and big data in higher education. We argue that higher education professionals must understand and consider the legal, moral, and ethical ramifications that arise from collecting unprecedented amounts of student data to inform institutional decision-making and practice.

Historical Origins of Artificial Intelligence

To understand the evolution of AI, we should first explore its origins. In 1943, Warren McCulloch and Walter Pitts published groundbreaking work that set the stage for deep neural networks and early AI models (McCulloch & Pitts, 1943). They introduced a concept that compared the logical processes of biological neurons in the human brain to neural networks in computational models. McCulloch and Pitts demonstrated that networks of artificial neurons could perform logical operations through simple input-output functions (Muthukrishnan et al., 2020). For example, an artificial neuron receives a Boolean logic input (e.g., true/false statement) and generates a binary output (e.g., 0 or 1) in response. This approach was foundational to AI, illustrating how artificial neural networks could model human brain processes in a simplified manner and produce logical outputs (McCulloch & Pitts, 1943).

The Turing Test (Turing, 1950, 2009), named after AI pioneer Alan Turing, later expanded upon simple input and output functions by measuring and comparing machine intelligence to that of humans. The Turing test posits that a machine exhibits humanlike intelligence if an individual interacts with a human and a machine but cannot distinguish the difference between the two. The

Turing Test was pivotal in the early stages of AI development and machine intelligence. Building on this momentum at the 1956 Dartmouth conference, John McCarthy, Marvin Minsky, Nathaniel Rochester, and Claude Shannon officially coined the term "artificial intelligence," highlighting its potential to efficiently and precisely simulate human intelligence. This conference is often considered the birthplace of AI as a field of study, sparking public interest in the powerful capabilities of intelligent machines (Muthukrishnan et al., 2020).

Despite initial enthusiasm for AI, there was a noticeable decline in interest and funding in AI in the 1970s and again in the 1990s, commonly referred to as the "AI winters" (Gonsalves, 2019). The decline in AI investment during these AI winters was largely caused by failure to meet unrealistic promises of machine intelligence due to hardware and software limitations and market downturns. Under-delivering on overhyped promises led to unmet expectations and investors pulling research funding. Although there was a considerable setback in AI development during these periods, public interest returned in the mid-1990s when IBM's chess-playing computer, Deep Blue, defeated the reigning world chess champion Garry Kasparov in 1997 (Kasparov, 2010). Although Kasparov defeated Deep Blue the year prior, IBM upgraded its computational power and strategic algorithms, leading to its victory in the rematch against Kasparov in 1997. This key event in the history of AI marked a turning point in the public perception of AI. Today, the excitement surrounding AI is at an all-time high. With widely accessible generative AI systems like OpenAI's ChatGPT, Google's Gemini, Microsoft's Copilot, Meta's Llama, and Anthropic's Claude, among others, the public has access to some of the most advanced and powerful technologies available.

Defining Artificial Intelligence and Big Data

What exactly are AI and big data? In this digital age, *artificial intelligence* and *big data* have become buzzwords. These terms tend to lack consistency and clarity among scholars, with little consensus on their working definitions, leading to increased misunderstanding and apprehension among potential users. AI can be broadly defined as using computer systems to simulate human intelligence to perform tasks. This goal is accomplished by collecting vast amounts of data to train systems to think and behave like humans through continuous learning, reasoning, and self-correction (Mukhopadhyay et al., 2019). However, definitions of AI vary among scholars. For instance, Baker and Smith (2019) describe AI as "computers which perform cognitive tasks, usually associated with human minds, particularly learning and problem-solving" (p. 10), while Russell and Norvig (2010) emphasize the aim of AI to "not just understand but also build intelligent entities" (p. 1). Similarly, Nilsson (2009) describes AI as an "activity devoted to making machines intelligent, and intelligence is that quality that enables an entity to function appropriately and with foresight in its environment" (p. 13).

Terms like *machine learning* (ML), *deep learning* (DL), and *natural language processing* (NLP) are frequently mentioned when considering the inner workings of AI as they are interrelated fields under the broader umbrella of AI. ML uses algorithms to train computers and develop predictive models from data, often used for data-driven decision-making (Alpaydin, 2020). Generative AI models (e.g., OpenAI's ChatGPT) use ML to create new outputs after training on existing data (Feuerriegel et al., 2024). DL is another subset of ML modeled after the neurons in the human brain and has the capability to identify learning patterns in large datasets. We often see this type of technology used in language translation (e.g., Google Translate), facial recognition, self-driving cars, and speech recognition (e.g., Siri and Alexa) (Pospíchal et al., 2015). Finally, NLP bridges computing and human language, allowing computers to interpret and understand human language (Chowdhary, 2020; Fanni et al., 2023). Chatbots and virtual assistants, speech-to-text, and text summarization rely on NLP to process and produce outputs from text.

Big data, a concept closely linked to AI, refers to large and complex datasets used to train such intelligent systems. Laney (2001) first defined big data in terms of "volume, velocity, and variety" given its massive scale, processing speed, and wide range of data types and formats. Over time, "veracity," or accuracy and trustworthiness of data, and "value," or benefits or insights from the data, have been added to the working definition of big data (Mucci & Stryker, 2024). Similarly, Kitchin (2013) describes big data as more than just massive datasets but as data that are "huge in volume . . . diverse in variety . . . exhaustive in scope, striving to capture entire populations or systems . . . fine-grained in resolution . . . indexical in identification, aiming to be as detailed as possible . . . relational . . . containing common fields that enable the conjoining of different data sets . . . flexible . . . can add new fields easily and scalability can expand in size rapidly" (p. 262).

Simply put, big data involves the process of inputting vast amounts of diverse, scalable, flexible, complex, and detailed data that traditional data analysis tools cannot handle (Mucci & Stryker, 2024). This data is fed into a learning algorithm, designed to enhance human efficiency and productivity (McAfee & Brynjolfsson, 2012). The amount of data humans produced every 2 days in 2014 was about the same amount produced between the dawn of civilization and 2003 (Lane & Finsel, 2014). Big data is characterized by the swift ability to both aggregate volumes of data and generate meaning from that information. Within the context of postsecondary institutions, examples of using big data include analyzing student ID card swipes, viewing how students search for classes on the online catalog, and monitoring student social networks. Further, Kitchin's (2013) definition includes how particular campus units surveil student behavior. Campus police departments, for example, use big data to analyze student behavior through facial recognition, vehicle parking patterns, and cell phone networks. Today, AI and big data are reshaping all aspects of our daily lives. This rise in faster, more powerful, and readily available information at our fingertips is transforming how we experience the world around us.

The Roles of Artificial Intelligence and Big Data in Higher Education

What are the ethical implications of AI and big data on higher education's duty to ensure student privacy, offer equitable university admissions, and safeguard academic integrity? These tools have the potential to benefit the field of higher education. By analyzing data and implementing AI-generated content, college and university personnel can make data-driven decisions, streamline time-intensive administrative processes, and improve student success (Nietzel, 2022; Newton, 2021). For example, a private midsize university used AI to increase enrollment by 15% by targeting prospective students with personalized calls and financial aid offers to influence enrollment decisions (Newton, 2021). Previously, admissions staff spent hours making personal phone calls to applicants, achieving a less than 10% yield rate. AI allowed the admissions officers to collect data, create an algorithm, and produce a streamlined procedure that increased enrollment (Nietzel, 2022).

ML also plays a critical role in university admissions by analyzing student data to predict student performance, calculate financial aid needs, and gauge the potential for future alum engagement (Dennis, 2018). Some universities require applicants to submit recorded videos as part of their application and use AI to evaluate applicants on personality characteristics like openness, motivation, agreeableness, and neuroticism. AI influences admissions decisions by quickly narrowing applicants based on predetermined criteria (Newton, 2021).

Further, AI can transform formal classroom settings into a blended learning environment that combines traditional instruction with self-paced, customizable learning that enhances the student learning experience (Schroeder, 2022). AI teaching assistants can assess students' understanding of course material and tailor instruction to address gaps in understanding (Bucea-Manea-Toni et al., 2022). Not restricted by time barriers, AI can provide constant support and feedback to students around the clock. If educators can use big data and AI to identify patterns and trends to understand best practices in the classroom, they can better meet the learning needs of their students (Schroeder, 2022).

AI and big data can revolutionize how universities interact with and make judgment calls about prospective and current students. So why should educators adopt an open yet cautious approach when considering ethical implications? Since computers cannot think independently, can we assume that AI-generated content is impartial, thus eliminating threats like human bias?

Unfortunately, that may not be the case. Data-driven decision-making using AI has been widely critiqued for reducing autonomy and transparency while compromising privacy due to the lack of public oversight (Zeide, 2017). Prior research highlights concern over student data privacy and security and the need for stronger safeguards and protocols (Florea & Florea, 2020; Jones et al., 2020; Yang & Beil, 2024). Issues such as data breaches (Huang, 2023) within remote exam proctoring (Marano et al., 2024) and data tracking (Jones et al., 2020) pose threats to the security of students' data. Similarly, institutional members must be on guard for biases found in outputs. AI algorithms are programmed by humans who may have implicit or unconscious biases that are potentially replicated in these algorithms. For instance, Amazon designed a recruitment tool to remove biases in the hiring process and select the best candidates. AI technology used data to match applicant characteristics to those of Amazon's most successful employees to narrow the pool of applicants. However, because men primarily occupy technical roles at the company, the algorithm reproduced gender bias to favor males and eliminate female applicants. Applicants who attended a women's college or included the word "woman" on their resume, as in "captain of the women's varsity soccer league," were immediately excluded (Hauser, 2020, para. 6).

Even seemingly helpful features of technology can have issues, such as using facial recognition technology in smartphones to track and identify persons suspected of committing crimes. Studies have shown that facial recognition is the least accurate for people of color (Grother et al., 2019; Kotwal & Marcel, 2025; Muthukumar et al., 2018). Law enforcement officers have wrongfully arrested and detained three black men for crimes they did not commit based on flawed facial recognition technology (Hill, 2020). Institutions of higher education are also active participants in the creation of racially biased algorithms used in technologies (e.g., Burke, 2020). For example, institutions that use AI and ML programs for admissions perpetuate the already documented bias in selecting applicants. The programs "learn" to create admissions models from previous admissions data and make recommendations that resemble previous biases. In 2020, the University of Texas at Austin abandoned an admissions program due to its inability to escape perpetuating historical inequities (Burke, 2020). As a result, AI has the potential to promote stigmatization and violate privacy, given its ability to access and process sensitive personal information.

Potential Impact of Artificial Intelligence and Big Data on Higher Education

Consider how AI and big data can specifically impact those in higher education. Higher education administrators and faculty have expressed concern about how instantaneous AI-generated content could hinder student learning. For example, *Forbes* commissioned ChatGPT, an AI chatbot auto-generative system created by OpenAI, to write two college admissions essays (Jump, 2023). The chatbot received a simple yet detailed prompt to write a 650-word essay from the perspective of an 18-year-old high school senior interested in majoring in business with a competitive swimming background and a broken shoulder medical history. His parents are from Bangalore, India, and now own a restaurant in Newton, Massachusetts. As a result, ChatGPT generated a grammatically correct, well-structured admissions essay in less than 10 minutes (Jump, 2023).

University administrators and faculty members fear AI will negatively impact academic integrity as students fail to develop fundamental reading, writing, and critical thinking skills to formulate thoughts and opinions and develop unique voices (D'Agostino, 2023).

What role will AI play in student recruitment and admissions? Its ability to filter applicants based on ethnicity, financial aid needs, and predicted academic performance raises additional ethical concerns (Dennis, 2018). Students from disadvantaged backgrounds could face greater discrimination if algorithms make decisions based on biases related to ethnicity, gender, or socioeconomic status. Further, given AI's vulnerability to cyberattacks, how will universities securely manage student academic and health records? What privacy considerations must universities adopt to ensure the confidentiality of sensitive information? AI systems are vulnerable to data breaches, so universities must consider enhanced security measures to safeguard students' private information.

How will universities and colleges protect students from foreseeable technological concerns? Following the case of University of California, Los Angeles (UCLA) student Katherine Rosen, who was attacked and stabbed by a classmate in her chemistry lab, the California Supreme Court established the *duty of care*, calling universities to protect students from foreseeable harm. University officials were monitoring Rosen's assailant, who exhibited disturbing behavior days leading up to the attack. This court ruling is gaining traction throughout the country as public institutions are being held responsible for protecting the safety of their student body (Dolan, 2018). Given the foreseeable privacy and equity concerns of AI and big data, what measures of caution, transparency, and accountability should universities implement as part of their existing duty of care for students?

Higher education professionals can be cautiously optimistic about AI's ability to target persistent problems and streamline educational processes. While it may seem like AI is thinking independently, it is not autonomous. AI simulates human intelligence, so human thinking ultimately drives outputs (Warner, 2023). A robot on its own accord cannot teach a class; however, a robot programmed by humans can. The aphorism "Garbage in, garbage out" explains how humans have existing biases and preferences (Bourne, 2019), and AI can perpetuate and amplify them. However, some scholars critique this metaphor for oversimplifying how biases are reproduced in AI systems (Powles & Nissenbaum, 2018). While this phrase illustrates how biased AI inputs can lead to biased outputs, it is important to understand that humans ultimately decide how data is collected, labeled, processed, and interpreted. AI models are tools, and humans are responsible for using them ethically to protect and evaluate vast amounts of data and should be held accountable for their use (Powles & Nissenbaum, 2018; Zeide, 2017). As AI and big data shape the future of higher education, educators must consider the moral and ethical implications that could arise to ensure equitable and safe outcomes for students.

Organization of Volume and Overview of Chapters

In this volume, we take a comprehensive view of the origins and ramifications of embracing artificial intelligence and big data in higher education. While this volume primarily focuses on implications for the U.S. higher education system, the transformative potential of AI in the field of higher education extends well beyond the U.S. While higher education governance and policies may differ, concerns related to data security, privacy, equitable admissions policies, and academic integrity are shared worldwide. The growth of AI is an international phenomenon, offering similar opportunities and challenges for higher education institutions around the world.

We divide the book into two parts, with each offering a breadth of perspectives from leading scholars in the field of higher education. The volume explores AI's potential and pitfalls, providing insights into how institutions can responsibly implement advanced technologies to support students and campus communities. These two parts fit together by first offering readers an understanding of legal, ethical, and philosophical critiques and considerations when using emerging technologies to enhance institutional practices and improve educational policies. The chapters in part I emphasize the importance of their responsible use and discuss potential impacts on higher education practices. Part II builds on these discussions by exploring practical examples of how AI and big data are used and misused to inform decision-making and practice in higher education. The chapters in part II examine the impacts of leveraging data-driven technologies to streamline institutional operations and enhance student success outcomes. Across both parts of the volume, chapters discuss legal and ethical challenges to fairness, social equity, and academic integrity. This volume emphasizes the importance of human-centered AI in improving the campus environment and the practical implications of AI and data ownership in higher education. Finally, this volume provides a critical perspective on policy, law, and ethics with practical insight on the responsible implementation of AI and big data, addressing the need for additional data to address inequalities in higher education.

Part I begins with chapter 2, "Algorithmic, Autonomous, and Artificial: How Big Data and Mediated Actions Reshape the Legal and Ethical Landscape of Academic Research," in which Sun examines AI in higher education through a survey of legal and ethical analyses, including privacy and publicity, products liability, security, harassment, free speech, intellectual property, and discrimination. In chapter 3, "The Impact of Artificial Intelligence on Higher Education: Opportunity, Risk, and Responsible Governance," Carleton and Knight address how the law is racing to catch up with the proliferation and evolution of AI on college and university campuses and how these pressures fit into the existing educational decision-making paradigm, including how AI use and misuse should be handled. In chapter 4, "Desiring Machines: The Sociotechnical Production of Datafication in Higher Education," Smithers outlines the form of power that produces big data, predictive analytics, AI, and their kin as common sense solutions to higher education problems. Chapter 5, "Making a Digital Record of Campus Life: The Student Data Warehouse and the Datafication of Student Records in U.S. Higher Education," Brown traces the emergence of student recordkeeping, its formalization through the construction of data warehouses, the public policy that makes data warehouses essential, and future directions for student-centered humanistic data storage.

Part II begins with chapter 6, "Putting AI in Practice: Applications for Serving Students and Campuses," where Hephner LaBanc and colleagues present case studies on the adoption and integration of AI technologies in campus policing, dining services, and student engagement. The authors provide perspectives from a student affairs lens on how emerging technologies are changing the profession and influencing everyday practice on college campuses. In chapter 7, "Predictive Policing in American Schools and Universities," Miller discusses the existing human racial and gender biases embedded in predictive analytics to determine human behavior and examines the ethical, legal, and social considerations and implications of using big data and AI in campus policing. In chapter 8, "Artificial Communication and Media Realism for College Admissions," Munoz-Najar Galvez and coauthors examine the college admissions holistic review process considering advancements in NLP and college admissions data. The authors explore the interconnections between social identity, social contexts, and fairness in NLP and discuss implications for higher education. In chapter 9, "Understanding Challenges Repaying Student Loans: An In-Depth Study Utilizing BERT Models for Emotion Recognition and Issue Classification," Yang and colleagues analyze the emotional experiences of student loan borrowers following the resumption of loan repayments. Utilizing advanced large language transformer techniques, they examine the emotions and emotional trajectories of student complaints over time, classifying them by topic to better understand the impact of policy changes on borrowers. In chapter 10, "Promising Applications for Promoting Disaster Resilience on College Campuses," Noorani and colleagues show how AI can be used to scrape and classify campus image data and then demonstrate how a web interface tool can be used to show campus stakeholders samples of image data and ask them to help identify vulnerabilities and safety concerns. Finally, in chapter 11, "Connecting Theory, Ethics, and Practice: Future Directions for AI and Big Data in Higher Education," Dean Divaker shares key takeaways from the volume and proposes directions for educational leaders to consider as they navigate the future of AI and big data in higher education.

This volume aims to help readers consider the ethical, legal, and practical implications of AI and big data to inform practice and decision-making. While part I gives readers a foundational understanding of critical perspectives to consider, part II focuses on successfully integrating AI and big data into higher education practices and policies. Together, readers will gain a comprehensive understanding of ethical considerations and practical applications of these technologies, allowing higher education administrators, scholars, practitioners, and graduate students to bridge the gap between theory and practice as they navigate the use of AI and big data in higher education. Using such innovative tools responsibly requires a deeper understanding of these key areas and a commitment to continued ethical and equitable practice.

References

Alpaydin, E. (2020). *Introduction to machine learning* (4th ed.). MIT Press.

Baker, T., & Smith, L. (2019, February). *Educ-AI-tion rebooted? Exploring the future of artificial intelligence in schools and colleges.* Nesta Foundation. https://media.nesta.org.uk/documents/Future_of_AI_and_education_v5_WEB.pdf

Bourne, J. (2019). Unravelling the concept of unconscious bias. *Race & Class*, *60*(4), 70–75. https://doi.org/10.1177/0306396819828608

Bucea-Manea-Țoniş, R., Kuleto, V., Gudei, S. C. D., Lianu, C., Lianu, C., Ilić, M. P., & Păun, D. (2022). Artificial intelligence potential in higher education institutions enhanced learning environment in Romania and Serbia. *Sustainability*, *14*(10), 1–18. https://doi.org/10.3390/su14105842

Burke, L. (2020, December 14). The death and life of an admissions algorithm. *Inside Higher Ed.* https://www.insidehighered.com/admissions/article/2020/12/14/u-texas-will-stop-using-controversial-algorithm-evaluate-phd

Cho, K. K. (2023, January 19). University of Texas at Austin bans TikTok from its networks. *Washington Post.* https://www.washingtonpost.com/nation/2023/01/18/ut-austin-bans-tiktok-greg-abbott/

Chowdhary, K. R. (2020). Natural language processing. In K. R. Chowdhary (Ed.), *Fundamentals of artificial intelligence* (pp. 603–649). Springer. https://doi.org/10.1007/978-81-322-3972-7_19

D'Agostino, S. (2023, January 12). ChatGPT advice academics can use now. *Inside Higher Ed.* https://www.insidehighered.com/news/2023/01/12/academic-experts-offer-advice-chatgpt

Dennis, M. J. (2018). Artificial intelligence and recruitment, admission, progression, and retention. *Enrollment Management Report*, *22*(9), 1–3. https://doi.org/10.1002/emt.30479

Dolan, M. (2018, March 22). In ruling for victim in UCLA attack, California Supreme Court says universities should protect students. *Los Angeles Times.* https://www.latimes.com/local/lanow/la-me-ln-ucla-stabbing-court-20180321-story.html

Fanni, S. C., Febi, M., Aghakhanyan, G., & Neri, E. (2023). Natural language processing. In M. E. Klontzas, S. C. Fanni, & E. Neri (Eds.), *Introduction to artificial intelligence* (pp. 87–99). Springer. https://doi.org/10.1007/978-3-031-25928-9_5

Fernandez, F., & Hutchens, N. H. (2023). Regulating research: IRBs, intellectual property, and governmental controls. In P. F. Lake (Ed.), *The Oxford handbook of U.S. higher education law*. Oxford University Press.

Feuerriegel, S., Hartmann, J., Janiesch, C., & Zschech, P. (2024). Generative AI. *Business & Information Systems Engineering*, *66*(2), 111–126.

Florea, D., & Florea, S. (2020). *Big data and the ethical implications of data privacy in higher education research. Sustainability*, *12*(20), 1–11. https://doi.org/10.3390/su12208744

Gonsalves, T. (2019). The summers and winters of artificial intelligence. In K. A. Patel (Ed.), *Advanced methodologies and technologies in artificial intelligence, computer simulation, and human-computer interaction* (pp. 168–179). IGI Global.

Grother, P., Ngan, M., & Hanaoka, K. (2019). *Face recognition vendor test (FRVT) part 3: Demographic effects* (NIST Interagency/Internal Report No. 8280). National Institute of Standards and Technology. https://doi.org/10.6028/NIST.IR.8280

Gurtu, A. (2021, June 2). Five industries reaping the benefits of artificial intelligence. *Forbes.* https://www.forbes.com/sites/forbestechcouncil/2021/06/02/five-industries-reaping-the-benefits-of-artificial-intelligence/

Hauser, R. (2020). Is our future equitable? *People and Strategy, 43*(1), 1–3.

Hill, K. (2020, December 29). Another arrest, and jail time, due to a bad facial recognition match. *The New York Times.* https://www.nytimes.com/2020/12/29/technology/facial-recognition-misidentify-jail.html

Huang, L. (2023). *Ethics of artificial intelligence in education: Student privacy and data protection. Science Insights Education Frontiers, 16*(2), 2577–2587. https://doi.org/10.15354/sief.23.re202

Hutchens, N. H., & Hulbert, A. (2016). Don't forget the fine print: MOOCs and student privacy. *New Directions for Institutional Research, 2015*(167), 57–68. https://doi.org/10.1002/ir.20154

Jones, K., Asher, A., Goben, A., Perry, M., Salo, D., Briney, K., & Robertshaw, B. (2020). *"We're being tracked at all times": Student perspectives of their privacy in relation to learning analytics in higher education. Journal of the Association for Information Science and Technology, 71*(9), 1044–1059. https://doi.org/10.1002/asi.24358

Jump, J. (2023, January 9). Ethical college admissions: "I am not a robot." *Inside Higher Ed.* https://www.insidehighered.com/admissions/views/2023/01/09/what-impact-will-chatgpt-have-college-essay-opinion

Kasparov, G. (2010, February 11). The chess master and the computer. *The New York Review of Books, 57*(2), 16–19. https://www.nybooks.com/articles/2010/02/11/the-chess-master-and-the-computer/

Kitchin, R. (2013). Big data and human geography: Opportunities, challenges and risks. *Dialogues in Human Geography, 3*(3), 262–267. https://doi.org/10.1177/2043820613513388

Kitchin, R. (2014). Big data, new epistemologies and paradigm shifts. *Big Data & Society, 1*(1), 1–11. https://doi.org/10.1177/2053951714528481

Kotwal, K., & Marcel, S. (2025, February 4). *Review of demographic bias in face recognition.* (arXiv:2502.02309v1 [cs.CV]). https://arxiv.org/abs/2502.02309

Lane, J. E., & Finsel, B. A. (2014). Fostering smarter colleges and universities. In J. E. Lane (Ed.), *Building a smarter university: Big data, innovation, and analytics* (pp. 3–26). State University of New York Press. https://doi.org/10.1515/9781438454542-005

Laney, D. (2001). *3D data management: Controlling data volume, velocity, and variety*. Gartner.

Marano, E., Newton, P. M., Birch, Z., Croombs, M., Gilbert, C., & Draper, M. J. (2024). *What is the student experience of remote proctoring? A pragmatic scoping review. Higher Education Quarterly*, *78*(3), 1031–1047. https://doi.org/10.1111/hequ.12506

McAfee, A., & Brynjolfsson, E. (2012, October). Big data: The management revolution. *Harvard Business Review*. https://hbr.org/2012/10/big-data-the-management-revolution

McCulloch, W. S., & Pitts, W. (1943). A logical calculus of the ideas immanent in nervous activity. *Bulletin of Mathematical Biophysics*, *5*(4), 115–133. https://doi.org/10.1007/BF02478259

Mucci, T., & Stryker, C. (2024, April 5). *What is big data analytics?* IBM. https://www.ibm.com/think/topics/big-data-analytics

Mueller, M. L., & Farhat, K. (2023). *TikTok and US national security*. Georgia Institute of Technology, School of Public Policy, Internet Governance Project. https://www.internetgovernance.org/wp-content/uploads/Tik-Tok-and-US-national-security-3-1.pdf

Mukhopadhyay, S., Iyengar, S. S., Madni, A. M., & Di Biano, R. (2019). The next generation of artificial intelligence: Synthesizable AI. In K. Arai, R. Bhatia, & S. Kapoor (Eds.), *Proceedings of the Future Technologies Conference (FTC) 2018: Volume 1* (pp. 659–677). Springer.

Muthukrishnan, N., Maleki, F., Ovens, K., Reinhold, C., Forghani, B., & Forghani, R. (2020). Brief history of artificial intelligence. *Neuroimaging Clinics of North America*, *30*(4), 393–399. doi.org/10.1016/j.nic.2020.07.004

Muthukumar, V., Pedapati, T., Ratha, N., Sattigeri, P., Wu, C.-W., Kingsbury, B., Kumar, A., Thomas, S., Mojsilovic, A., & Varshney, K. R. (2018). *Understanding unequal gender classification accuracy from face images*. (arXiv:1812.00099). https://arxiv.org/abs/1812.00099

Nieto-Rodriguez, A., & Vargas, R. V. (2023, October 27). *The opportunities at the intersection of AI, sustainability, and project management. Harvard Business Review*. https://hbr.org/2023/10/the-opportunities-at-the-intersection-of-ai-sustainability-and-project-management

Nietzel, M. T. (2022, October 1). How colleges are using artificial intelligence to improve enrollment and retention. *Forbes*. https://www.forbes.com/sites/michaeltnietzel/2022/10/01/colleges-are-turning-to-artificial-intelligence-to-improve-enrollment-and-retention/

Newton, D. (2021, April 26). *Artificial intelligence is infiltrating higher ed, from admissions to grading*. The Hechinger Report. http://hechingerreport.org/from-admissions-to-teaching-to-grading-ai-is-infiltrating-higher-education/

Nilsson, N. J. (2009). *The quest for artificial intelligence: A history of ideas and achievements*. Cambridge University Press.

Pospíchal, J., & Kvasnička, V. (2015). 70th anniversary of publication: Warren McCulloch & Walter Pitts: A logical calculus of the ideas immanent in nervous activity. In P. Sinčák, P. Hartono, M. Virčíková, J. Vaščák, & R. Jakša (Eds.), *Emergent trends in robotics and intelligent systems* (Advances in Intelligent Systems and Computing, Vol. 316). Springer. https://doi.org/10.1007/978-3-319-10783-7_1

Powles, J., & Nissenbaum, H. (2018, December 7). *The seductive diversion of "solving bias" in artificial intelligence.* One Zero. https://onezero.medium.com/the-seductive-diversion-of-solving-bias-in-artificial-intelligence-890df5e5ef53

Rooksby, J. H. (2020). Understanding IP considerations regarding online instruction. *Campus Legal Advisor*, *20*(12), 1–8. https://onlinelibrary.wiley.com/doi/pdf/10.1002/cala.40295

Rowan-Kenyon, H. T., & Alemán, A. M. M. (2016). *Social media in higher education* (ASHE Higher Education Report, 42[5]). John Wiley & Sons.

Kenyon, H. T., Martínez Alemán, A. M., & Savitz-Romer, M. (2018). *Technology and engagement: Making technology work for first generation college students.* Rutgers University Press.

Russell, S. J., & Norvig, P. (2010). *Artificial intelligence: A modern approach.* Pearson Education.

Schroeder, R. (2022, November 2). AI transforming education. *Inside Higher Ed.* https://www.insidehighered.com/digital-learning/blogs/online-trending-now/ai-transforming-education

Tidy, J. (2024, March 18). Is TikTok really a danger to the West? *BBC News.* https://www.bbc.com/news/technology-64797355

Tolentino, D. (2023, January 18). These are all the public universities that have instituted TikTok bans. *NBC News.* https://www.nbcnews.com/tech/tiktok-bans-public-universities-list-rcna66185

Turing, A. M. (1950). Computing machinery and intelligence. *Mind, 59,* 433–460. https://doi.org/10.1093/mind/LIX.236.433

Turing, A. M. (2009). Computing machinery and intelligence. In R. Epstein, G. Roberts, & G. Beber (Eds.), *Parsing the Turing test.* (pp. 23–65). Springer.

Warner, J. (2023, January 4). How about we put learning at the center? *Inside Higher Ed.* https://www.insidehighered.com/blogs/just-visiting/how-about-we-put-learning-center

Webber, K. L., & Zheng, H. (2020). *Big data on campus: Data analytics and decision making in higher education.* Johns Hopkins University Press.

Yang, E., & Beil, C. (2024). *Ensuring data privacy in AI/ML implementation. New Directions for Higher Education,* 2024(207), 63–78. https://doi.org/10.1002/he.20509

Zeide, E. (2017). The structural consequences of big data-driven education. *Big Data, 5*(2), 164–172. https://doi.org/10.1089/big.2016.0061

Part I

Legal, Ethical, and Philosophical Considerations

2

Algorithmic, Autonomous, and Artificial

How Big Data and Mediated Actions Reshape the Legal and Ethical Landscape of Academic Research

Jeffrey C. Sun

Artificial intelligence (AI) has roots in higher education and government research labs. In the late 1940s and early 1950s, Dr. Alan Turing presented and wrote about various developments about integrated actions involving a machine's processing in a manner that models cognitive processing (Copeland, 2004). As captured in an edited collection (Copeland, 2004), Turing's scholarly dissemination referenced the Automatic Computing Engine (1947), Intelligent Machinery (1948), and Computing Machinery and Intelligence (1950). In the later piece, Turing (1950) raised the inquiry, "Can machines think?" as he described the "imitation game" in which machines would process a series of question–response prompts to make certain conclusions. Soon after, other scholars saw the possibilities of machines outperforming humans. Realistically framing the current hurdle as human-based, McCarthy et al. (1955) presented the sole problem with machines not being able to outperform humans at the time, but "the major obstacle is not lack of machine capacity but our inability to write programs taking full advantage of what we have" (para. 3). Today, that perceived hurdle has been reduced largely because of increases in data capacity.

Recent developments have accelerated these data-driven capabilities even further. The Stanford University Human-Centered Artificial Intelligence (HAI) 2025 AI Index Report documents that the number of foundation models released in 2024 exceeded 200, and there are training datasets now regularly comprising trillions of tokens drawn from diverse sources including academic literature, social media, and specialized domain knowledge (Stanford HAI, 2025). This explosion in model capacity and training data scale has profound implications for academic researchers, who must navigate unsettled and complex legal and ethical frameworks, while trying to develop, deploy, or utilize these powerful AI systems.

Data are key to the expansion of AI in higher education. Data storage alone is a major consideration. One only needs to consider changes just over two decades ago with data-volume levels during which the unit of digital measurement as processing moved from gigabytes to terabytes to petabytes to exabytes to zettabytes to yottabytes. For academic researchers, the exponential increases in power present more opportunities for massive analyses and prediction. Given the characteristics of big data as a function of AI systems, matters of legal, policy, and ethical parameters around data collection, mining, storage, processing, analytics and interpretation, application, and destruction become reified elements for academic research.[1]

Consider, for instance, how AI research typically draws on large datasets, which may include personally identifiable information (PII) or other sensitive data sources. Already, academic researchers have developed AI systems that draw on college students' education records to construct personalized learning (Rouhiainen, 2019; Sun, 2024c) and patient healthcare/medical records to offer, in many instances, quicker diagnoses (e.g., identifying distinct pathologies) and other precision medicine approaches (Murdoch, 2021). Likewise, these systems draw on various forms of information such as medical clinical notes and observations of patients with psychiatric disorders (Richter et al., 2021) and emotional analyses (Bhatt et al., 2023); data examinations related to critical infrastructure and national security protections (Congressional Research Service, 2020; Duffy & Fendorf, 2024); and other detailed and sensitive information. Nonetheless, the data processing may be generated from piecemealing details, which are not readily available, through a disclosure mishap, such as masked email addresses, corporate secrets, and a person's genetic marker (see, e.g., White, 2023).

Centering on the data, there are practical concerns and potential legal considerations associated with data violations, such as when the data are potentially stolen, impermissibly exposed, sloppily handled, improperly disposed of, exploited and sold, and intentionally or unintentionally hacked. Given the data sensitivity and possible data violations, universities and academic researchers engaged with PII and other sensitive data are faced with addressing data privacy protocols, determining degrees of consent, identifying forms of protections, and constructing action plans in case of breaches.

Complicating this matter, AI and computational outputs based on data predictions have emerged with greater accuracy and speed given increased computational power, larger datasets, more sophisticated algorithms, better autonomous systems, and complex layered neural networks. At the same time, the design, development, implementation, or use of AI systems by academic researchers raises increasing concerns about legal and ethical issues that involve human decisions, which may include defaulting to the AI system as the ultimate decision maker. Accordingly, this chapter illuminates legal and ethical matters from the perspective of academic researchers.

Drawing on the framework used in Sun and Baez (2009), this chapter examines the intersecting components of the legal parameters, technological advancements, and competing interests to illuminate the established law under set conditions, draw on corollary legal sources as a way to present patterns and emergent analyses of legal direction, and identify clear gaps in the law. Because this chapter takes the perspective of legal and ethical concerns when academic researchers' design, develop, implement, or use AI systems, the focus resides with big data treatment within the AI systems. Specifically, this chapter unpacks academic researchers' considerations and decisions around privacy, algorithmic fairness, intellectual property, security and controls, and safety and harms.

Privacy

Education Records

Data are at the center of AI systems, but in some instances, they are protected or subject to protocols to reach consent. For instance, data drawn from students' educational records are governed by the Family Educational Rights and Privacy Act (FERPA, 1974). That federal law prohibits educational institutions from releasing education records absent written consent or not falling within one of the exceptions (e.g., accreditation reporting, response to issued subpoena, or health or safety emergency). Under the law, education records generally include student disciplinary records containing PII (*United States v. Miami University*, 2002). At times, masking the data sufficiently protects college students' privacy. One court acknowledged that "confidentiality of a Title IX [sexual harassment] disciplinary proceeding may sometimes — but not always — furnish grounds for finding an exceptional case warranting pseudonymity" (*Doe v. Massachusetts Institute of Technology*, 2022, p. 74). The issue is ultimately how much disclosed data leads to PII, and court cases have examined the extent to which culled data may lead to that identification. Thus, in one federal case, the court deemed the requested data as "somewhat minimal information" when the requestor sought "grade point average, test scores, race, gender, and ethnicity" because the data were "not sufficient, by itself, to trace the identity of an applicant" (*Osborn v. Board of Regents of the University of Wisconsin System*, 2002, p. 171).

Besides the data type as an examination to determine release, data access offers another level of analysis. Unauthorized disclosure of educational records has been presented in less obvious ways, such as data arrangements with interstate compacts, enrollment management consultants, outsourced online program managers, cloud-based data storage units, and state longitudinal data system offices. Further, the complexities of interagency relationships may seem, at first, permissible. Yet in a matter involving the University of Massachusetts, which had an online presence in the state of Maryland, the consent and protocol processes required a bit of untangling (Sun, 2014).

The Maryland Higher Education Commission (MHEC), the state's coordinating board for higher education institutions, mandated all universities interacting with Maryland residents to file their data with the Maryland Longitudinal Data System (MLDS) Center, the state agency responsible for data services, including data collection and management of education records and related data from early childhood to higher education to the workforce. After careful analysis, the U.S. Department of Education's Family Policy Compliance Office informed the University of Massachusetts that submission of Maryland students' education records to the MLDS Center would be impermissible unless MHEC and the MLDS Center had a written agreement (i.e., memorandum of understanding) authorizing MLDS as a third party to act on MHEC's behalf. Absent a written agreement holding MLDS accountable and compliant, the data sharing of education records would be impermissible under the law.

Although college students have privacy rights available, the U.S. Supreme Court ruled in *Gonzaga University v. Doe* (2002) that FERPA offers no personal recourse for individuals to collect any financial damages from any university violations of students' privacy. Instead, the potential penalties under the law are limited to the violating university losing its federal financial aid. As an additional protection, state laws, in many instances, reinforce or increase students' rights of privacy over their educational records, potentially adding opportunities to collect financial damages from university privacy breaches (see, e.g., Ky. Rev. Stat. § 164.283 [2025]; Ohio Rev. Code § 3319.321 [2025]; Va. Code § 23.1-405(C) [2025]).

While FERPA compliance, including the technicalities associated with third-party educational providers, continue as an important safeguard, at the end, there is a more fundamental concern about student privacy laws. Elana Zeide (2016) contends that legal frameworks like FERPA are inadequate for governing predictive and behavioral data systems. These regimes emphasize procedural formalities, particularly providing notice and consent, rather than the substantive impacts that data use has on student autonomy, equity, and development. Given these conflicting approaches, Zeide recommends refashioning student privacy laws around principles. For instance, she suggests principles of purpose limitations in which the data are only used for legitimate, pedagogically sound objectives; minimal invasiveness provisions so data are not employed for unnecessary or intrusive data collection; pedagogical integrity purposes so technologies enhance rather than displace meaningful learning relationships; and developmental appropriateness checks so data practices align with the cognitive, emotional, and social needs of students. In other words, she proposes privacy of student data to center around educational goals rather than institutional efficiency or commercial interests. As AI applications and acceptance increases, this reframing of FERPA and state-level student privacy policies will likely be required so the laws work to advance, rather than unduly stifle, educational goals under this new environment.

Protected Health Information

Academic researchers also engage with medical and other health-related research employing AI models for predictive and generative outputs. Similar to FERPA and educational records, the Health Insurance Portability and Accountability Act (HIPAA) offers safeguards against unauthorized release of protected health information (PHI). PHI encompasses any information that can identify an individual and relates to their health condition, healthcare provision, or healthcare payment.

Not all patient or healthcare records fall within HIPAA. The federal law offers a safe harbor provision for de-identified health information. Specifically, the law outlines information lacking qualified identifiers (e.g., name, address, social security number) as not PHI. At the same time, "limited datasets" qualify as potentially permissible uses for academic research under strict monitoring and access conditions. The protocols include Institutional Review Board (IRB) standards restricting data access and levels of de-identification. IRB protocols apply HIPAA and research ethics standards, adding a potential layer of considerations, so the proposed AI research offers data clearances, additional masking, or data elimination to prevent unauthorized identifiable PHI. Further, academic researchers using limited datasets agree to data use agreement (DUA) terms, which follow HIPAA requirements, with the covered entity. Nonetheless, distinguishing between acceptable and risky uses remains a nuanced issue, and AI usage has complicated the line between acceptable and risky use.

A well-publicized case dealing with academic research using patient electronic health records for AI predictive modeling provides an illustrative example. In this case, the question arose about the injury that the patient sustained through the health provider data disclosures for a collaborative project with a technology company and a research university running big data analytics (*Dinerstein v. Google*, 2023). The case, involving this collaboration between the University of Chicago and Google on healthcare prediction using AI, was dismissed on procedural grounds, but it highlights the concerns regarding the anonymity of data used in AI as well as the risks of re-identifying individuals. Even when data are sufficiently de-identified, AI algorithms have the potential to predict and link identities, as the platform may draw on multiple data types and sources, allowing for identification narrowing to a small group or specific person. Accordingly, HIPAA incorporates a "minimum necessary rule" that limits data access to only the essential amount of data needed for the research. Furthermore, also like FERPA, state laws governing health privacy present potentially additional parameters applicable to academic research using AI.

Records Impacting International Reach

Numerous international laws apply to U.S.-based academic research that reaches other nation-states and international regions (Sun, 2023). Notably, the European Union's General Data Protection Regulation (GDPR) presents significant complexities for U.S. academic researchers employing AI, especially when handling information pertaining to E.U. citizens. Although the GDPR does not directly govern in the United States, its influence stretches to research activities involving personal data of individuals residing in the E.U., thus presenting substantial compliance challenges and potential impediments to research advancement.

The GDPR emphasizes the importance of transparency and fairness when organizations use automated decision-making. A provision within the GDPR, the right to explanation, mandates that researchers be able to disclose the operational processing of complex AI models. For instance, academic researchers might create an automated system that makes decisions about mental health interventions or design plans leading to robots performing advanced manufacturing production activities (Sun & Pratt, 2024). Regardless of the AI system, these types of automated systems potentially impact individuals. Given the human impact, the GDPR permits an individual in the E.U. to request an explanation of the decision, and the explanation requires the user of the organization relying on the automated system to outline the factors the system drew upon and to define the logic behind those decisions.

In essence, there is an available interrogation behind the AI system almost akin to a food package label or a patent application disclosure describing the technology. This requirement presents a complication, however, to the degree of research transparency and research comprehension, because the data trailing and analyses using AI are not easy to present, track, or explain. Moreover, the GDPR describes the requirement indicating that the requestor receive "meaningful information" about the logic involved with the automated system's output. The determination of the information sufficiency to arise to the "meaningful" standard may present questions, fears, and assumptions from U.S. academic researchers. While the GDPR appears to offer end users an opportunity to comprehend and trust the AI results and output, it may also offer a false sense of data trustworthiness and usefulness posed as an effort to increase AI transparency.

Algorithmic Biases and Other Errors

Data Biases

The use of AI algorithms in higher education, especially by academic researchers, presents a series of legal, ethical, and practical challenges centered on potential biases and their discriminatory effects. Already, human nature leads to various forms of biases, whether intentional or unintentional, and these biases may affect algorithms and structured designs, leading to biases and discriminatory effects from the AI platform. For instance, the AI may perform design-bias outputs when assumptions or anchored sources are introduced during the design phase of a tool or process. These design biases may reflect the assumptions, preferences, or oversights of the designers and developers. Likewise, the AI may perform skewed outputs through data biases when the data drawn for the training or other performed analyses are not representative of the broader population or when they are missing key variables, artifacts, samples, or principles. Beyond the AI, human interpretation of the output may occur too. Interpretation bias may manifest through different understandings of the outputs, biases imputed into the output data, and experiences that better explain or omit details about the outputs.

Significantly, empirical research already demonstrates identity-based biases, including from academic researchers in fields representative in the AI developer and usage fields (Eaton et al., 2019). Illustrating this embedded concern, Eaton et al. (2019) found biases in the evaluation process that contribute to the underrepresentation of minoritized populations, particularly based on gender and race, in STEM fields within the academy. Among the findings, the researchers uncovered significant gender bias within physics departments, where male candidates were consistently rated as more competent and hireable compared to female candidates, even when qualifications were identical. Equally troublesome, the findings revealed that biology and physics faculty demonstrated racial biases, with candidates who were perceived as White or Asian receiving higher ratings for competence and hireability compared to those perceived as Black or Latinx. Further, the impact of intersecting gender and racial identities showed that Black and Latinx women, as well as Latinx men, faced the most significant disadvantages in hireability ratings, especially in physics. While these findings illuminate statistically significant demonstrations of evaluation biases, the literature also establishes identity-based harms present through practices, policies, and laws applicable to educational settings (see, e.g., Daniel & Sun, 2022; Sun & Daniel, 2023; Sun, 2024b).

Legislative Responses

From a legal challenge analysis, the United States has adopted very few AI targeted laws addressing biases and discrimination (Sun & Bruton, 2023). At the federal level, Congress has entertained a bill, the Algorithmic Accountability Act (2023), for several sessions. The bill would offer organizational guardrails to assess and mitigate bias and discriminatory impacts from AI platforms. The proposed AI law would create disclosure and testing elements inquiring about algorithm training, data source disclosures, approaches to the AI response, and protections against harms. Dozens of statehouses have also passed or entertained bills addressing bias audits (Zhu, 2023). In 2024 and 2025, California considered AB-2930, AB-331, AB316, SB 295, and SB 640 to assess and report impacts associated with AI decisions as well as establish liability and disclosures.

Connecticut's SB 2, Hawaii's SB 59, Illinois' HB 5116, and Oklahoma's HB 3835 offered similar reporting requirements on developers when AI serves as a controlling factor over consequential decisions. Hawaii proposed firmer rules simply prohibiting algorithmic discrimination via HB 1607 and SB 2524. So far, few states have enacted comprehensive legislation. Signed into law in May 2024 and effective in June 2026, Colorado's Artificial Intelligence Act (2025) is a major state law that tackles algorithmic discrimination, documentation and disclosure requirements, and governance and impact assessments associated with AI systems.

Several states have more focused policies. For instance, in 2024, the Illinois Artificial Intelligence Video Interview Act (2025) enacted provisions governing employment law. Effective in January 2026, the law prohibits an employer from using AI when the system demonstrates discriminatory effects onto employees within protected classes or ZIP code discriminators. Also, a 2020 law in Maryland requires applicant consent for facial recognition analysis using AI to analyze employment video interviews. Maryland also has regulatory provisions over state agency procurement and deployment of AI.

Absent direct legislation over AI biases, other legal sources where AI biases and discrimination claims may arise from academic researcher development and usage may be available. Generally, these laws would revolve around potential violations of civil rights laws, specifically those related to nondiscrimination. For instance, Title VI of the Civil Rights Act of 1964 prohibits discrimination on the basis of race, color, or national origin in programs and activities receiving federal financial assistance, and Title IX of the Education Amendments of 1972 presents a similar civil rights law based on sex; correspondingly, Title VII prohibits discrimination on the basis of race, color, national origin, or sex in employment regardless of federal funding. Given these federal provisions, if an AI platform is developed or used to adversely impact programs or activities at a university based on race, color, national origin, or sex — or impacts employment based on race, color, national origin, or sex — a civil rights claim under the federal law may become a viable concern. Similarly, Title IX of the Education Amendments of 1972 prohibits discrimination on sex, including gender identity and transgender status, in programs and activities receiving federal financial assistance.

Adding to these human-centered errors, empirical evidence exists that AI has fostered biases and discriminatory errors. Buolamwini and Gebru (2018) revealed that facial recognition technologies have produced higher error rates for darker-skinned women. Biases in AI research raise questions of fairness beyond an exclusionary and sorting function. Obermeyer et al. (2019) identified a healthcare algorithm that outputted adverse racial biases. The effect led to Black patients receiving less attention than equally sick White patients because the algorithm inaccurately predicted the health needs of the minorized population. In short, as the Eaton et al. (2019) study and the literature on AI biases suggest, design, data, and decision points may lead to unfair outputs and outcomes for minoritized persons within the academy.

Although race- and gender-based biases are potentially prevalent, other AI biases are also possible, such as discrimination based on disability pursuant to the Americans with Disabilities Act of 1990 and Section 504 of the Rehabilitation Act of 1973; religion pursuant to various constitutional and civil rights laws, including the First Amendment, Fourteenth Amendment, and Civil Rights Act of 1964; age pursuant to the Age Discrimination in Employment Act (1967); pregnancy status pursuant to the Pregnancy Discrimination Act (1978) and Title IX of the Education Amendments (1972); genetic information under the Genetic Information Nondiscrimination Act (2008); credit reporting pursuant to the Equal Credit Opportunity Act (1974); military status pursuant to the Uniformed Services Employment and Reemployment Rights Act (1994); housing under the Fair Housing Act (1968); and a variety of state-law-based claims, such as contract law.

This list is not exhaustive, and the circumstances and technology may mediate emergence of other legal arguments that could even identify other nontypical discrimination allegations. It is possible, for example, that the AI system colludes against certain groups restricting interstate commerce and competition in the marketplace. If so, the Sherman Antitrust Act (1890) may present a viable claim. Likewise, there may be unfair trade practices that lead to claims under the Federal Trade Commission Act (1914).

Administrative Responses

Outside of legal sources, federal and state agencies offer guidance or exploratory research about AI fairness. For instance, the National Science Foundation launched its Fairness in Artificial Intelligence program, a $20 million collaboration with Amazon to support research on addressing AI ethical issues, including fairness and transparency through just and equitable AI systems. AI, social policy, and legal researchers have also proposed frameworks to avoid discriminatory algorithms. Notably, Kleinberg et al. (2018) proposed actions to include increased transparency with algorithms; standardization and equity efforts with fairness embedded into the design and implementation; rigorous regulation and oversight that include audits, improved data quality, and assurances associated with algorithm training; and an agile legal framework that adapts to algorithms and changing technologies.

Legal scholars have proposed other recommendations toward policy reform to manage algorithmic biases since complete elimination is likely not possible. Bambauer and Zarsky (2025) identify two persistent problems in the current AI regulatory landscape. One is that regulators fail to provide clear guidance, so there is an abdication problem. The other is that the critics publicly condemn AI systems even when developers make sincere efforts to act fairly, so there is a persistent ad hoc criticism problem. Taking these two problems into account, the authors argue that fairness in AI should not be measured solely by adherence to any single technical standard or by meeting every conceivable normative demand. Instead, policies should recognize that an AI system should be considered "fair enough" if it transparently and intentionally makes context-sensitive trade-offs among competing fairness goals. The article encourages AI governance structures to focus less on achieving perfection and more on documenting decision-making processes, clarifying the fairness objectives pursued, and justifying trade-offs in light of the application's context. Although seemingly harmful, Bambauer and Zarsky's (2025) "fair-enough" framework reframes the regulatory environment to advance resilience and practical accountability. This approach resists paralysis or overreaction in the face of imperfection, and it fosters more innovation and construction of reasonable algorithmic systems.

Intellectual Property

Ownership or Inventorship

While federal and state lawmakers have attributed AI system biases to developers, implementers, and potentially owners of the AI, the rights and property protections associated with AI systems is less clear. Intellectual property (IP) challenges, particularly when it comes to ownership and attribution of AI-generated works and availability of protected works in a variety of ways, especially in the AI training process, has not boded well for innovation efforts. A primary issue revolves around determining who, if anyone, can claim inventorship or creator status for works produced by AI. The legal landscape in this area remains relatively undeveloped, with only a few cases providing guidance. This section presents discussion elements about federal IP protections, such as copyright, patents, trade secrets, and related claims associated with a right of publicity.

One federal court answered the inventorship question. In 2022, a federal appellate court ruled that AI systems cannot qualify as inventors for the purposes of patent registration (*Thaler v. Vidal*, 2022). This ruling came after Stephen Thaler, the developer of the AI system at issue, attempted to patent inventions created by his AI system, named DABUS, by listing it as the inventor. The U.S. Patent and Trademark Office rejected these applications, leading to a legal challenge that culminated in a decision affirming that only natural persons can be named as inventors on patents. This decision aligns with other rulings, such as the notable case where a monkey took a selfie, and the court determined that nonhuman entities, including animals, cannot hold or claim copyright status (*Naruto v. Slater*, 2018). Since then, other legal sources, such as those from the U.S. Copyright Office, continue to reinforce that machine-generated outputs do not qualify for copyright protections under current interpretations of federal law, which specify that an identifiable human creator is required. For instance, the Copyright Office has denied claims involving works created by nonhumans, such as murals painted by elephants or digital transformations performed by machines.

Fair Use or Infringement

Current legal decisions about AI raise critical questions about the nature of AI in the realm of IP, focusing on who owns the data used to train AI systems and how these data should be licensed. The issue extends to the management of data privacy and the establishment of protocols for handling sensitive information during AI development and research. This is especially pertinent when considering aggregated data from multiple sources, where consent and proper data usage protocols become increasingly complex.

Indeed, several court cases have begun to explore these issues. For example, in 2023, a lawsuit against GitHub and associated companies addressed whether AI systems that scraped and utilized copyrighted program codes, without proper attribution or respecting copyright notices, constituted copyright infringement (*Doe 1 v. GitHub*, 2023). The plaintiffs argued that the AI systems actively disregarded copyright management information potentially setting a precedent for how IP laws apply to AI-generated content. More specifically, the 2023 trial court ruled that a violation only happens if someone uses an identical copy of the original material. The plaintiffs disagreed. They contended that the law does not actually require copies to be exactly identical to violate Digital Millennium Copyright Act (DMCA). They argued that the intent and effect still violated DMCA, particularly a section that deals with removing or altering copyright information (Section 1202). The trial court opened the case for further factual details, which were reviewed in 2024. In that case review, the federal court denied the plaintiffs' motion to reconsider the earlier dismissal of these claims (*Doe 1 v. GitHub*, 2024). The court reaffirmed that the plaintiffs failed to show that AI outputs were identical to the copyrighted code, which centered again on whether the DMCA actually requires "identical" copy to demonstrate a violation. Ultimately, if the DMCA requires a showing of identical copies in order to establish a violation for the removal or alteration of copyright management information, then this ruling basically left open whether the law should apply to modified or transformed outputs generated by AI trained on copyrighted data (*Doe 1 v. GitHub*, 2025).

Another case from 2023 involved Stability AI and other companies that used AI to create text-to-image generators trained on copyrighted images without obtaining permission from the original artists (*Andersen v. Stability AI*, 2023). Although the case is currently still unresolved, preliminary comments from the judge suggest that the sheer volume of data used by these AI systems may complicate claims of direct copyright infringement. Likewise, a case involving questions about copyright infringement using plaintiffs' books to train the AI platform, with plaintiffs as the authors and copyright holders of those books, ruled in favor of the AI research organization. The court concluded that the AI training did not lead to similar works and there was no intentional removal or alteration of copyright management information (*Tremblay v. OpenAI*, 2024).

The law permits transformative uses of copyrighted materials as a basis of fair use. Thomson Reuters, the company behind the legal database Westlaw, sued Ross Intelligence for copying and using thousands of its editorial summaries of court cases, which are referred to as headnotes (*Thomson Reuters v. Ross Intelligence*, 2025). Ross Intelligence drew on the headnotes to train its AI-powered legal research tool. The court found that these headnotes involved enough original work to be protected by copyright. Given that copyright protection, Ross Intelligence's use of the headnotes was unfair because it helped create a competing service. The federal trial court in Delaware noted that this kind of copying did not arise to a "transformative" work because it did not add new meaning or function (*Thomson Reuters v. Ross Intelligence*, 2025). According to the court, Ross Intelligence simply replaced what Westlaw already offered.

Other cases are suggesting similar outcomes. In a consolidated case, The New York Times (2025) and other parties such as the Daily News alleged that OpenAI and Microsoft used the news media journalism without permission in order to train the defendants AI models. These news media outlets claim that these AI tools can now produce parts of their articles almost word-for-word when prompted. They contend that the technology companies' AI violates copyright law. In March 2025, a federal court allowed the case to move forward. The judge ruled that the news media companies made a strong enough case that OpenAI and Microsoft may have copied and used news media works unlawfully (*New York Times Company v. Microsoft Corporation*, 2025).

Chegg, an educational technology company that provides study aids and other learning resources, filed an antitrust lawsuit against Google (*Chegg, Inc. v. Google*, 2025). According to Chegg, Google's AI-generated search republishes Chegg's educational content without its permission. By doing so, Google diverts traffic and harms Chegg's subscription-based business. Rather than relying on copyright law, the case challenges Google's practices under antitrust law. With this alternative legal claim, this case potentially sets a precedent for how generative AI companies use and negotiate access to publishers' content.

The legal interpretations of these cases portend the future of intellectual property rights of AI-generated works and works in which AI-generated or AI-trained approaches draw upon items or processes potentially covered under a filed intellectual property protection. These decisions shape ongoing academic research of AI technologies and their integration in higher education. For now, the law is grappling with these new challenges, highlighting the need for updated legal frameworks that consider the unique aspects of AI and its ability to independently create or utilize existing IP. For instance, Villasenor (2024) argues that IP law, particularly copyright, patent, and trade secret regimes, can and should play a central role in shaping how AI is developed, governed, and held accountable. He proposes reframing IP law as a regulatory tool that can promote public interest outcomes in AI systems. According to Villasenor (2024), IP law serves as an incentivized-based policy, but if strategically restructured, IP protections could be used also to enforce transparency, ensure fairness, and prevent unchecked corporate control over AI technologies. He illustrates how trade secret protections, while attractive to private firms, limit public scrutiny by shielding algorithms and training data from disclosure. As a result, these practices allow companies to control powerful technologies without democratic oversight. Yet, IP law could condition IP protections on a developer's willingness to provide public disclosures of how AI systems are trained and function, especially when such systems are used in high-impact domains like education. The law could also incentivize open-source models for certain datasets and algorithms. This policy is particularly valuable for those AI systems developed with public funding or deployed in essential services. Until greater legal clarity exists or new model regimes are adopted, IP challenges involving academic researchers are likely to continue.

Security and Controls

Federal Data Security

Academic researchers developing and using AI inevitably raises the legality around data security and protections associated with the processing and analysis of large data sets (Sun, 2014). This dependency on big data brings to the forefront numerous legal concerns in the realm of data security and data controls. This section highlights the interplay of key federal laws and security breaches within the context of AI design, development, implementation, and usage by academic researchers. Specifically, this section addresses data security from the applications of the Electronic Communications Privacy Act (ECPA, 1986) and its subparts, which include the Wiretap Act (1968), the Stored Communications Act (SCA, 1986), and the Clarifying Lawful Overseas Use of Data Act (CLOUD Act, 2018), as well as potentially other federal and state laws governing incidents of cybercrimes, such as the Computer Fraud and Abuse Act (1986; Losavio et al., 2022).

The ECPA, which includes the Wiretap Act and the SCA, provides an overarching legislative framework for the federal-level electronic communication privacy and security protections applicable to AI and the academic research context. However, the law has, at times, struggled to keep pace with rapid technological advancements. For instance, in a data access dispute associated with a search warrant, Microsoft, as the provider of web-based email services in a dispute, challenged a U.S. warrant seeking email disclosures when the email servers resided in Ireland. In reviewing this jurisdictional data access and rights matter under SCA, a federal circuit court ruled in favor of Microsoft, declining to extend the extraterritoriality of the law. According to a federal appellate court, data of interest and the SCA language refer to places, and data have a "discernible physical location" (Matter of Warrant to Search, 2016, p. 220, n28).

Not all judges agreed with that strict conception of data "location." In a subsequent review of the case, a federal judge commented on the outdated approach that judges might make in taking narrow interpretations of the law and not considering modern technology. Circuit Judge Dennis Jacobs explained, "Localizing the data in Ireland is not marginally more useful than thinking of

Santa Claus as a denizen of the North Pole. Problems arise if one over-thinks the problem, reifying the notional: Where in the world is a Bitcoin? Where in my DVR are the images and voices? Where are the snows of yesteryear?" (Matter of Warrant to Search, 2017, p. 62).

Later, Congress passed the CLOUD Act as an amendment to the ECPA, making the case moot by removing the territorial constraints and allowing data disclosures (*United States v. Microsoft Corp.*, 2018). Nonetheless, this case illustrates potentially applicable law and challenges associated with the law or its interpretation based on outdated anchored conceptions. In this instance, the case addressed the realities associated with globally distributed data storage and processing technologies, which are often used in academic research, drawing on AI development and applications.

International Export Controls

Similarly, oversight of international exchanges of academic research are governed by federal export controls. Federal laws, such as those enforced under the Export Administration Regulations and the International Traffic in Arms Regulations, are designed to prevent the dissemination of technology that could be used in ways that might threaten national security. For academic researchers, these regulations mean that certain AI technologies, particularly those with potential dual-use capabilities in military applications, could require licenses before they can be shared internationally or with foreign nationals. For instance, in 2021, the United States fined Princeton University for export violations based on controlled strains and recombinant animal pathogens that the university sent to foreign research facilities without proper protocols and clearances (Trager, 2021). This event demonstrates the required filings and restrictions as well as the possibility of errors. More recently, the U.S. Department of Defense awarded Princeton, along with an industry technology company, a project with the design and testing of lower energy microchips for AI processing, which inherently has a national security concern (Lyon, 2024).

Export controls as applied to higher education have mixed support because they tug at the ends between scientific openness and innovation to scientific protections and national security. For instance, Thomsen (2018) argued that export control measures have been previously counterproductive in information technology development, in terms of both their effectiveness and their impact, and those effects are likely to continue as applied to academic research of AI.

Thomsen's arguments are framed around specific instances where export controls aimed at AI-related technologies, like neural network circuits, did not prevent the technology's progress or adoption outside of the United States. Instead, he posited that the targeted controls may have inadvertently prompted further innovation through unregulated areas or other countries, for which he argued that export controls lead to counterproductivity.

Crandall (2023) was less inclined to dismantle legal restrictions, but she advocated for greater legal practitioner engagement in the operational level of applicable laws and policies. She posited that more practitioner insights would improve safeguards around safety and IP from foreign governments. Thus, she called for legal practitioners to navigate the challenges and conflicts in hopes of better defining responsive policies and laws. Similarly, Kop et al. (2024) illustrated how advanced technologies stall innovation and pose safety threats, which would negatively impact the nation and academic researchers, without a responsible innovation framework that would inform policymakers about quantum computing. The authors advocated for a more nuanced approach based off the Safeguarding, Engaging, and Advancing (SEA) framework as a way to balance technological innovation with ethical and social responsibilities. As the literature presents, policies and laws around AI and export controls require a significant interplay of scientific and societal principles to process.

Safety Measures and Anticorruption

The incorporation of AI into academic research introduces a spectrum of other potential or perceived safety violations surrounding concerns of conflicts of interest, bribery, and other unethical practices. These concerns become especially significant given the lucrative potential of AI technologies, which may tempt individuals to prioritize personal or corporate gains over scholarly integrity and objectivity. For instance, the federal Anti-Kickback Statute (1986), the False Claims Act (1863), and the Foreign Corrupt Practices Act (1977) provide a legal framework intended to prevent such misconduct by imposing severe penalties on those who attempt to manipulate research outcomes for improper benefit. Conflicts of interest may also arise when researchers receive undisclosed funding from AI corporations, potentially leading to biased research that could mislead public policy and commercial practices (Dukie et al., 2023). Although IRB protocols and university conflict of interest policies offer avenues to enforce ethical standards, left unchecked or without significant discussions around applications to AI academic research, external influences may stray academics and institutions from good judgment.

Furthermore, there are other external influences that may be rare yet have practical considerations, such as instances of bribery in the academic AI landscape, which can complicate the transparency and reliability of research findings. A notable criminal situation that highlights the broader implications of such ethical breaches involves Harvard University's department chair of chemistry and chemical biology (*United States v. Lieber*, 2022), where the head of the chemistry department was charged under the False Claims Act for failing to disclose a conflict of interest with a foreign government and company, allegedly influencing his research agenda and outputs. This case underscores the necessity for stringent enforcement of conflict of interest policies and regular audits to uphold the integrity of AI research. Universities and research institutions must adopt clear guidelines and training programs to ensure that all collaborations and sponsorships are fully transparent and do not compromise the ethical standards essential to scholarly work and public trust in AI advancements (see, e.g., Fleischman, 2024; University of California Presidential Working Group on AI, 2021).

Individual Safety and Harms

Fair Use or Infringement

Deepfakes, which is "deep learning" and "fake" representation, refers to AI-generated media (e.g., images, videos, or voice clones) designed to deceive. Within the AI context, this technological deception raises legal issues applicable to academic researchers, including effects onto IP rights and potential damages, such as reputational harm to universities and others (Sun, 2024a).

Typically, the use of AI to create deepfakes can lead to the manipulation of visual and audio content, such as manipulating endorsers of a product or service, creating perceptions of universities' brands and the integrity of their communication, or altering messages about research and advancing disinformation. For instance, AI-generated deepfakes may distort university logos or the likenesses of prominent faculty, thereby misleading audiences about actual research findings that feed into an agenda, unproven outcome, or counternarrative about consensus science. Such activities may trigger claims under federal copyright law, as the unauthorized removal or alteration of copyrighted material for training AI could be considered an infringement unless deemed a transformative work. In *Andersen v. Stability AI* (2023), the court posited that generative AI might not infringe on copyrights if the AI-generated output shows no substantial similarity to the original works, potentially qualifying it under the fair use doctrine. In other words, the originally copyrighted work had been transformed taking on a different expression, so it falls within a copyright exception, eligible for fair use.

The transformative use argument is unsettled, however, and this legal argument could shift if legislative changes specifically address implications of deepfakes aimed to deceive or harm, as some states have done. Although many state laws limit deepfake prohibitions to election fraud, revenge porn, and commercial value alterations, demonstrating that such manipulations cause reputational damage could be crucial in legal challenges in higher education (Sun, 2024a). For example, altered trademarks like brand names or logos through deepfakes have led to trademark infringement claims under the Lanham Act, based on the likelihood of confusion or deception regarding the source or endorsement of goods and services.

Moreover, deepfakes can infringe on the "right of publicity," which involves the unauthorized commercial use of an individual's name, image, and likeness.

Although generally treated as a tort, in some jurisdictions this is also viewed as an IP right. A pivotal case concerning this in academia was *National Collegiate Athletic Association v. Alston* (2021), where the U.S. Supreme Court found the NCAA's restrictions on college athletes benefiting from their own image and likeness to be anticompetitive under the Sherman Antitrust Act.

Further, a new federal crime may apply. In May 2025, the U.S. president signed the Tools to Address Known Exploitation by Immobilizing Technological Deepfakes On Websites and Networks Act ("TAKE IT DOWN" Act). The law requires online platforms to remove nonconsensual intimate images (NCII), and it made violation a federal crime. The law amends multiple federal provisions such as the Communications Act of 1934 (47 U.S.C. § 223) and the Federal Trade Commission Act (15 U.S.C. § 57a[a][1][B]) to outline legal requirements and support enforcement via the Federal Trade Commission (FTC). Significantly, the law extends the FTC's jurisdiction, under matters of NCII, to nonprofit organizations such as private universities, which are not usually covered by the FTC.

The TAKE IT DOWN Act provides platforms until May 19, 2026, to establish compliant notice-and-takedown systems, which must be in-place one year from enactment. Once implemented, platforms must remove reported NCII within 48 hours and make reasonable efforts to identify and remove identical copies. The Act includes a safe harbor provision, which protects platforms from liability for good-faith removal of content believed to constitute NCII, even if that determination proves incorrect. Criminal penalties range from fines and up to 2 years imprisonment for violations involving adults, with enhanced penalties of up to 3 years for violations involving minors. The Act specifically exempts from criminalization: disclosures for law enforcement purposes, disclosures for medical treatment, disclosures in judicial proceedings, and journalistic publication serving a legitimate public interest (47 U.S.C. § 223(h)(4)). For academic researchers, particularly those studying AI-generated content or conducting research that involves intimate imagery, the Act's criminal provisions and platform obligations establish several legal parameters to consider. For instance, research protocols involving NCII, even for legitimate academic purposes such as studying deepfake detection, must incorporate safeguards that include compliance with the Act's notice-and-removal requirements and criminal prohibitions.

Unfair and Deceptive Practices

The Federal Trade Commission Act also comes into play, protecting against unfair or deceptive practices that might involve AI-generated content, such as the dissemination of false endorsements or derogatory and false representations of university figures. Yet, a significant challenge in legal accountability arises; that is, identifying the liable party, whether it be the AI tool, its owner, the user, or the distributor. These concerns apply to state consumer protection laws. In essence, these considerations highlight the evolving legal landscape, as AI technologies, particularly deepfakes, become more integrated into academic research and communication. Universities must navigate these complex issues, ensuring they protect their IP and manage the potential legal risks associated with the use of sophisticated AI technologies in educational settings.

Products Liability

Similarly, products liability laws present another legal liability concern for academic research involved in the design, development, implementation, or use of AI systems. These laws typically hold manufacturers, distributors, and sellers accountable for product defects causing harm. As AI systems become more autonomous or human oversight is abdicated to the AI, there may be unforeseen consequences, including harm to users or third parties. Whether through design defects, manufacturing defects, or failure to warn, products liability law may hold academic researchers, who could participate in AI production at any critical stage, as a viable party to litigation, along with the university having a stake in the invention or product at issue in a lawsuit. Further, a good deal of proposed state legislation has included rather broad language holding organizations participating in the design, development, implementation, or use of AI systems as potentially liable for any harm these systems create. Notably, several states have considered bills offering protections to individuals based on any foreseeable impacts, whether intended or unintended, or uses of unsafe or ineffective AI systems (e.g., California, Connecticut, Louisiana, and Vermont). Yet, as the IP discussion above has noted, the IP rights and protections are not as clear, especially when the AI system is created by iterations of AI systems.

Conclusion

In late spring and summer of 2023, Congress sought to learn more about AI. Taking a perspective of developing guardrails but not inhibiting innovation, several bills were proposed, though none were passed. In October 2023, the Biden-Harris administration issued an executive order titled Safe, Secure, and Trustworthy Development and Use of Artificial Intelligence, which was intended to raise consciousness around responsible AI systems. Further, the Trump administration has issued two executive orders with messages of advancing AI (Exec. Order No. 14,179, 2025; Exec. Order No. 14,277, 2025). Paralyzed by the federal stalemate from the technological complexity, industry influences,[2] and legal territoriality, state houses have entertained their own bills, and some new laws have been enacted. Nonetheless, legal gaps and academic researcher directions remain open, potentially fostering confusion, conflating protections, and operating with ignorance.

While the laws present knowledge gaps about AI, which demonstrate that it is woefully behind the technology, the technology to manage the technology is also under-conceived or unavailable (potentially in progress and sometimes in beta mode for the blue team as defensive examiners or the red team as simulated attackers to test). The reality is that technological responses to AI systems such as ChatGPT, Gemini, Copilot, and Claude require a technological development of AI detectors. Similarly, quantum and block chain technology require more sophisticated chips and technology designs.

Further, the National Institute of Standards and Technology (NIST; 2024) draws attention to identifying, evaluating, and mitigating risks specific to generative AI, such as large language models and image-generation systems. It outlines 12 categories of risks unique to or exacerbated by generative AI. These risks range from confabulation and data privacy violations to IP infringement, environmental impacts, and misuse for chemical, biological, radiological, or nuclear threats. Although a voluntary approach, the NIST standards may influence how courts, policymakers, and university leaders consider policy construction and implementation. The guided approach may lead these policy bodies to contemplate principles of trustworthy, transparent, and lawful design and deployment of AI technologies.

In the end, a continuous interaction between technology and policy that focuses on a more systematical approach should be adopted. One way to accomplish this focus is taking a multiagency effort with industry, higher education, and interest groups at the table. For instance, with the Explainable AI (XAI) initiatives underway to offer clear AI explanations and recommendations, the policymaking and scientific communities are challenged with managing their interactive responsibilities so that innovation, law, and ethics are balanced in a manner that considers industry, higher education (especially the insights of academic researchers), and interest group perspectives that align with a national investment and strategy in AI and related emerging technologies.

Notes

1 While academic research offers a clear context and motivation around the growth of AI, Meredith Whittaker (2021) argues that today's most celebrated AI advances are not rooted in breakthrough science. Instead, a handful of tech companies drawing on massive, centralized corporate resources shaped AI development by controlling access to data, computing power, and funding. Framing this environment as an historical parallel to how the U.S. military shaped scientific research during the Cold War, Whittaker warns that tech firms similarly punish dissent and co-opt academic institutions. Given the power dominance, she calls for organized resistance from both academic and tech workers to protect independent research, permit critical inquiry, and allow democratic and public interests within this currently corporate controlled environment.

2 Oremus and Jiménez (2025) report on states along with some members of congress opposing federal halting of state AI laws. The federal legislation (H.R. 1, 2025) rationalizes its state-level AI prohibitions because they become a "patchwork" of different laws on AI, and they present a regulatory nightmare for U.S. tech firms.

References

Age Discrimination in Employment Act, 29 U.S.C. §§ 621 et seq. (1967).

Algorithmic Accountability Act, H.R. 5628. 118th Cong., 1st sess. (2023).

Ali, S., Abuhmed, T., El-Sappagh, S., Muhammad, K., Alonso-Moral, J. M., Confalonieri, R., Guidotti, R., Del Ser, J., Díaz-Rodríguez, N., & Herrera, F. (2023). Explainable artificial intelligence (XAI): What we know and what is left to attain trustworthy artificial intelligence. *Information Fusion, 99*, Article 101805. https://doi.org/https://doi.org/10.1016/j.inffus.2023.101805

Americans with Disabilities Act, 42 U.S.C. §§ 12101 et seq. (1990).

Andersen v. Stability AI, Civ. No. 3:23-cv-00201 (N.D. Cal. Jul. 19, 2023) (hearing).

Anti-Kickback Statute, 42 U.S.C. § 1320a-7b(b) (1986).

Bambauer, J. R., & Zarsky, T. Z. (2025). Fair-enough AI. *Yale Journal of Law & Technology, 27*(1), 1–52.

Bhatt, P., Sethi, A., Tasgaonkar, V., Shroff, J., Pendharkar, I., Desai, A., Sinha, P., Deshpande, A., Joshi, G., Rahate, A., Jain, P., Walambe, R., Kotecha, K., & Jain, N. K. (2023). Machine learning for cognitive behavioral analysis: Datasets, methods, paradigms, and research directions. *Brain Informatics, 10*(1), Article 18. https://doi.org/10.1186/s40708-023-00196-6

Buolamwini, J., & Gebru, T. (2018). Gender shades: Intersectional accuracy disparities in commercial gender classification. *Proceedings of Machine*

Learning Research, 81, 1–15. http://proceedings.mlr.press/v81/buolam-wini18a/buolamwini18a.pdf

Chegg, Inc. v. Google LLC, No. 5:25-cv-02489 (N.D. Cal. May 1, 2025), Complaint at 1-4.

Civil Rights Act, 42 U.S.C. § 2000e et seq. (1964).

Clarifying Lawful Overseas Use of Data Act, 18 U.S.C. § 2523 (2018).

Colorado Artificial Intelligence Act, Colo. Rev. Stat. § 6-1-1701 et seq. (2025).

Computer Fraud and Abuse Act, 18 U.S.C. § 1030 et seq. (1986).

Congressional Research Service. (2020). *Artificial intelligence and national security* (Report No. R45178). https://sgp.fas.org/crs/natsec/R45178.pdf

Conroy, G. (2024, September 20). Do AI models produce more original ideas than researchers? *Nature.* https://doi.org/10.1038/d41586-024-03070-5

Copeland, B. J. (Ed.). (2004). *The essential Turing: Seminal writings in computing, logic, philosophy, artificial intelligence, and artificial life.* Oxford University Press.

Crandall, C. (2023). Protecting federally-funded research and development: A primer on National Security Decision Directive 189 for legal practitioners. *Jurimetrics Journal, 63*(4), 325–354. https://www.americanbar.org/content/dam/aba/publications/Jurimetrics/summer-2023/protecting-federally-funded-research-and-development-a-primer-on-national-security-decision-directive-189-for-legal-practitioners.pdf

Daniel, P. T. K., Gee, E. G., Sun, J. C., & Pauken, P. D. (2025). *Law, policy, and higher education: Cases and materials* (2nd ed.). Carolina Academic Press.

Daniel, P. T. K., & Sun, J. C. (2022). Two cases, two different freedoms: Student free speech through social media and the rights of minoritized students. *Texas Journal on Civil Liberties and Civil Rights, 27(2), 179–215.*

Dinerstein v. Google, LLC, 73 F. 4th 502 (7th Cir. 2023).

Doe 1 v. GitHub, Inc., 672 F. Supp. 3d 837 (N.D. Cal. 2023).

Doe 1 v. GitHub, Inc., 672 F. Supp. 3d 837 (N.D. Cal. 2023).

Doe 1 v. GitHub, Inc., No. 24-7700 (9th Cir. Apr. 9, 2025), Brief for Appellants at 3.

Doe v. Massachusetts Institute of Technology, 46 F.4th 61 (1st Cir. 2022).

Duffy, K., & Fendorf, K. (2024). *In the age of AI, personal data security is national security.* Council on Foreign Relations. https://www.cfr.org/article/age-ai-personal-data-security-national-security

Dukie, A., McMullan, C. K., Pipes, S., & Wilder, A. (2023). *Sanctions, export controls, anti-bribery: The ever-changing landscape.* The National Association of College and University Attorneys.

Eaton, A. A., Saunders, J. F., Jacobson, R. K., & West, K. (2019). How gender and race stereotypes impact the advancement of scholars in STEM: Professors' biased evaluations of physics and biology post-doctoral candidates. *Sex Roles, 82*(3–4), 127–141. https://doi.org/10.1007/s11199-019-01052-w

Electronic Communications Privacy Act, 18 U.S.C. §§ 2510 et seq. (1986).

Equal Credit Opportunity Act, 15 U.S.C. §§ 1691 et seq. (1974).

Exec. Order No. 14,110, 88 Fed. Reg. 75191 (Oct. 30, 2023).

Exec. Order No. 14,179, 90 Fed. Reg. 8741 (Jan. 15, 2025).

Exec. Order No. 14,277, 90 Fed. Reg. 17519 (Apr. 23, 2025).

Fair Housing Act, 42 U.S.C. §§ 3601 et seq. (1968).

False Claims Act, 31 U.S.C. §§ 3729–3733 (1863).

Family Educational Rights and Privacy Act, 20 U.S.C. § 1232g (1974).

Federal Trade Commission Act, 15 U.S.C. §§ 41–58 (1914).

First Amendment, U.S. Const. amend. I.

Fleischman, T. (2024). Task force offers guidance to researchers on use of AI. *Cornell Chronicle.* https://news.cornell.edu/stories/2024/01/task-force-offers-guidance-researchers-use-ai

Foreign Corrupt Practices Act of 1977, *15 U.S.C. §§ 78dd-1* et seq. (2024).

Fourteenth Amendment, U.S. Const. amend. XIV.

Genetic Information Nondiscrimination Act, 42 U.S.C. §§ 2000ff et seq. (2008).

Gonzaga University v. Doe, 536 U.S. 273 (2002).

H.R. 1, 119th Cong. ("One Big Beautiful Bill Act") (2025) (as passed by House, May 22, 2025).

Illinois Artificial Intelligence Video Interview Act, 820 ILCS 42 (which also amends the Illinois Human Rights Act, 775 ILCS 5/2-101 and 775 ILCS 5/2-102 regarding employment discrimination).

Kleinberg, J., Ludwig, J., Mullainathan, S., & Sunstein, C. R. (2018). Discrimination in the age of algorithms. *Journal of Legal Analysis, 10,* 113–174. https://doi.org/10.1093/jla/laz001

Kop, M., Aboy, M., De Jong, E., Gasser, U., Minssen, T., Cohen, I. G., Brongersma, M., Quintel, T., Floridi, L., & Laflamme, R. (2024). Towards responsible quantum technology: Safeguarding, engaging and advancing quantum R&D. *UC Law Science and Technology Journal, 15*(1), 63–94. https://doi.org/10.48550/arXiv.2303.16671

Losavio, M. M., Sun, J. C., Kerrick, S. A., Elmaghraby, A. S., Purdy, C., & Johnson, C. (2022, March 17–18). Integrating democratic cybersecurity: Empowerment of traditional law enforcement and democratic public safety. In R. P. Griffin, U. Tatar, & B. Yankson (Eds.), *17th international yearbook on cyber warfare and security* (pp. 155–165). Academic Conferences International. https://doi.org/10.34190/iccws.17.1.37

Lyon, S. (2024). *New chip built for AI workloads attracts $18M in government support.* Princeton University. https://www.princeton.edu/news/2024/03/06/new-chip-built-ai-workloads-attracts-18m-government-funding-revolutionary-tech

Maryland Use of Facial Recognition Services Prohibited, Consent by Applicant, Md. Code, Lab. & Empl. § 3-717 (2025).

Maryland State Finance and Procurement Article, Md. Code, State Fin. & Proc. § 3.5-801 et seq. (2025).

Matter of Warrant to Search a Certain E-Mail Account Controlled and Maintained by Microsoft Corporation, 829 F.3d 197 (2d Cir. 2016).

Matter of Warrant to Search a Certain E-Mail Account Controlled and Maintained by Microsoft Corporation, 855 F.3d 53 (2d Cir. 2017) (Jacobs, J., dissenting).

McCarthy, J., Minsky, M. L., Rochester, N., & Shannon, C. E. (1955). *A proposal for the Dartmouth summer research project on artificial intelligence.* https://www-formal.stanford.edu/jmc/history/dartmouth/dartmouth.html

Murdoch, B. (2021). Privacy and artificial intelligence: Challenges for protecting health information in a new era. *BMC Medical Ethics*, *22*, Article 122. https://doi.org/10.1186/s12910-021-00687-3

Naruto v. Slater, 888 F.3d 418 (9th Cir. 2018).

National Collegiate Athletic Association v. Alston, 594 U.S. 20 (2021).

National Institute of Standards and Technology. (2024). *Artificial intelligence risk management framework: Generative artificial intelligence profile* (NIST AI 600-1). U.S. Department of Commerce. https://doi.org/10.6028/NIST.AI.600-1

New York Times Company v. Microsoft Corporation, Civ. Nos. 23-cv-11195 (SHS), 24-cv-3285 (SHS), 24-cv-4872 (SHS) (S.D.N.Y. Apr. 4, 2025).

Obermeyer, Z., Powers, B., Vogeli, C., & Mullainathan, S. (2019). Dissecting racial bias in an algorithm used to manage the health of populations. *Science*, *366*(6464), 447–453. https://doi.org/10.1126/science.aax2342

Oremus, W., & Jiménez, A. (2025, June 3). State lawmakers to Congress: Don't stop us from regulating AI. *Washington Post*. https://www.washingtonpost.com/politics/2025/06/03/ai-regulation-moratorium-state-lawmakers-letter/

Osborn v. Board of Regents of the University of Wisconsin System, 647 N.W.2d 158 (Wisc. 2002).

Pregnancy Discrimination Act, 42 U.S.C. § 2000e(k) (1978).

Rehabilitation Act, 29 U.S.C. § 794 (1973)

Richter, T., Fishbain, B., Richter-Levin, G., & Okon-Singer, H. (2021). Machine learning-based behavioral diagnostic tools for depression: Advances, challenges, and future directions. *Journal of Personalized Medicine*, *11*(10), 957–974. https://doi.org/10.3390/jpm11100957

Rouhiainen, L. (2019, October 14). How AI and data could personalize higher education. *Harvard Business Review*. https://hbr.org/2019/10/how-ai-and-data-could-personalize-higher-education

Sherman Antitrust Act, **15 U.S.C. §§ 1–7 (1890).**

Stanford University, Human-Centered Artificial Intelligence. (2025). Artificial intelligence index report 2025. https://hai.stanford.edu/ai-index/2025-ai-index-report

Stored Communications Act, 18 U.S.C. §§ 2701–2712 (1986).

Sun, J. C. (2014). Legal issues associated with big data in higher education: Ethical considerations and cautionary tales. In J. E. Lane (Ed.), *Building a smarter university: Big data, innovation, and ingenuity* (pp. 27–56). State University of New York Press.

Sun, J. C. (2023). Gaps, guesswork, and ghosts lurking in technology integration: Laws and policies applicable to student privacy. *British Journal of Educational Technology, 54*(6), 1604–1618. https://doi.org/10.1111/bjet.13379

Sun, J. C. (2024a). Generative creations, code, and data: How intellectual property rights over ownership, use, and image apply to higher education. In X. Lin, R. Y. Chan, S. Sharma, & K. Bista (Eds.), *ChatGPT and global higher education: Using artificial intelligence in teaching and learning* (pp. 159–178). STAR Scholars Press.

Sun, J. C. (2024b, March 4–5). *Identity bans: Legalized restrictions on college learning and development* [Keynote speech]. Texas Higher Education Law Conference, Denton, TX, United States.

Sun, J. C. (2024c, April 16). *Democratized learning: Engagement of the professor, learner, and the content* [Keynote speech]. Spotlight on Learning Conference, Athens, OH, United States.

Sun, J. C., & Baez, B. (2009). *Intellectual property in the information age: Knowledge as commodity & its legal implications for higher education.* Jossey Bass. https://doi.org/10.1002/aehe.3404

Sun, J. C., & Bruton, C. R. (2023, October 25–28). *Avoiding non-artificial discrimination claims from college students: AI and higher education* [Paper presentation]. Education Law Association 69th Annual Meeting, Reno, NV, United States.

Sun, J. C., & Daniel, P. T. K. (2023, April 13–16). *Policy bans on race and gender identity: A critical and liberating policy analysis* [Paper presentation]. Annual Meeting of the American Educational Research Association, Chicago, IL, United States.

Sun, J. C., & Pratt, T. L. (2024, June 25). *Processing (AI language tools), plug-ins, and privacy* [Poster presentation]. Army University Learning Symposium, Leavenworth, KS, United States.

Thaler v. Vidal, 43 F.4th 1207 (Fed. Cir. 2022), cert. denied 143 S. Ct. 1783 (2023).

Thomsen, R. C., II. (2018). Artificial intelligence and export controls: Conceivable, but counterproductive? *Journal of Internet Law, 22*(5), 1; 15–24. https://t-b.com/wp-content/uploads/2019/01/AI-and-Export-Controls-Journal-of-Internet-Law-Article.pdf

Thomson Reuters Enterprise Center GMBH v. Ross Intelligence, 765 F. Supp. 3d 382 (D. Del. 2025).

Thomson Reuters Enterprise Center GMBH v. Ross Intelligence, No. 1:20-cv-613-SB, 2025 WL 1488015 (D. Del. May 23, 2025) (certified appeal granted).

Title IX of the Education Amendments of 1972, 20 U.S.C. §§ 1681 et seq. (1972).

Tools to Address Known Exploitation by Immobilizing Technological Deep-fakes on Websites and Networks Act (TAKE IT DOWN Act), amending Communications Act of 1934, 47 U.S.C. § 223 et. seq. and Federal Trade Commission Act, 15 U.S.C. § 57a(a)(1)(B) (2025).

Trager, R. (2021, March 1). Princeton fined for export violations involving controlled pathogens. *Chemistry World*. https://www.chemistryworld.com/news/princeton-fined-for-export-violations-involving-controlled-pathogens/4013318.article

Tremblay v. OpenAI, Inc., Civ. Case Nos. 23-cv-03223-AMO, 23-cv-03416-AMO (N.D. Cal. 2024).

Uniformed Services Employment and Reemployment Rights Act, 38 U.S.C. §§ 4301 et seq. (1994).

United States v. Lieber, 626 F. Supp. 3d 310 (D. Mass. 2022).

United States v. Miami University, 294 F.3d 797 (6th Cir. 2002).

United States v. Microsoft Corp., 138 S. Ct. (2018).

University of California Presidential Working Group on AI. (2021). *Responsible artificial intelligence: Recommendations to guide the University of California's artificial intelligence strategy*. University of California. https://www.ucop.edu/ethics-compliance-audit-services/compliance/uc-ai-working-group-final-report.pdf

Villasenor, J. (2024). Artificial intelligence, trade secrets, and the challenge of transparency. *North Carolina Journal of Law & Technology*, *25*(3), 495–536.

White, J. (2023, December 22). How strangers got my email address from ChatGPT's model. *New York Times*. https://www.nytimes.com/interactive/2023/12/22/technology/openai-chatgpt-privacy-exploit.html

Whittaker, M. (2021). The steep cost of capture. *Interactions*, *28*(6), 50–55. https://doi.org/10.1145/3488666

Wiretap Act, 18 U.S.C. §§ 2510-2522 (1968).

Zeide, E. (2016). Student privacy principles for the age of big data: Moving beyond FERPA and FIPPS. *Drexel Law Review*, *8*(2), 339–394.

Zhu, K. (2023, August 3). *The state of state AI laws: 2023*. Electronic Privacy Information Center. https://epic.org/the-state-of-state-ai-laws-2023/

3

The Impact of Artificial Intelligence on Higher Education

Opportunity, Risk, and Responsible Governance

Melissa M. Carleton and Jeffrey Knight

Artificial Intelligence (AI) isn't new, and certainly not new on the college campus, but something about the introduction of generative AI (GAI) at this speed and scale *feels* different. Different for students, who are suddenly dealing with myriad ways to either enhance learning or find shortcuts to do the same (Koczera & Pushard, 2023). Different for faculty, who are not only trying to stay a step ahead of students but also managing GAI as it impacts their livelihood (see, e.g., Pettinato Oltz, 2023). And different for campus leaders, who are tasked with thoughtfully implementing GAI systems while simultaneously developing policies to harness its benefits and mitigate its risks (Muscanell & Robert, 2023).

This round of AI, the one that now brings GAI, is nothing short of a transformation in higher education. From intelligent tutoring systems to predictive analytics, AI-powered tools have begun permeating virtually every aspect of the campus experience and university operations (Trumbore, 2023). While AI holds immense potential to improve learning, research, and institutional efficiency, integrating these rapidly advancing technologies into the academic context also raises profound ethical, legal, and social implications. As AI capabilities approach or exceed human intelligence in certain areas, difficult questions arise around data privacy, algorithmic bias, academic integrity, liability, and the role of educators in general. Institutions of higher education are almost always bastions of technological progressivism.[1] AI and GAI are here to stay.[2] As a result, institutions must respond to both AI's possibilities and its perils through purposeful governance, oversight, and an eagerness to understand and address how this automation amplifies inequities and bias.

Our intent is to explore the current and potential future applications of AI across campus through a legal and risk-identification lens. After all, we're practicing lawyers. However, in so doing, we will endeavor to highlight the deeply human impact that AI and GAI bring to the table because the human issues — whose job is impacted, which students are admitted and which are not, whether a student gained an unfair advantage in the classroom — have proven to be as central to our discussions with clients as any legal issue. Along the way we'll explore some use cases and identify the attendant risks, and we'll gently propose a framework for campus leaders to consider as AI and GAI become further enmeshed in the academic landscape.

The Opportunities and Risks of AI

It is difficult to properly articulate the risks, much less liability, that AI and GAI pose on the college campus without also exploring the opportunities they bring. Though in writing this article we are limited to using words, we often counsel leaders to spend time physically exploring space on their campus in order to appreciate AI integrations and their associated risks and rewards. We'll invite the reader to do the same.

First, look to the academic buildings. Intelligent tutoring systems have the potential to revolutionize academic support by providing personalized and adaptive instruction tailored to each student's strengths, weaknesses, and pacing (Trumbore, 2023). Such a model can increase engagement, comprehension, and retention, especially for challenging material. However, improperly designed systems could disadvantage or even exclude students with certain disabilities (McMurtrie, 2023).

Now turn to admissions, and the significant resources that support recruitment and engagement. Chatbots and virtual assistants are creating new channels for delivering information and interacting with students (Viano, 2023). These chatbots are no longer limited to simple logic or virtual flowcharts. Now they can also handle queries about registration and financial aid, keeping prospective students engaged and freeing up human staff capacity. However, chatbots are also a source of significant risks — risks of inaccurate, or even potentially dangerous, information (see Gold & Fischer, 2023, describing "injection attacks"); risks of cold or flippant responses to calls for help (Metz, 2023). Chatbots need to be trained, tested, and updated regularly. And, as their deployment becomes more widespread, they need to be accompanied by the type of transparency that is meaningful and practical to the end user. A simple "powered by ChatGPT" can leave end users — students or their families — feeling frustrated or, worse, misled. After all, hallucinations — plausible but false responses — are a significant concern (IBM, n.d.-a).

Turn now toward residence halls, one of the most hallowed but riskiest ventures on campus per capita. We already know that GAI has taken campus by storm. While it has been slowly increasing its presence in our day-to-day lives (auto-completion of emails and text messages, for example), easily available GAI systems can now help automate basic writing tasks and produce solid drafts. Now, the enterprising student is going to understand the significant need to write and rewrite GAI-produced content. But not every student will — some are going to submit as-is (Barnett, 2023). Can this be stopped? Not likely and certainly not easily. Even GAI-powered "plagiarism detectors" are considerably fallible (Epstein-Gross, 2023). So, how does the campus leader work to ensure academic integrity in an age where GAI tools are producing content in droves? Unfortunately, there is no one-size-fits-all method, which we'll explore in more detail below.

Now zoom in. Look at the building entrances and hallways. Notice the robust and interconnected system of cameras and software that powers them, designed with the hope of 24/7 security in mind. They watch, record, and inform. But what happens when those cameras have the ability to know, or suggest? For instance, what if your visitor management system is matching guests — or anyone — against databases of known sex offenders (Raptor Technologies, n.d.)? What happens when a match is suggested? Expanded monitoring brings expanded risk — risk of a mismatch or, worse, risk of harm to someone who is mismatched. And what of the risk of reliance on such technology when it fails to identify a predator? While camera systems with face recognition, behavioral analysis, and anomaly detection can help quickly identify threats, these AI tools rely on collecting sensitive personal information that could be misused, be deep-faked, or expose the university to lawsuits if not governed properly.

Before turning to the legal issues and how those issues dovetail with known use cases, the opportunities and risks can be summarized as follows: AI offers automation potential to streamline processes, reduce costs, and improve decision-making. AI can generate data analytics to inform resource allocation, detect financial risks, and increase operational efficiency. However, AI can over-automate. Its decision-making can be flawed and it can deskill and demoralize a workforce. Responsible campus governance entails understanding these risks and opportunities at a molecular level.

Key Legal Issues

The integration of AI, particularly GAI, systems into higher education raises myriad legal challenges for campus leaders. As campuses increasingly utilize AI in areas like personalized learning platforms, predictive analytics, automated administrative processes, and generative content creation, thorny issues around data privacy, discrimination, liability, accessibility, and copyright infringement emerge. Rather than a survey of each of the above, we dig into two — student data privacy and the potential for discrimination and bias — because the approach to these two may inform the approach to many other issues. At bottom, however, is the ever-present risk that the failure to implement policies and protocols addressing these AI-amplified risks may leave institutions vulnerable to lawsuits, regulatory actions, and reputational damages (Steiger & Horres, 2022).

Student Data Privacy

Student data privacy protections are driven in large part by the 1974 Family Educational Privacy Rights Act (FERPA), a 1970s-era law designed to protect "education records" at a time when such records were maintained in filing cabinets. Its application to anything post–internet age is fraught, at best. Nevertheless, it's the law.

FERPA, a sector-specific privacy statute, does essentially two things. First, it allows for access and amendment rights. Students (or parents, until the student turns 18 or enters postsecondary study) may inspect, copy, and seek correction of "education records." Second, it offers some minimally complex disclosure controls. Personally identifiable information (PII) from those records cannot be disclosed without prior written consent unless a regulatory exception applies. Everything else — data security, algorithmic fairness, de-identification standards, vendor accountability — is not in the statute. Those guardrails must be supplied by contract, institutional policy, or other laws.

In the digital age, student information is often stored and managed through various educational technologies, which can pose significant privacy risks. These technologies often collect vast amounts of data, some of which may not (read: almost certainly not) be adequately protected under FERPA's current provisions (Rhoades, 2021). We see this most frequently with EdTech- and school-issued devices, and now we're seeing it with AI and GAI technological advancements.

Put differently, and somewhat plainly, if a school uploads homework files, learning management system discussion threads, or advising notes (i.e., "education records") to fine-tune a large language model, that transfer is a FERPA disclosure. The only viable path is the school official exception, coupled with a contract that imposes direct control and bars secondary uses.

Use Case: AI and the Privacy of Student Mental Health Records

Perhaps the most sensitive personal information that can be collected are our innermost thoughts — not just the conscious dialogue we may be able to articulate, but the unconscious behaviors and mannerisms that may become clues to our mental health. It is exactly this information that has begun to create a new foundation for diagnosing and treating depression, anxiety, and other issues that college students face, raising new questions about how to protect one's privacy in the meantime.

It is no secret that the pandemic accelerated an already developing pattern of mental health concerns among traditional college aged students. The pandemic not only created barriers to socializing in the form of lockdowns, but it also created barriers to receiving therapy, which then exacerbated the underlying issues. Institutions of higher education across the country turned to teletherapy services to assist students off campus, but even these more flexible services were apparently not enough to tamp down the burgeoning crisis (Carrasco, 2021).

The increase in patients to be served, when coupled with a decrease in mental health providers to serve them, created an urgent need for additional, and perhaps more creative, service delivery models. Students were given more access to online screening to assist them in determining whether services were needed. Access to self-help resources — and apps — proliferated. Teletherapy services began to be offered not only through real-time video services but also via text message (O'Hara, 2019). Consistent with the world around, these services began to be delivered in a "wherever, whenever" model that could meet patients in the midst of crisis, or simply fit their busy schedules.

However, even this rapid development was not enough. While campuses tried to meet their students where they were and provide services as needed, student affairs professionals found themselves meeting regularly to discuss the increasing number of students displaying concerning behaviors and how to help avert their crises and help them continue to engage in the campus community at large. The challenge became to identify students sooner, before they were in crisis, to get services at the earliest possible point to maximize success.

Technology attempted to deliver in the form of two methods. First, teletherapy chatbots came to the fore. Second, smartphone behavioral monitoring applications were developed to act as advanced warning systems. Campuses turning to either of these scenarios should consider not just the efficacy of the services, which is still very much under study, but also the considerable privacy implications. These implications are addressed below.

Teletherapy Chatbots. A chatbot is a computer program, typically embedded in a website or phone application, that is designed to interface with a user on a particular topic (IBM, n.d.-b). It recognizes and can respond to certain questions in a conversational format. While often used in a custom service capacity to provide basic information, chatbots are increasingly used to connect individuals to mental health resources. For example, an application called Woebot can assist individuals with exploring current feelings, tracking, and journaling, and connecting them to mindfulness and other tools to assist them with their mental state as they are experiencing it, instead of during a preset appointment (Woebot Health, 2021).

As GAI becomes more sophisticated, it creates the opportunity for more complex interactions, in real time, using natural language — which in turn creates the opportunity for more data, and more thoughts, to be collected. Where does this user information go, and what protects it from disclosure?

Institutions of higher education that use such chatbots will want to ensure that, as with any data collection, users are given information about the nature of the data that will be collected, the purpose for which the data will be collected, whether the data will be stored by the institution (perhaps linked to the student's medical or mental health records), and, importantly, whether the institution will be monitoring the results. For example, if a student discloses suicidal ideation, will the institution receive information necessary to perform a wellness check? If a student discloses depression due to a sexual assault, will information be provided to the Title IX coordinator to do intake and offer supportive measures?

Often, the answer with chatbots is no. While the chatbot might provide resources in these situations, the dialogue is not routinely monitored by the institution (Huang, 2023; Viano, 2023). This increases the privacy for the student and limits potential breaches of the information, but also can decrease the ability of the institution to intervene in the midst of a crisis. If that is the case, students may be more inclined to interact with the chatbot, which may ultimately mean that more individuals access services.

Academic Chatbots. The authors are also aware of the growing prevalence of chatbots outside of the health or telehealth space. Indeed, according to the 2025 EDUCAUSE AI Landscape Study: Into the Digital AI Divide, "37% of colleges and universities provide institution-wide licenses for chatbots, and 14% have their own homegrown bots." (Hennick, 2025). In other words, it certainly appears as if chatbots — telehealth or otherwise — have crossed the "early adopter" chasm, meaning for these institutions, the FERPA, accessibility, and bias questions (discussed below) are live, operational issues, and not future tech-speculation. But a nontrivial 14% are developing in-house, meaning they are directly inheriting the custody of their usage logs and their attendant FERPA requirements, IP ownership issues, and workforce competence and training, as well as patching, pen-testing, and model-drift monitoring responsibilities.

Returning to FERPA, imagine a scenario where a student is able to ask a chatbot — whether licensed or developed in-house — why they lost 7 points on their latest quiz. Such an innocuous prompt triggers three immediately paramount data flows, each with its own FERPA considerations. First, the chatbot may only be able to answer if it can reach into the appropriate information system to understand the point deduction. The moment it does so, presuming a third party operates the model, there is a FERPA disclosure. Second, the chatbot responds, saying, perhaps, that points were lost because of an imprecise definition on the quiz. Now, this response, generated by AI, may not be an education record, but what happens when the professor copies it or otherwise maintains it in their records? Third, what happens to the log of this interaction? Where is it maintained and, if it is outside of the school, by whom is it maintained and according to what standard?

Because FERPA never anticipated conversational AI, compliance has become contractual craftsmanship plus risk engineering. Until SPPO — or Congress — writes AI-specific regulations, the practical safeguard is to force the vendor into the role FERPA already understands: a tightly controlled "school official," watched as closely as any human with similar access.

Digital Phenotyping. If a chatbot is the overt data collection regarding mental health, then digital phenotyping is its latent opposite. Digital phenotyping apps work to collect data about smartphone use in the background, tracking phone use, website visits, scrolling, language patterns, and other information (Marks, 2021). That data is then run through various algorithms to determine whether the user's risk is higher for various mental health concerns, such as depression or suicidal ideation. The monitoring system can then notify campus officials, or others, of developing and immediate concerns. Consent is obviously key to this system, as tracking this information without consent would seriously undermine any commitment to data transparency (Marks, 2021, p. 1053).

This idea is a powerful way to address mental health matters even before they are recognized by the individuals themselves. But taking the subconscious and giving it a name can be intrusive, and more importantly, it can be incorrect. AI is only as good as its programming and the data that it uses for analysis, and technology is not yet at a point where the determinations are fail-safe. Students may be over-identified as concerning, which raises its own set of problems, or under-identified, which could be catastrophic, especially if the student is relying on the monitoring program to act as their cry for help.

Further, because the technology is changing, the possession of this data could form the basis of powerful understanding regarding a student's inner psyche that could be used or misused for other purposes. For example, can data predict when another is about to commit a crime, and if so, what is the appropriate intervention? Those campuses that choose to participate in digital phenotyping gather a broad data set that may be too powerful to justify in the end, and that can actually change the nature of the institution's legal obligations to the students themselves.

Use Case: Student Surveillance and Exam Taking

Old-fashioned exam-taking surveillance typically involved a bored proctor at the front of a room of well-spaced, quietly working students. When the pandemic occurred, suddenly "well-spaced" could not be spaced far enough, and many institutions began looking at virtual proctoring to ensure that students were not cheating (Ryznar, 2023). The practice quickly spread, with many bar examinations and other professional examinations being offered in an at-home setting.

Taking an exam through a virtual proctoring service means complying with a list of requirements that vary based on the institution (Ryznar, 2023). The computer in use must have a camera, which must be trained on the exam taker at all times. It is common to request that the examination be taken on a clean desk where no books are within reach, and often the exam taker is required to use their camera to show the entirety of the workspace or room to identify any potential security concerns. Anything more than one monitor is often prohibited, with any extra monitors needing to be disconnected or potentially even removed from the desktop.

Traditional webcams simply record. Modern proctoring suites layer GAI vision models that interpret the feed — flagging "multiple faces," estimating gaze direction, even generating written narratives of what the student appears to be doing and "flags" certain behaviors (Ryznar, 2023). Some flags may result in a live proctor connecting with the exam taker to do a visual scan of the desk space while the exam is ongoing (Swaak, 2022).[3] In other cases, exam takers may not know they have been "flagged" until after the exam, leading to additional test anxiety that exam takers could suddenly fail for some unknown microbehavior.

Students taking exams through virtual proctors have raised concerns about constitutional violations. For example, in one recent case, a student of a public institution was required to show the proctor the room he was sitting in — his bedroom — before he was permitted to take an exam (*Ogletree v. Cleveland State Univ.*, 2022). In this case, the student had no other options to take his examination except through a virtual proctor in the privacy of his home. The court held that the student had a reasonable expectation of privacy in his own bedroom and that the room scan constituted a "search" that violated the student's privacy (p. 614). The court issued an injunction against requiring any room scan in connection with an exam without either offering a reasonable alternative or without receiving the student's express consent. In the wake of the decision, public institutions began ensuring that alternative testing locations were available that did not invoke a reasonable expectation of privacy while still allowing students to take a test in their private space, provided they were willing to consent to the room scan. Others have encouraged the development of examinations that do not require proctoring at all.

Of course, students are not just on camera during their exams these days. Rarely is a campus not peppered with all manner of surveillance, including cameras, card swipes, and even biometric scanning devices (Hattersley, 2022). When investigating conduct cases, administrators can track students across campus, often to the minute, to compile detailed timelines of a night in question. Even this, however, is not as robust as the technology allows. Smartphone data can help search engines estimate how many people are on a particular road, in a particular area, or at a particular restaurant to assist searchers in determining the best routes to take or places to go. That data could be harvested to give campus officials even more information, to the point of adjusting staffing levels for certain public points of contact during certain times of the day or sending security to monitor unanticipated crowds or handle traffic accidents on campus. Individual data could be gathered to assist students who have been directed to have "no contact" to move apart from each other when they get close, and to track student movement for a period of time after such alerts are issued.

Do these types of surveillance also raise concerns regarding the Fourth Amendment? Where data is not personally identifiable and is used to identify general trends, perhaps not. But in cases where an individual student can be identified and monitored, the question is typically whether the student has a "reasonable expectation of privacy" in the situation, in which case the right to be free from unreasonable search and seizure will apply. Reasonable is, of course, in the eye of the beholder, and it is a moving target in these days where regular privacy intrusions are more common than ever before. Generally speaking, publicly observable locations are less likely to have such a reasonable expectation of privacy than are movements in a more private space, such as one's one home or a public restroom (Electronic Privacy Information Center, n.d.).

Federal law requires that surveillance footage not include audio unless at least one person in the conversation consents to being recorded; state laws may be even more restrictive and require all parties to the conversation to consent to the recording (Reporters Committee for Freedom of the Press, n.d.). This generally protects the substance of student conversations as they move through campus, at least from recording. But where it is legal to capture other data, is it intrusive? As new methods for capturing and analyzing data develop, how are campuses communicating to students about this data collection and use?

Discrimination and Bias

Beyond student data privacy, there are considerable risks around AI-enabled bias and discrimination against protected classes. Though perhaps unintentional, biases encoded in training data or algorithms may lead AI to disproportionately harm minorities, women, students with disabilities, and other marginalized groups (Lazaro, 2022). Though, again, there is no shortage of examples to draw upon, we'll focus on a few that pertain to enrollment.

AI and GAI introduce new capabilities for institutions to enhance and personalize their student recruitment (Abdous, 2023; McCarty Carino, 2023). As noted previously, chatbots with natural language processing can engage prospective applicants, answering common (and uncommon) questions and guiding them through the admissions process 24/7 (see, e.g., Kelly, 2022). Before even working with a prospective student, institutions can use AI and GAI to better target marketing to individual interests based on analysis of online behavior, texts, and social media profiles. GAI could even create customized video pitches using images and voices tailored to each applicant (see, e.g., Moody, 2023).

While these innovations can boost engagement and enrollment numbers, risks abound. Targeting could exclude underrepresented groups if historical biases are baked into algorithms — and, given that enrollment data is, in part, driven by historical information, the risk is considerable. Put differently, as of this writing, the authors are unaware of an automated system that is reliably being used to weed out and adjust for bias in its dataset. Though it's a glib conclusion, and perhaps one that will soon be rectified, if an AI system is trained on data from a historically and predominantly white institution, it almost certainly will not effectively serve students from diverse backgrounds without significant intervention.

But it's not enough to know that this can occur. The most technologically progressive (and risk-avoidant) institutions will know how to spot whether historical biases are present in the algorithms that they use in their recruitment and enrollment efforts (Walch, 2021; Walker, 2018). If they use algorithms developed in-house, they will have coders who can work to ensure that biases are mitigated. If they use third parties with AI/GAI tools, they will know the questions to ask and the answers to strive for.

Buying Down Risk Through Responsible Campus AI Governance

Realizing AI's benefits in higher education while navigating its multifaceted risks requires holistic governance frameworks. These frameworks should balance enabling innovation with precaution, codifying AI ethics institutionally, and promoting responsible design, development, and deployment through collaborative oversight. Easier said than done.

We presume that most campus leaders who read the previous paragraph likely balked at the ease with which we suggested a process that presumes all or most stakeholders are paddling in the same direction, or even paddling at all. To get to the point where an AI governance framework is even being considered likely takes a herculean effort that the authors have frequently observed but can rarely break into its component parts.

Nevertheless, while we leave the nitty gritty (read: mission critical) to the on-campus leaders, we suggest considering the following principles in any AI governance model:

> *Transparency*: Campus stakeholders should understand an AI system's capabilities, limitations, data sources, and logic. Though it is occasionally still fashionable for campus leaders to plead ignorance with technology, it cannot be the case with AI. Speaking while on mute during a Zoom call is one thing. Using a chatbot to gather data hand-over-fist from incoming students is another entirely.
>
> *Human Oversight*: Critical decisions affecting people's lives require human judgment. AI assists but does not replace human discretion. In our line of work we say "AI will not replace lawyers. Lawyers who use AI will replace lawyers who do not. And lawyers who use AI well will replace those who use it to check a box." The same may be said of campus leaders.
>
> *Accountability*: Mechanisms must exist to address inappropriate or harmful AI uses. Ethical lapses or harms merit appropriate consequences through clear policies. These mechanisms must not be drawn entirely from the boilerplate that can be found online with a simple search. Rather, they must match your institution's ethic of care. What fits the large research university will not fit the small liberal arts college — though the risks of an ill-fitting policy are similar with both.
>
> *Purpose Limitations*: Restrain AI systems to uses consistent with your mission and your ethic of care. Avoid uses that exceed your comfort (and your applicable liability policies). When in doubt, know that use cases that involve tracking or surveilling students, or those that involve a failure of complete transparency, are likely those that will be scrutinized the closest.
>
> *Equity and Inclusion*: Whether you are using in-house systems or those provided by a vendor, they must be carefully evaluated for biases, with continuous audits on AI outputs and outcomes. As a corollary, they must be evaluated by those who understand what they are looking for.

One area worthy of particular exploration is the development and empowerment of an AI governance committee, comprising campus leaders, students, faculty, and legal/compliance officers[4] — a multidisciplinary group that could be empowered to propose campuswide AI policies, review proposals for AI projects and systems, perform risk-benefit analyses, and govern or halt deployment of high-risk AI applications. An Institutional Research Board, of sorts, with a broader mandate.

Building this out, the authors are mindful of the ever-present considerations of shared governance. Though the task of harnessing AI on campus is lofty, there is no reason to deviate from those considerations. And, in many ways, an AI governance committee that is mindful of the principles of shared governance could be positioned for long-term success, and perhaps insulated from the tendency to act, or react, in a knee-jerk manner. Faculty would maintain primary responsibility over academic matters (e.g., the integration of AI in the classroom and appropriate use for assignments), administrators would maintain authority over business operations (e.g., the whole-of-campus approach to AI and AI-powered solutions in recruitment, retention, the disbursement of financial aid), and staff and students would have a voice on matters that impact them (e.g., for staff in particular, how the automation of certain tasks impacts their day-to-day workload).

A Risk-Based Campus AI Governance Framework

Continuing with the theme started in the previous section — a framework for AI governance — we turn finally to our gentle suggestion that any framework be tied to a risk-based approach, à la what the European Parliament is working through on a grand scale. For readers that aren't Parliament watchers, the European Union's Artificial Intelligence Act entered into force as of August 1, 2024, and certain provisions regarding "unacceptable-risk" AI systems were enforceable as of early 2025. Other provisions, including those that apply to "high-risk" AI systems, will become enforceable in 2026 (see European Commission, 2024, AI Act; European Parliament, 2023). The AI Act, at its conceptual core, is straightforward: different rules for different levels of risk. AI technologies will be classified according to the level of risk they pose to the health, safety, or fundamental rights of a person. At present, the risk tiers include unacceptable, high, and limited/minimal.

Unacceptable-risk AI systems include cognitive behavioral manipulation of people or specific vulnerable groups, like children (European Parliament, 2023). Think voice-activated toys that encourage dangerous behavior. Other unacceptable-risk AI systems include those that involve social scoring and real-time and remote biometric identification systems.

High-risk AI systems are divided into two main categories: (1) those integrated into products regulated under the EU's existing product safety laws, such as toys, medical devices, aviation, and automobiles; and (2) those used in eight specific sectors, including biometric identification, critical infrastructure, education, employment, essential private and public services, law enforcement, migration, and legal interpretation. These high-risk systems must undergo strict assessments before they can be placed on the market and throughout their life cycle to ensure they meet the necessary requirements for safety, data quality, transparency, human oversight, and risk management. High-risk AI systems will be assessed before going to market and throughout their life cycle (European Parliament, 2023).

Limited-risk AI systems, too broad of a category to be defined here, are basically those that must comply with transparency requirements in order to allow users to make informed decisions (European Parliament, 2023).

Though critics of the AI Act fairly note that an AI risk taxonomy is both laborious and will likely stifle innovation, its application in a campus environment *may* be better received. A risk-based approach would allow campuses — typically, though not always, more nimble than a partnership of 27 countries — the flexibility to innovate with AI while managing potential downsides that can be tailored to their unique living/learning environments. That flexibility, though not unlimited, allows campus leaders the ability to be initially permissive when it comes to the adoption of AI and GAI tools.

Without suggesting a one-size-fits-all taxonomy, consider the following:

> • Unacceptable-risk AI systems might include real-time surveillance of students on campus, or surveillance with an end goal of producing a dataset that might suggest students who are in need of academic intervention based on time spent at academic locations versus other locations on campus. (For an example from the K–12 environment, see K–12 Dive [2023].)
>
> • High-stakes applications — like admissions, hiring, and student discipline — while potentially allowable, warrant the most stringent governance. Prior to deployment, such systems must be rigorously audited for biases and tested extensively. Automated decisions must be subject to human review. Perhaps an entirely human appeal may be necessary. Similarly, other high-stakes applications for student-facing services, like personalized tutors or mental health chatbots, must be vetted initially and regularly.
>
> • Lower-risk applications in operations, facilities management, or communications enable more flexibility. Nevertheless, bias audits, privacy impact assessments, impact reviews, and staff training remain prudent for any institutional deployment.

Overall, while precaution is not one-size-fits-all, a flexible, risk-based approach may empower campus leaders to encourage AI innovation while still providing oversight and due diligence to stakeholders.

From here, it may be helpful to pivot from the AI Act's high-level compass toward the National Institute of Standards and Technology's AI Risk Management Framework (AI RMF), a voluntary framework that helps all sectors manage risks beyond cybersecurity. Without getting unnecessarily detailed, where the AI Act provides insight into which systems need the strictest oversight, the AI RMF gives more detail into how that oversight should look: *governing* the program (policy, roles, accountability), *mapping* the context (purpose, data lineage, affected groups), *measuring* performance (accuracy, bias, security, accessibility), and *managing* the life cycle (incident response, retraining, retirement).

Conclusion

We end where we began. AI is here to stay and it's quickly working its way into all facets of campus life.[5] Risks and opportunities abound, but prudence, and sound risk management, dictates that institutions of higher education move efficiently toward establishing a governance structure, identifying a framework (perhaps risk-based) that matches their institutional ethic of care with their desire to innovate and tolerate risk, and incentivizing AI fluency across all business units.

Notes

1   This is not by accident. It's by design. ARPANET, the precursor to today's internet, originally connected schools within the University of California system. UNIX variants emerged from U.C. Berkeley. The web browser Mosiac was developed at the University of Illinois Urbana-Champaign. The Human Genome Project benefited mightily from contributions from MIT, Stanford, and Baylor researchers. The histories of Google and Facebook are other well-known examples.

2   Our goal is not to suggest that *artificial intelligence* and *generative artificial intelligence* are synonymous, though they are occasionally referred to interchangeably in the zeitgeist. Instead, our intent is to highlight AI, generally, and call out those specific instances when GAI will have a more marked or immediate impact.

3   Anecdotally, the authors can speak to similar experiences in obtaining a recent professional credential awarded by, ironically, a leading privacy organization.

4   The authors are aware of institutions of higher education pursuing such endeavors and aren't endorsing any one method over another from a risk-mitigation standpoint. For a primer on AI governance, see Mucci & Stryker, 2023.

5   "Here to stay" is not meant to suggest that there is room for AI in every corner of campus. It's also not meant to be fatalistic. Rather, it's a pragmatic acknowledgment that AI — not unlike the internet itself — has crossed from novelty to tool. But it's people who will decide where, when, and how AI Is used. In that sense, "here to stay" is the beginning, not the end.

References

Abdous, M. (2023, March 22). How AI is shaping the future of higher ed. *Inside Higher Ed*. https://www.insidehighered.com/views/2023/03/22/how-ai-shaping-future-higher-ed-opinion

Barnett, S. (2023, January 30). ChatGPT is making universities rethink plagiarism. *Wired*. https://www.wired.com/story/chatgpt-college-university-plagiarism/

Carrasco, M. (2021, September 19). Colleges expand mental health services for students. *Inside Higher Ed*. https://www.insidehighered.com/news/2021/09/20/colleges-expand-mental-health-services-students

Electronic Privacy Information Center. (n.d.). *Fourth Amendment*. Epic.org. https://epic.org/issues/privacy-laws/fourth-amendment/

Epstein-Gross, C. (2023, July 26). OpenAI abruptly shuts down ChatGPT plagiarism detector — and educators are worried. *Observer*. https://observer.com/2023/07/openai-shut-ai-classifier/

European Commission. (2024, July 12). *The Artificial Intelligence Act*. https://artificialintelligenceact.eu/the-act/

European Parliament. (2023, July 12). *EU AI Act: First regulation on artificial intelligence*. https://www.europarl.europa.eu/news/en/headlines/society/20230601STO93804/eu-ai-act-first-regulation-on-artificial-intelligence

Family Educational Rights and Privacy Act. 20 U.S.C. § 1232g; 34 CFR Part 99.

Gold, A., & Fischer, S. (2023, February 21). Chatbots trigger next misinformation nightmare. *AXIOS*. https://www.axios.com/2023/02/21/chatbots-misinformation-nightmare-chatgpt-ai

Google. (n.d.). *Perspectives on issues in AI governance* [White paper]. https://ai.google/static/documents/perspectives-on-issues-in-ai-governance.pdf

Hattersley, R. (2022, November 16). Survey shows diversity, depth of video surveillance system use on campus. *Campus Safety Magazine*. https://www.campussafetymagazine.com/news/2022-campus-safety-video-surveillance-survey-results/

Hennick, C. (2025, May 13). How three universities developed their chatbots. *EdTech*. https://edtechmagazine.com/higher/article/2025/05/how-three-universities-developed-their-chatbots

Huang, K. (2023, January 16). Alarmed by A.I. chatbots, universities start revamping how they teach. *The New York Times*. https://www.nytimes.com/2023/01/16/technology/chatgpt-artificial-intelligence-universities.html

IBM. (n.d.-a). *What are AI hallucinations?* https://www.ibm.com/topics/ai-hallucinations

IBM. (n.d.-b). *What is a chatbot?* https://www.ibm.com/topics/chatbots

K–12 Dive. (2023, August 28). *AI in Edtech: Helping pave the way for personalized education*. https://www.k12dive.com/spons/ai-in-edtech-helping-pave-the-way-for-personalized-education/691328/

Kelly, R. (2022, March 4). University of Illinois uses AI chatbot to grow student recruitment for online MBA program. *Campus Technology*. https://campustechnology.com/articles/2022/03/04/university-of-illinois-uses-ai-chatbot-to-grow-student-recruitment-for-online-mba-program.aspx

Koczera, P., & Pushard, R. (2023, July 5). AI has arrived in higher education. Now what? *EdTech*. https://edtechmagazine.com/higher/article/2023/07/ai-has-arrived-higher-education-now-what

Lazaro, G. (2022, May 17). Understanding gender and racial bias in AI. *ALI Social Impact Review*. https://www.sir.advancedleadership.harvard.edu/articles/understanding-gender-and-racial-bias-in-ai

Marks, M. (2021). Emergent medical data: Health information inferred by artificial intelligence. *UC Irvine Law Review, 11*(4), 995–1066. https://scholarship.law.uci.edu/ucilr/vol11/iss4/7

McCarty Carino, M. (2023, January 16). AI used for hiring and recruitment can be biased. But that's changing. *Marketplace*

Tech. https://www.marketplace.org/shows/marketplace-tech/ai-used-for-hiring-and-recruitment-can-be-biased-but-thats-changing-2/

McMurtrie, B. (2023, May 26). How ChatGPT could help or hurt students with disabilities. *The Chronicle of Higher Education*. https://www.chronicle.com/article/how-chatgpt-could-help-or-hurt-students-with-disabilities

Metz, C. (2023, February 26). Why do A.I. chatbots tell lies and act weird? Look in the mirror. *The New York Times*. https://www.nytimes.com/2023/02/26/technology/ai-chatbot-information-truth.html

Moody, K. (2023, May 18). LinkedIn recruiter will use AI to craft personalized candidate messages. *HR Dive*. https://www.hrdive.com/news/linkedin-recruiter-AI-messages/650646/

Mucci, T., & Stryker, C. (2023, November 28). *What is AI governance?* IBM. https://www.ibm.com/topics/ai-governance

Muscanell, N., & Robert, J. (2023, February 14). EDUCAUSE Quick-Poll results: Did ChatGPT write this report? https://er.educause.edu/articles/2023/2/educause-quickpoll-results-did-chatgpt-write-this-report

O'Hara, R. E. (2019, June 6). Healthier college students through texting. *Psychology Today*. https://www.psychologytoday.com/us/blog/nudging-ahead/201906/healthier-college-students-through-texting

Ogletree v. Cleveland State Univ., 647 F. Supp. 3d 602 (N.D. Ohio 2022).

Pettinato Oltz, T. (2023). ChatGPT, professor of law. *University of Illinois Journal of Law, Technology, & Policy*, 23(1), 207–221. http://dx.doi.org/10.2139/ssrn.4347630

Raptor Technologies. (n.d.). Visitor management systems for schools. https://raptortech.com/protect-your-school/raptor-visitor-management-system/

Reporters Committee for Freedom of the Press. (n.d.). *Introduction to the reporter's recording guide*. https://www.rcfp.org/introduction-to-reporters-recording-guide/

Rhoades, A. (2021). Big tech makes big data out of your child: The FERPA loophole EdTech exploits to monetize student data. *American University Business Law Review*, 9(3) 446–474. https://digitalcommons.wcl.american.edu/aublr/vol9/iss3/4/

Ryznar, M. (2023). Exams in the time of ChatGPT. *Washington and Lee Law Review Online*, 80(5), 305–322. https://scholarlycommons.law.wlu.edu/wlulr-online/vol80/iss5/3

Steiger, D. A., & Horres, S. (2022, May 26). Incorporating AI into today's risk management processes. *Westlaw Today*. https://today.westlaw.com/Document/Ia19fba21dd0411ec9f24ec7b211d8087/View/FullText.html?transitionType=Default&contextData=%28sc.Default%29

Swaak, T. (2022, August 24). Online tests are invasive. Now a judge agrees. *The Chronicle of Higher Education*. https://www.chronicle.com/article/students-say-room-scans-during-online-tests-are-invasive-now-a-judge-agrees

Trumbore, A. (2023, February 22). ChatGPT could become a personal tutor to millions of students if it learns lessons from the robot teachers that came before. *Fortune.* https://fortune.com/2023/02/22/chatgpt-ai-openai-educatoin-tutor-teaching-school/

Viano, A. (2023, February 9). How universities can use AI chatbots to connect with students and drive success. *EdTech.* https://edtechmagazine.com/higher/article/2023/02/how-universities-can-use-ai-chatbots-connect-students-and-drive-success

Walch, K. (2021, May 6). How to detect bias in existing AI algorithms. *EnterpriseAI.* https://www.techtarget.com/searchenterpriseai/feature/How-to-detect-bias-in-existing-AI-algorithms

Walker, C. (2018). *Student predictions, student protections* [Google slides]. https://docs.google.com/presentation/d/1SM-CIZfHlwp7_utSk3NpCeFwTcHFinCxxjGG-xI0sCL8/htmlpresent

Woebot Health. (2021). *Woebot Health Copilot.* https://woebothealth.com/

4

Desiring Machines

The Sociotechnical Production of Datafication in Higher Education

Laura Smithers

This chapter is not about the details of particular "big data" or artificial intelligence (AI) solutions in higher education (Hammond et al., 2022), but rather the sociotechnical systems in higher education that mark these modes of datafication as solutions. Of all the ways societies can value higher education, and of all the problems societies can figure higher education to have, what makes it such that the value of higher education in American and many Westernized societies is understood through outputs, and their problems (and attendant solutions) take the form of data?

Big data and AI are two of many modes that sociotechnical systems of datafication produce. To understand the social force that fuels our desire for datafication as a solution to trenchant higher education problems is to understand that there is nothing necessary or inevitable about datafication as a solution. Breaking this notion of datafication as a mere product of progress breaks open the horizon of actions that responsible higher education actors can take to create value. Understanding this notion of value is the subject of this chapter.

This chapter follows the assumption that all we take to be individual in our world are individualized productions of social forces of ordering and desire (Braidotti, 2013; Deleuze & Guattari, 2009; Keeling, 2019; McKittrick, 2021; Seigworth & Pedwell, 2023; van der Tuin, 2019). As such, this chapter focuses on the social forces that make modes of datafication, including big data and AI, possible in higher education. The directionality here is important. I use current practice surrounding data use in higher education to imagine the system from which these practices come — a whole that is greater than the sum of its parts, a whole that we ultimately cannot imagine but we will experiment toward here anyway.

A sociotechnical analysis acknowledges in its naming that society and technology are imbricated in each other (Brown & Klein, 2020; Jarke & Macgilchrist, 2021; Williamson, 2017b). There is no technology that can be understood separate from the society that makes it possible and there is no society that can be understood separate from its technologies, or tools of extension (Deleuze,

1992; Deleuze & Guattari, 2009; la paperson, 2017). Jarke and Breiter (2019) put it thusly: "[D]ata do not provide a 'window' to the social world, but rather the relationship between data and what they are meant to represent is recursive: Data are not 'natural' by-products of social actions, but must always be understood in the context of their origin and the affordances of the respective digital infrastructure" (p. 5). Technology is the product and producer of sociotechnical networks (Perrotta & Williamson, 2018), themselves made of "technical components, social relations, people, policies, funding arrangements, expert knowledge, and discourse" (Williamson, 2017, p. 61). To analyze datafication as a sociotechnical system, this chapter concerns itself with an intensely practical question: What problems are created in the image of data in higher education, and therefore where does data present itself as solution?

In two major sections, this chapter explores the desiring machine that produces modes of datafication as common sense solutions to higher education problems. The first section outlines the social theory of *desiring machines* (Deleuze & Guattari, 2009). The second section details datafication, the sociotechnical system produced by desiring machines that makes the denizens of higher education desire machines. This sociotechnical system is a composition of power that produces higher education's overwhelming desire for technological and data solutionism (Deleuze & Guattari, 2009; Perrotta & Williamson, 2018; Witzenberger & Gulson, 2021).

Desiring Machines: Creating Social Impulses in Higher Education

Desiring machines as a term is doubled throughout this chapter. It refers both to the social theory in use and to our modern desire for machines, or datafication. I begin with a discussion of desiring machines as social theory.

Desire, Machines, Desiring Machines

Desire is the motor of both stasis and change. It is the connective force that creates systems of thought and movement that we take to be the self-evident sociotechnical organization of the world. Desire is not limited to this, though, as it also contains a connective force unbound by current sociotechnical configurations. In this second expression, desire contains our capacities for reconfiguration and change beyond what we can imagine. Desire is not a force that is limited to humans; desire configures all existing things (Deleuze & Guattari, 2009).

Desire is usually experienced in the first expression: as captured by existing sociotechnical arrangements. The force of desire is pre-individual. Desire forms individual subjects; it is not formed by them (Evans et al., 2022). Humans do not fully shape the social world; in fact, we are mostly shaped by it. In contemporary higher education, desire creates and connects all sorts of individuals through data, including ambition (Thompson & Prinsloo, 2022), certainty (Complete College America, 2021), responsible action (Whitman, 2020), efficiency and productivity (Brasca et al., 2022; Clark & Noone, 2018), culture (Webber & Zheng, 2020), capital (Hall, 2020), truth (Schwartz et al., 2018), students (Harrison et al., 2020), faculty (Duin & Tham, 2020; Ovetz, 2021), staff (Hubbard, 2019), the past (Hosch, 2020), and the future (Smithers, 2020; Witzenberger & Gulson, 2021). Desire composes higher education settings soaked, yet never soaked enough, with data. Desire also opens subjects up to new connections, both unthought and unexperienced. Transformation happens when we individuated individuals connect in ways not determined by our sociotechnical arrangements (Barad, 2003). In experimentation, we compose new ways of being (St. Pierre, 2015).

If desire is the force of creation, machining is creation itself. In this social theory, everything is production, production is immediately consumption, and there can be no understanding of outcome that is not in its first instance process (Deleuze & Guattari, 2009). This has an immediate consequence for thinking about datafication: Data of all kinds are not points along a system (be they inputs, environmental variables, outputs, outcomes, or otherwise) — they are processes. Data are not data *for all times, for all people;*[1] our particular sociotechnical arrangement abstracts processes into data. To machine is to create individuals and connections that determine the world in particular ways through "attach[ing] to, accumulat[ing], and creat[ing] other machines" (la paperson, 2017, p. 14). That technologies proliferate and share commonalities within a sociotechnical arrangement reflects their common source (Raunig, 2016). A desiring machine is the force that creates the world, both the world of possibilities and the world "under determinate conditions" (Deleuze & Guattari, 2009, p. 29) — here, datafication.

The Sociotechnical Apparatus of Datafication

There is nothing au courant about data, no matter how it hangs onto an of-the-moment vibe across its various expressions (e.g., J. C. Scott, 1998). Datafication in what becomes the United States begins to come into its own in the late 1700s through technologies of ledgers; it is kickstarted in the late 1800s with census competitions to build a machine capable of reducing the work of counting the national population every 10 years (Hollerith, 1894; Reid-Green, 1989). These developments in American society are mirrored in higher education. Ledgers, while in existence in the earliest colonial colleges, gain sophistication in the beginning of the 1800s (Holden, 1976). Harvard develops a scale of merit designed to combine in one score attendance and performance evaluations of all manner (Morison, 1936). Course grades come into existence in this time in various unstandardized configurations (Stibal, 1959). The elective system — the creation of majors — revolutionizes the student experience as well as institutional configurations beginning in the mid-1800s. Systems to track student progress across their choice of degree programs are now necessary. When the elective system also produces the ability for students to take elective courses within nascent majors, the need for appropriate data tracking systems intensifies (Stibal, 1959). Among other technologies, higher education takes up the technology produced to increase the efficiency of the Census Bureau's work, Hollerith's punch card system (Preinkert, 2005). Data becomes the tool through which institutions know students, staff, and faculty.

When knowing students becomes equated with gathering data about students, datafication takes on a colonizing mode of operation. The mission of higher education becomes overdetermined by efficiency and productivity. There is never enough data to properly know institutional actors; therefore, the task of institutions is to gather more data in this quest for knowledge, productivity, and optimization (Hoskin, 1996). Data becomes the source of efficiency and progress. The digitization of data increases the speed at which already datafied higher education transforms (Williamson, 2017a). Problems of higher education, now defined in terms of data, seek data as solution, fueling a data imaginary of technological solutionism and inevitability (Beer, 2019).

While datafication long predates our current age, there are some markers about this production of datafication that distinguish it from datafications of the past. First, the technical apparatus that supports datafication now allows for the near-real-time production of metrics. This is a key aspect of big data (Williamson, 2017a). AI tools enter this sociotechnical field with the promise to supercharge productivity (Gardner, 2018). I collapse big data and AI into datafication on these grounds: They are two of several expressions of the same sociotechnical system, and if we are to learn how to do education differently, we must focus on the system that makes them possible. Next I explore four interlocking truths (Foucault, 2002) that datafication produces: human capacity is measurable; preemption; a limit might be student cheating; and datafication is never enough.

Desiring Productions

Datafication produces particular higher education worlds that actors, especially those invested in cultures of data, consider to be independent and self-evident truths. These are truths that responsible actors must desire, spread across their realms, and work to reproduce ad infinitum. I detail four of these major truths of datafication below.

Truth: Human Capacity Is Measurable

An early and critical truth of datafication is that human capacity can be measured. Human attributes lend themselves to measurement of course, as units like the *foot* are the roots of measurement in cultures across the globe (Kaaronen et al., 2023; Vincent, 2023). Human capacity refers to the actions and desires that become possible through us. These are definitionally not objects to be measured here and now. Human capacities are the "potential modes of knowing, relating, and attending to things [that] are already somehow present in them in a state of potentiality and resonance" (Stewart, 2013, p. 3). Capacity's capture by measurement makes possible the scientific production of datafied students. It also marks the beginning of the end of higher education's "devotion to truth and wisdom" (Hoyt, 1965, p. 47), to be replaced by the secular religion of productivity (Gregg, 2018).

Measurements of capacity mark the dawn of the student personnel age in American higher education. The student personnel point of view crystallizes a movement to individualize higher education and use new horizons in statistics to measure capacities of students to develop "to the limits of his potentialities and in making his contribution to the betterment of society" (American Council on Education, 1937, p. 3; gendered pronoun used in original). The student personnel movement does many things, including bringing the new measurements of the day into higher education to predict the development of students, and producing a series of cumulative record forms to standardize the data collected by colleges and universities and its format of collection (Stibal, 1959). These technologies allow student data to be fastened to students, through which college students become their data (Koopman, 2019).

Measurements of student capacity are just the product that today's EdTech profiteers and earnest true believers in data-informed education alike see as the proper orientation of higher education institutions. When the problem in need of immediate attention is framed as "How can colleges get more students to graduate faster?" (e.g., Jones, 2015), solutions come in knowing which students are capable of graduating from which institutions (e.g., Smith et al., 2013) in which majors (e.g., EAB, 2016) in the allotted time or less (Poliakoff, 2020), and so on. The logic of productivity is old, the orientation of productivity to the data-engineered production of graduates is newer, and the technological capacity and imaginary that measurements of success can be engineered in near-real-time for entire populations of students is the new era of datafication.

Truth: Preemption

A century of investment in the measurement of human capacity combined with new technology and the effects of fear and anxiety have produced the desire for and practice of preemption in higher education. The two major data movements in American higher education of the last 15 years center not just data but anxiety and fear. The completion agenda has, for over a decade, insisted that low on-time graduation rates are a moral failing and that more and better data pave the path to solutions (Complete College America, 2011; see also Parkes et al., 2020). More recently, discourse around a projected impending enrollment cliff cite and project an existential crisis for institutions, as to not act in data-informed ways to reform your institution now is to doom its future irreparably

(McKinsey & Company, 2020). Acting on a fear of the future — a future graduation rate, future catastrophic drops in enrollment, or otherwise — produces the feared future as true in the present, as "an *effect* of the preemptive action taken. The reality-based community wastes time studying empirical reality, the Bushites said: 'We *create* it.' And because of that, 'we' the preemptors will always be right" (Massumi, 2015, p. 14). Our modern data imaginary fuels preemption (Beer, 2019). Data analytics provide the "governing of educational futures" (Webb et al., 2020, p. 285) that preemption requires. Future problems as defined by the completion agenda (future graduation statuses) and enrollment cliff (decreases in future enrollment) become true for current students and current institutions through their anticipation (Adams et al., 2009; Groves, 2017; Rahm, 2023), and modes of datafication stand ready as solutions.

Datafication provides the solutions preemption requires, in no small part because the message of our modern data imaginary "is founded upon an ability to grasp the future and use it in the present" (Beer, 2019, p. 27). The sociotechnical apparatus of datafication produces "a fully recursive arrangement where . . . the data produce the learner as much as the learner produces the data" (Williamson, 2016, p. 139). Completion and enrollment are both data problems to be solved through data, and preemption "determines the conditions that lead to the desired future and simultaneously enacts a series of interventions to reach it" (Witzenberger & Gulson, 2021, p. 420). The crisis of completion is one where urgent action is required now through data insights to preempt future undesirable graduation rates (Complete College America, 2011, 2014; Hammond et al., 2022). The crisis of enrollment is one where urgent action is required now through data insights to preempt financial crashes from "a sizeable reduction in the number of available students" (Grawe, 2021, p. 81). Modes of datafication promise future-proofing through proper anticipation and real-time data intervention (Beer, 2019; Lane, 2018; Webb et al., 2020; Williamson, 2016; Witzenberger & Gulson, 2021). Preemption not only produces its own reality, it also produces the continued desire for datafication as a cure for these problems that are not real.

Truth: A Limit of Datafication Might Be Student Cheating

What does the disconnect in the reception of student versus institutional use of generative AI say about the functioning of datafication? Widespread use of AI through the public release of technologies like OpenAI's ChatGPT (GPT-4) has changed the tenor of some conversations about datafication. In a world where datafication is entrenched and preemption defines moral action, generative AI presents a particular issue: Should humans turn over human spheres to machines whose operations cannot by definition be scrutinized, leading to data-driven solutions taking on a life of their own? Here I discuss two related developments in AI: the moral panic over undetectable student cheating with the public release of ChatGPT, and the monetization and feeding of institutional datafication desires through EdTech's embrace of AI.

The use of generative AI by students to cheat on assignments in undetectable ways generated near-instant moral panic and backlash among faculty and staff. At least two messy camps have emerged: those who see AI as a direct threat to student learning and the purpose of higher education, and those who see student use of AI as both inevitable and desirable (D'Agostino, 2023b; Horowitch, 2023; McMurtrie, 2023). The moral panic camp warns against embracing generative AI and thus enabling most or all students to learn none of the knowledge or habits otherwise required to earn a college degree (e.g., Keegin, 2023; I. Scott, 2023). The inevitability camp calls for the strategic (Brassett, 2021) integration of AI into teaching and learning (e.g., Bala & Colvin, 2023; Mowreader, 2023; Schroeder, 2023). According to this camp, faculty and administration should incorporate AI in all areas of higher education, including in student work, with an "inclusive focus on equitable student value" (Dolan & Yasin, 2023, para. 6). In this view, since AI's impact on teaching and learning is a question of "how — not if" faculty and staff should "experiment, not panic" (D'Agostino, 2023a, para. 4). AI in the hands of students has produced a break, even if not total, in higher education's investment in datafication.

In other higher education applications, AI is embraced by university actors for this same effect — the supercharging of productivity — wielded differently (Abdous, 2023; Ellucian, 2023b; Hubbard, 2019). Major EdTech vendors are advertising the addition of AI to their current products, debuting new AI-centric solutions and cultivating an audience to desire this new horizon of digital transformation (Coffey, 2023; EAB, 2023; Ellucian, 2023a; Hodges & Ocak, 2023; Londono & Sengupta, 2023; Salesforce, 2023; Swaak, 2023b). Notably in this group is the response from the plagiarism end of the EdTech sphere, whose business model is shot without a solution to sell. Plagiarism checkers like Turnitin and others have risen to this task, though it is unclear how anyone would be able to judge if these work (Knox, 2023; Surovell, 2023; Williams, 2023). The faculty resistance that exists to generative AI seems to be the loudest resistance to a form of datafication in American higher education than has taken place in recent memory. Will this crack in datafication this debate shows change the course of datafication?

Interlude: Datafication Works Only When It Breaks

There is another important part of how a sociotechnical machine works: It only works when it breaks (Deleuze & Guattari, 2009; la paperson, 2017; Raunig, 2016). This, admittedly, is a head-scratcher at first thought. For Deleuze and Guattari (2009), the social machine "can operate only by fits and starts, by grinding and breaking down, in spasms of minor explosions. The dysfunctions are an essential element of its very ability to function. . . . [S]ocial machines make a habit of feeding on the contradictions they give rise to, on the crises they provoke, on the anxieties they *engender*, and on the infernal operations they regenerate" (p. 151). Machines are forces that produce the determinate world but are not themselves points within them. Therefore, they must stay on the move in order to remain forces (Deleuze & Guattari, 2007). They cannot become so stable as to become an identifiable point in the world — so they break and flow, and in breaks and flows retain the broad orientation of their force without becoming captured and immobilized within the world.

Truth, Continued

The use of generative AI by students has produced a rupture in datafication. The break, however, is not simply lodged in conversations among faculty and administrators. Evidence of the break is also, and importantly, in the scramble by EdTech to produce a solution. In fact, these solutions are ubiquitous: EdTech and other capitalist forces (e.g., consultants) in higher education exist to sell solutions to problems. Problems are the coin of the realm. Each problem is a break in datafication — if the existing datafications worked, there would be no need for the next product or even the next system upgrade. Yet EdTech solutions are ubiquitous. Problems abound. Datafication breaks all around us, daily, and its consistent inability to work requires constant reinvestments in datafication to address.

Truth: Datafication Is Never Enough

This leads us to our final truth about datafication, at least for this chapter: Datafication is never enough to satisfy the productivity desires it produces (Hoskin, 1996). Datafication is variously described as "an arms race" (Merisotis, 2023, para. 16), a "need for speed" (Dolan & Yasin, 2023, para. 7), improvements that your campus will not survive without (Kim, 2023), and an unyielding desire for "better data faster" (Cohen-Vogel, 2018, p. 20). Continued investments in datafication past the point of today's solutions will write the future of higher education (Ellucian, 2023b; Hodges & Ocak, 2023; McCredie, 1983) and differentiate C-suite leaders who *get it* from those who do not (Complete College America, 2011; Ness et al., 2021; Porter, 1992). Datafication has colonized higher education (Webb et al., 2020). Even the digital datafication and big EdTech-ification of higher education is not that new. Legacy student information system vendors, for example, have been selling their solutions to campuses for decades (e.g., Delf, 1982). Relative upstarts have become virtually un-entanglable from campus operations (Swaak, 2023a).

With all of these longstanding, deeply interwoven, and very expensive solutions circulating on campus, why have they not worked? Why do we continue to have a need for digital transformation? Given that datafication works when it breaks, its solutions working would mark the demise of datafication as an organizing force in higher education. To the extent this would mark the ability of students, faculty, and staff to dump the secular religion of datafied productivity in favor of processes of learning and productions of indeterminate futures, this is something to fight for.

You've Gotta Fight for Your Right to Indeterminate Futures

When we problematize the sociotechnical production of AI, big data, and all modes of datafication past and future, problems and solutions take a different form.[2] Solutions to the problems that datafication creates that are themselves modes of datafication (e.g., calls for increased privacy or democratic adoption processes) simply perpetuate datafication. A broken datafication keeps working to fix itself. Datafication as a sociotechnical system is not a problem because data are inherently problematic; it is a problem because it rewrites our futures and our present in its image within a system that boundlessly consumes every corner of human capacity toward a valueless productivity. Some call for acceleration of datafication to break its dominance (Webb et al., 2020). Others call for us, as parts of systems ourselves, to wield technologies to dismantle colonial universities, or universities that are "machine[s] for accumulation and expansion" (la paperson, 2017, p. 37) for decolonial purposes from within (see also Harney & Moten, 2013). These actions might not be all that distinct. Paradoxically, datafication *must* be addressed from within it — we are all made by it — in ways that escape its sociotechnical hold on us. We must escape datafication even if it will not leave us alone to be re-formed by desire unbound.

Desiring machines do not just produce sociotechnical systems. They contain our collective possibilities, our capacities that exceed measurement and data. To reach these possibilities through datafication, in defiance of datafication, to finally let datafication work and then lay it to rest, is how to wield a desiring machine to produce higher education otherwise. Data will likely be with us for a while. Datafication does not have to be. Sociotechnical systems make us and are made by us. We must exploit the agency we have within this system to change its terms and focus higher education on the production of the immeasurable values of learning and progress.

Notes

1   Shout-out to the motto of the metric system, an early enabler of datafication and "a turning point for humanity" (National Institute of Standards and
Technology, 2018).
2   Section titled with respect and apologies to the Beastie Boys (1986).

References

Abdous, M. (2023, March 21). How AI is shaping the future of higher ed.
Inside Higher Ed. https://www.insidehighered.com/views/2023/03/22/
how-ai-shaping-future-higher-ed-opinion

Adams, V., Murphy, M., & Clarke, A. E. (2009). Anticipation: Technoscience,
life, affect, temporality. *Subjectivity, 28,* 246–265. https://doi.org/10.1057/
sub.2009.18

American Council on Education. (1937). *The student personnel point of view.*
American Council on Education.

Bala, K., & Colvin, A. (2023). *Generative artificial intelligence for education
and pedagogy.* Center for Teaching Innovation, Cornell University.

Barad, K. (2003). Posthumanist performativity: Toward an understanding of
how matter comes to matter. *Signs: Journal of Women in Culture and
Society, 28*(3), 801–831. https://doi.org/10.1086/345321

Beastie Boys. (1986). Fight for your right [song]. On *Licensed to Ill.* Def Jam;
Columbia.

Beer, D. (2019). *The data gaze: Capitalism, power and perception.* SAGE
Publications.

Braidotti, R. (2013). *The posthuman.* Polity Press.

Brasca, C., Kaithwal, N., Krishnan, C., Lam, M., Law, J., &
Marya, V. (2022). *Using machine learning to improve student success in higher education.* McKinsey & Company.
https://www.mckinsey.com/industries/education/our-insights/
using-machine-learning-to-improve-student-success-in-higher-education#/

Brassett, J. (2021). Anticipating the work to be done. *Futures, 134,* Article
102851. https://doi.org/10.1016/j.futures.2021.102851

Brown, M., & Klein, C. (2020). Whose data? Which rights? Whose power? A
policy discourse analysis of student privacy policy documents. *Journal of
Higher Education, 91*(7), 1149–1178. https://doi.org/10.1080/00221546.2
020.1770045

Clark, C., & Noone, D. (2018, October 23). The future(s) of public higher
education: Five new models for state university success. *Deloitte
Insights.* https://www2.deloitte.com/us/en/insights/industry/public-sector/
future-of-public-higher-education-study.html

Coffey, L. (2023, October 12). AI buzz dominates annual ed-tech
conference. *Inside Higher Ed.* https://www.insidehighered.

com/news/tech-innovation/artificial-intelligence/2023/10/12/
ai-buzz-dominates-annual-ed-tech-conference

Cohen-Vogel, D. R. (2018). Higher education decision support: Building capacity, adding value. In J. S. Gagliardi, A. R. Parnell, & J. Carpenter-Hubin (Eds.), *The analytics revolution in higher education: Big Data, organizational learning, and student success* (pp. 15–30). Stylus Publishing.

Complete College America. (2011). *Time is the enemy: The surprising truth about why today's college students aren't graduating . . . And what needs to change.* https://files.eric.ed.gov/fulltext/ED536827.pdf

Complete College America. (2014). *Four-year myth: Make college more affordable. Restore the promise of graduating on time.* https://files.eric.ed.gov/fulltext/ED558792.pdf

Complete College America. (2021). *No room for doubt: Moving corequisite support from idea to imperative.* https://files.eric.ed.gov/fulltext/ED611851.pdf

D'Agostino, S. (2023a, January 11). ChatGPT advice academics can use now. *Inside Higher Ed.* https://www.insidehighered.com/news/2023/01/12/academic-experts-offer-advice-chatgpt

D'Agostino, S. (2023b, September 13). Why professors are polarized on AI. *Inside Higher Ed.* https://www.insidehighered.com/news/tech-innovation/artificial-intelligence/2023/09/13/why-faculty-members-are-polarized-ai

Deleuze, G. (1992). Postscript on the societies of control. *October, 59*(1), 3–7. https://www.jstor.org/stable/778828

Deleuze, G., & Guattari, F. (2007). *A thousand plateaus: Capitalism and schizophrenia.* University of Minnesota Press.

Deleuze, G., & Guattari, F. (2009). *Anti-Oedipus: Capitalism and schizophrenia.* Penguin Books.

Delf, R. M. (1982). How to shop for a student information system. *American School & University, 54*(12), 18–20.

Dolan, D., & Yasin, E. (2023, March 21). A guide to generative AI policy making. *Inside Higher Ed.* https://www.insidehighered.com/views/2023/03/22/ai-policy-advice-administrators-and-faculty-opinion

Duin, A. H., & Tham, J. (2020). The current state of analytics: Implications for learning management system (LMS) use in writing pedagogy. *Computers and Composition, 55*, Article 102544. https://doi.org/10.1016/j.compcom.2020.102544

EAB. (2016, July 26). How meta-majors guide students toward on-time graduation. *Daily Briefing.* https://web.archive.org/web/20240420012202/https://eab.com/insights/daily-briefing/student-success/how-meta-majors-guide-students-toward-on-time-graduation/

EAB. (2023, September 14). EAB adds artificial intelligence to popular student recruitment and retention technology [Press release]. https://eab.com/about/newsroom/press/eab-adds-artificial-intelligence-to-popular-student-recruitment-and-retention-technology/

Ellucian. (2023a). *Artificial intelligence, machine learning, big data: Taking predictive analytics to the next level.* https://web.archive.org/web/20211204005302/https://www.ellucian.com/resources/webinar/artificial-intelligence-machine-learning-big-data-taking-predictive-analytics

Ellucian. (2023b). *The roadmap to higher education 4.0.* https://www.ellucian.com/blog/higher-education-roadmap-40-efficiencies

Evans, S., Harrison, M., & Rousell, D. (2022). Teaching in the afterward: Undoing order-words and affirming transversal alternatives. *Discourse: Studies in the Cultural Politics of Education, 43*(5), 785–803. https://doi.org/10.1080/01596306.2021.1996695

Foucault, M. (2002). Truth and power. In J. D. Faubion (Ed.), *Power: Essential works of Foucault, 1954–1984* (pp. 111–133). The New Press.

Gardner, L. (2018, April 8). How A.I. is infiltrating every corner of the campus. *The Chronicle of Higher Education.* https://www.chronicle.com/article/how-a-i-is-infiltrating-every-corner-of-the-campus/

Grawe, N. D. (2021). *The agile college: How institutions successfully navigate demographic changes.* Johns Hopkins University Press.

Gregg, M. (2018). *Counterproductive: Time management in the knowledge economy.* Duke University Press.

Groves, C. (2017). Emptying the future: On the environmental politics of anticipation. *Futures, 92,* 29–38. https://doi.org/10.1016/j.futures.2016.06.003

Hall, R. (2020). The hopeless university: Intellectual work at the end of the end of history. *Postdigital Science and Education, 2*(3), 830–848. https://doi.org/10.1007/s42438-020-00158-9

Hammond, L., Adams, P., Rubin, P. G., & Ness, E. C. (2022). A rhetorical analysis of intermediary organization documents on college completion policy. *Educational Policy, 36*(2), 377–406. https://doi.org/10.1177/0895904819888231

Harney, S., & Moten, F. (2013). *The undercommons: Fugitive planning and black study.* Minor Compositions. https://www.minorcompositions.info/wp-content/uploads/2013/04/undercommons-web.pdf

Harrison, M. J., Davies, C., Bell, H., Goodley, C., Fox, S., & Downing, B. (2020). (Un)teaching the "datafied student subject": Perspectives from an education-based masters in an English university. *Teaching in Higher Education: Critical Perspectives, 25*(4), 401–417. https://doi.org/10.1080/13562517.2019.1698541

Hodges, C., & Ocak, C. (2023, August 30). Integrating generative AI into higher education: Considerations. *EDUCAUSE Review.* https://er.educause.edu/articles/2023/8/integrating-generative-ai-into-higher-education-considerations

Holden, H. P. (1976). Student records: The Harvard experience. *The American Archivist, 39*(4), 461–467. https://www.jstor.org/stable/40291918

Hollerith, H. (1894). The electrical tabulating machine. *Journal of the Royal Statistical Society, 57*(4), 678–689. https://doi.org/10.2307/2979610

Horowitch, R. (2023, August 7). Here comes the second year of AI college. *The Atlantic.* https://www.theatlantic.com/ideas/archive/2023/08/ai-chatgpt-college-essay-plagiarism/674928/

Hosch, B. J. (2020). Big data and the transformation of decision making in higher education. In K. L. Webber & H. Y. Zheng (Eds.), *Big data on campus: Data analytics and decision making in higher education* (pp. 30–49). Johns Hopkins University Press.

Hoskin, K. (1996). The "awful idea of accountability": Inscribing people into the measurement of objects. In R. Munro & J. Mouritsen (Eds.), *Accountability: Power, ethos and the technologies of managing* (pp. 265–282). International Thomson Business Press.

Hoyt, D. P. (1965). *The relationship between college grades and adult achievement. A review of the literature.* American College Testing Program. https://files.eric.ed.gov/fulltext/ED023343.pdf

Hubbard, C. (2019, September 11). Technology won't replace advisors, but it can help us do our jobs better. *EAB Insights.* https://eab.com/insights/blogs/community-college/technology-wont-replace-advisors-but-it-can-help-us-do-our-jobs-better/

Jarke, J., & Breiter, A. (2019). Editorial: The datafication of education. *Learning, Media and Technology, 44*(1), 1–6. https://doi.org/10.1080/17439884.2019.1573833

Jarke, J., & Macgilchrist, F. (2021). Dashboard stories: How narratives told by predictive analytics reconfigure roles, risk and sociality in education. *Big Data & Society, 8*(1), 1–15. https://doi.org/10.1177/20539517211025561

Jones, S. (2015). The game changers: Strategies to boost college completion and close attainment gaps. *Change, 47*(2), 24–29. https://doi.org/10.1080/00091383.2015.1018085

Kaaronen, R. O., Manninen, M. A., & Eronen, J. T. (2023). Body-based units of measure in cultural evolution. *Science, 380*(6648), 948–954. https://doi.org/10.1126/science.adf1936

Keegin, J. M. (2023, May 23). ChatGPT is a plagiarism machine. *The Chronicle of Higher Education.* https://www.chronicle.com/article/chatgpt-is-a-plagiarism-machine

Keeling, K. (2019). *Queer times, Black futures.* New York University Press.

Kim, J. (2023, September 29). "All in on AI" and the university. *Inside Higher Ed.* https://www.insidehighered.com/opinion/blogs/learning-innovation/2023/09/29/all-ai-and-university

Knox, L. (2023, April 3). Can Turnitin cure higher ed's AI fever? *Inside Higher Ed.* https://www.insidehighered.com/news/2023/04/03/turnitins-solution-ai-cheating-raises-faculty-concerns

Koopman, C. (2019). *How we became our data: A genealogy of the informational person.* University of Chicago Press.

la paperson. (2017). *A third university is possible.* University of Minnesota Press. https://doi.org/10.5749/9781452958460

Lane, J. E. (2018). Examining how the analytics revolution matters to higher education policy makers: Data analytics, systemness, and enabling student success. In J. S. Gagliardi, A. R. Parnell, & J. Carpenter-Hubin (Eds.), *The analytics revolution in higher education: Big data, organizational learning, and student success* (pp. 155–171). Stylus Publishing.

Londono, H., & Sengupta, A. (2023, February 1). Avoiding the college enrollment cliff with AI. *EDUCAUSE Review*. https://er.educause.edu/articles/2023/2/avoiding-the-college-enrollment-cliff-with-ai

Massumi, B. (2015). *Ontopower: War, powers, and the state of perception.* Duke University Press.

McCredie, J. W. (Ed.). (1983). *Campus computing strategies.* Digital Press. http://archive.org/details/bitsavers_decBooksDiampusComputing Strategies1983_22727590

McKinsey & Company. (2020, March). *Perspective on university transformation: A conversation with Paul Pastorek* [Video]. https://www.mckinsey.com/Videos/video?vid=6237535803001&plyrid=IzQolWCsY

McKittrick, K. (2021). *Dear science and other stories.* Duke University Press.

McMurtrie, B. (2023, March 6). ChatGPT is everywhere. *The Chronicle of Higher Education*. https://www.chronicle.com/article/chatgpt-is-already-upending-campus-practices-colleges-are-rushing-to-respond

Merisotis, J. (2023, February 27). In the age of artificial intelligence, we need our human skills to keep it real. *Forbes*. https://www.forbes.com/sites/jamiemerisotis/2023/02/27/in-the-age-of-artificial-intelligence-we-need-our-human-skills-to-keep-it-real/

Morison, S. E. (1936). *Three centuries of Harvard, 1636–1936.* Harvard University Press.

Mowreader, A. (2023, September 28). Academic success tip: Establish guidelines for AI use. *Inside Higher Ed*. https://www.insidehighered.com/news/student-success/academic-life/2023/09/28/report-three-ways-address-generative-ai-college

National Institute of Standards and Technology. (2018). A turning point for humanity: Redefining the world's measurement system. *SI Redefinition*. https://www.nist.gov/si-redefinition/turning-point-humanity-redefining-worlds-measurement-system

Ness, E. C., Rubin, P. G., & Hammond, L. (2021). Becoming a "game changer": Complete College America's role in U.S. higher education policy fields. *Higher Education, 82*(1), 1–17. https://doi.org/10.1007/s10734-020-00619-x

Ovetz, R. (2021). The algorithmic university: On-line education, learning management systems, and the struggle over academic labor. *Critical Sociology, 47*(7–8), 1065–1084. https://doi.org/10.1177/0896920520948931

Parkes, S., Benkwitz, A., Bardy, H., Myler, K., & Peters, J. (2020). Being more human: Rooting learning analytics through resistance and reconnection with the values of higher education. *Higher Education Research and*

Development, 39(1), 113–126. https://doi.org/10.1080/07294360.2019.16
77569

Perrotta, C., & Williamson, B. (2018). The social life of learning analytics:
Cluster analysis and the "performance" of algorithmic education. *Learning, Media and Technology, 43*(1), 3–16. https://doi.org/10.1080/1743988
4.2016.1182927

Poliakoff, M. B. (2020, July). *A three-year bachelor's degree.* American
Enterprise Institute. https://www.luminafoundation.org/wp-content/
uploads/2020/08/a-three-year-bachelors-degree.pdf

Porter, J. H. (1992, December 1–4). *Introducing technology to senior executives: Theory and Practice — A case study* [Paper]. CAUSE92, Dallas,
TX, United States. https://www.educause.edu/ir/library/text/CNC9213.txt

Preinkert, A. H. (2005). *The work of the registrar: A summary of principles
and practices in American universities and colleges 1910–1939.* American Association of Collegiate Registrars and Admissions Officers.

Rahm, L. (2023). Education, automation and AI: A genealogy of alternative
futures. *Learning, Media and Technology, 48*(1), 6–24. https://doi.org/10.
1080/17439884.2021.1977948

Raunig, G. (2016). *Dividuum: Machinic capitalism and molecular revolution*
(A. Dcricg, Trans.). Semiotext(e).

Reid-Green, K. S. (1989). The history of census tabulation. *Scientific American, 260*(2), 98–103. https://www.jstor.org/stable/24987147

Salesforce. (2023). *Higher education in an AI-powered world.* https://www.
salesforce.com/video/4640720/

Schroeder, R. (2023, March 14). AI is impacting education, but
the best is yet to come. *Inside Higher Ed.* https://www.inside-
highered.com/digital-learning/blogs/online-trending-now/
ai-impacting-education-best-yet-come

Schwartz, C. M., Phillippe, K., Kowalski, D., & Polec, A. (2018). Evolving
from reflective to predictive: Montgomery County Community College
and analytics. In J. S. Gagliardi, A. R. Parnell, & J. Carpenter-Hubin
(Eds.), *The analytics revolution in higher education: Big data, organizational learning, and student success* (pp. 173–188). Stylus Publishing.

Scott, I. (2023, April 18). Yes, we are in a (ChatGPT) crisis. *Inside Higher
Ed.* https://www.insidehighered.com/opinion/views/2023/04/18/
yes-we-are-chatgpt-crisis

Scott, J. C. (1998). *Seeing like a state: How certain schemes to improve the
human condition have failed.* Yale University Press.

Seigworth, G. J., & Pedwell, C. (2023). A shimmer of inventories. In G. J.
Seigworth & C. Pedwell (Eds.), *The affect theory reader 2: Worldings,
tensions, futures* (pp. 1–59). Duke University Press.

Smith, J., Pender, M., & Howell, J. (2013). The full extent of student–college
academic undermatch. *Economics of Education Review, 32*(1), 247–261.
https://doi.org/10.1016/j.econedurev.2012.11.001

Smithers, L. (2020). Student success as preemption: Predictive constructions of futures-to-never-come. *Futures*, *124*, 1–10. https://doi.org/10.1016/j.futures.2020.102639

St. Pierre, E. A. (2015). Practices for the "new" in the new empiricisms, the new materialisms and post qualitative inquiry. In N. K. Denzin & M. D. Giardina (Eds.), *Qualitative inquiry and the politics of research* (pp. 75–95). Routledge.

Stewart, K. (2013). *Ordinary affects*. Duke University Press.

Stibal, W. O. (1959). The historical development of student personnel records in colleges and universities. *The Emporia State Research Studies*, *8*(2). https://esirc.emporia.edu/bitstream/handle/123456789/475/61.pdf

Surovell, E. (2023, April 3). A plagiarism detector will try to catch students who cheat with ChatGPT. *The Chronicle of Higher Education*. https://www.chronicle.com/article/a-plagiarism-detector-will-try-to-catch-students-who-cheat-with-chatgpt

Swaak, T. (2023a, February 22). Education dept. shocks ed-tech experts and colleges with expansion of oversight. *The Chronicle of Higher Education*. https://www.chronicle.com/article/education-dept-shocks-ed-tech-experts-and-colleges-with-expansion-of-oversight

Swaak, T. (2023b, August 7). First came ChatGPT. Then came the over-the-top sales pitches. *The Chronicle of Higher Education*. https://www.chronicle.com/article/first-came-chatgpt-then-came-the-over-the-top-sales-pitches

Thompson, T. L., & Prinsloo, P. (2022). Returning the data gaze in higher education. *Learning, Media and Technology*, *48*(1), 1–13. https://doi.org/10.1080/17439884.2022.2092130

van der Tuin, I. (2019). On research "worthy of the present." *SFU Educational Review*, *12*(1), 8–20. https://doi.org/10.21810/sfuer.v12i1.860

Vincent, J. (2023). *Beyond measure: The hidden history of measurement from cubits to quantum constants*. W. W. Norton & Company.

Webb, P. T., Sellar, S., & Gulson, K. N. (2020). Anticipating education: Governing habits, memories and policy-futures. *Learning, Media and Technology*, *45*(3), 284–297. https://doi.org/10.1080/17439884.2020.1686015

Webber, K. L., & Zheng, H. Y. (2020). Data analytics and the imperatives for data-informed decision making in higher education. In K. L. Webber & H. Y. Zheng (Eds.), *Big data on campus: Data analytics and decision making in higher education* (pp. 3–29). Johns Hopkins University Press.

Whitman, M. (2020). "We called that a behavior": The making of institutional data. *Big Data & Society*, *7*(1), 1–13. https://doi.org/10.1177/2053951720932200

Williams, T. (2023, February 6). Inside the post-ChatGPT scramble to create AI essay detectors. *Times Higher Education*. https://www.timeshighereducation.com/depth/inside-post-chatgpt-scramble-create-ai-essay-detectors

Williamson, B. (2016). Digital education governance: Data visualization, predictive analytics, and "real-time" policy instruments. *Journal of*

Education Policy, *31*(2), 123–141. https://doi.org/10.1080/02680939.201
5.1035758

Williamson, B. (2017a). *Big Data in education: The digital future of
learning, policy and practice*. SAGE Publications. https://doi.
org/10.4135/9781529714920

Williamson, B. (2017b). Learning in the "platform society": Disassembling
an educational data assemblage. *Research in Education*, *98*(1), 59–82.
https://doi.org/10.1177/0034523717723389

Witzenberger, K., & Gulson, K. N. (2021). Why EdTech is always right: Students, data and machines in pre-emptive configurations. *Learning, Media
and Technology*, *46*(4), 420–434. https://doi.org/10.1080/17439884.2021
.1913181

5

Making a Digital Record of Campus Life

The Student Data Warehouse and the Datafication of Student Records in U.S. Higher Education

Michael Brown

During a recent interview, I asked a senior vice president for information technology if they could identify where and how their institution stored data about students on her campus. After fumbling around with papers on her desk for a moment, she pulled out a diagram illustrating several tools and technologies that collected data about students: the learning management system, card swipe access points at various campus buildings, and interactions with the registrar, financial aid office, and academic advisors. I discussed the campus Wi-Fi system and what kind of information it stored about IP addresses and user access. The VP acknowledged the hastily sketched diagram was the result of conversations about protecting institutional data assets: "We compiled this over concerns about cyber security. We wanted to know where data was being inputted, and how and where that data might be insecure."

At the center of the diagram was a small box labeled "SDW," for student data warehouse. Every interaction with the data system had either its starting or ending point in the SDW. A student might, for example, log on to the learning management system to see their next homework assignment. This log-on (what's often termed *trace data*) is recorded in the SDW, and the SDW sends back information about what courses that student is enrolled in for the term. Since initial digitalization efforts — like the advent of campus learning management systems (Krumm, 2012) and card swipe access points (Bowman et al., 2019) — campuses have increasingly relied on the SDW to facilitate the digital architecture that supports campus life.

The SDW is the fulcrum technology of a process Ben Williamson (2018) calls the invisible architecture of datafication, and its emergence reflects how postsecondary institutions in the United States actually respond to technological innovation. After disruptive cycles of hype, tools that are widely adopted become mundane and opaque (Brown, 2016). Rather than because of substantive conversations about their configuration and implementation, the SDW became widespread because the practices it makes possible proliferated across campus with little policy documentation or guidance (Brown & Klein, 2020). The SDW does respond to a practical need in campus environments: Institutions needed a data archive that can organize educational records for institutional audits (Brown et al., 2023). Its configuration has changed to such an extent in the last decade that it is potentially implicated in all institutional activities.

A central data repository makes it easier to track who has access to student data and how people are using the data. It also makes it easier to act on student data. Through learning and academic analytic initiatives, the SDW allows data representations of students to circulate around campus, facilitating decision-making and action (Cox et al., 2017). Institutions have always needed to record and maintain information about students and their accomplishments. The SDW is simply the latest incarnation of a long-time practice. But as data about students proliferate, the SDW scales accordingly.

In this chapter, I provide a brief overview of the SDW, including the history of its emergence and evolution as an institutional system, and I identify how the SDW configures into contemporary debates around datafication and data justice in U.S. higher education. I conclude with guiding questions for research and practice. My goal is to encourage a broader dialogue about how the SDW can be reconfigured to support collaborative democratic governance activities.

What Is a Student Data Warehouse?

In conceptualizing the SDW, I draw a distinction between the system of student information, which includes the people, policies, practices, and relationships that allow information to circulate within institutions, and the student data warehouse, which is a technology that centralizes student data, in its myriad forms, to ease the use of data as an asset. The SDW may contain a variety of data assets, but its historical purpose has been to provide administrative recordkeeping related to students' academic careers. In most contemporary postsecondary institutions, the primary purpose of the SDW is to aggregate, organize, extract, and archive student data to support organizational functions.

As the technologies of information classification and documentary identity change, so too does the SDW. The SDW links data collection and extraction technologies with organizational and archival tools. Its increased automation allows data work to occur in ways that are opaque to institutional actors and data subjects. The SDW potentially governs students and instructors through involvement in predictive analytical tools and systems of judgment. Individual actors still need to act upon these tools; however, as I illustrate below, the accumulation and exercise of power through informatics (see Brown et al., 2023) originates in the automated work of the SDW.

A Very Brief History of Recordkeeping in U.S. Higher Education

There are three key periods in the lifespan of the SDW that have shaped its development and implementation, which in turn have made possible different kinds of work within the institution. Each period reflects the needs of the institution for information. Early on, information about students is maintained for the purposes of verification and credentialing. As the federal government increases reporting requirements, and as computational capacity for storage and analysis increases, the SDW grows and changes. It transitions from a static archive to a dynamic technology with the potential to inform organizational futures.

The first period, *data inputs*, spans from the institution's founding through the expansion of undergraduate and graduate education as part of the GI Bill and onward to the passage of the Family Educational Rights and Privacy Act (FERPA). The second period, *data processes*, is largely driven by government intervention and focuses on how the student information system is systematized to protect the rights of students as data subjects, reduce institutional risk for data disclosure, and meet institutional reporting needs after the creation of the Integrated Postsecondary Data System (IPEDS). This period spans the late 1970s through the early 2000s and includes the passage of the Jeanne Clery Act. The final period, *data extraction*, involves the expansion of digital technologies in the organization and administration of higher education institutions, including the widespread use of learning management systems (LMS; e.g., Krumm, 2012) and the construction of the data warehouse.

During the era of data inputs, the informatics of documentary bookkeeping are developed and technologies of documentary identity become stable (Koopman, 2019). For example, at the end of the 19th century through the early 20th century, the U.S. government begins to provide social security cards, which allow individuals to demonstrate their identities and assert their rights to things like veterans benefits after the Civil War (Koopman, 2019). Higher education institutions are increasingly expected to develop their own documentary bookkeeping to aid individuals in documenting their earned credentials and to keep track of entitlements like the GI Bill. The institutional student data system involves an ad hoc network of physical records stored in various physical locations without standardized requirements. During this period, the student information system is often treated as a burdensome and costly network of people and technologies — because it is mostly composed of human beings reading and summarizing records. This period ends with the passage of FERPA in 1974, which provides students with specific rights to control their data representations and requires institutions to formalize their bookkeeping practices.

As a consequence, the SDW shifts from an input-focused archive to a process-focused network. Federal reporting requirements increase alongside policy mandates that place a burden on institutions to protect student data (and to ensure that that data are accurate). State and federal policies require the institution to develop a regular reporting system, the baseline for which is generally mandated through the annual IPEDS survey. The IPEDS survey goes beyond previous accreditation and reporting requirements to set a national template for what kinds of student information need to be archived and retrieved. During this period, the institution's ability to store information also increases substantially with the development of computational power and the construction of digital storage systems on campus. The institution invests substantial resources in the movement from what stakeholders call the "miles of tape" system to digital and cloud-based storage. Specialized staff are hired to maintain new data infrastructure and to manage new reporting and archiving requirements. In the same period, changes to Title IX and the passage of the Clery Act increase institutional reporting requirements.

In the final period, data extraction, the SDW transitions from liability to asset. Institutional leaders, previously frustrated by the burdensome investments required to maintain the SDW, are now looking for strategic ways to capitalize on student data, both to improve teaching and learning activities and to better position the institution in competitive student choice markets. The student information system (SIS) now includes a set of unified technologies, often purchased from an outside vendor, that make extraction and storage of data from multiple interoperable systems possible with little human involvement. The SIS now feeds the SDW as their virtual environment where millions of educational records are stored on servers. This data warehouse is no longer located on campus, and the work that is done within and through the warehouse is mostly opaque to students, faculty, and staff. Traces of this work show up in digital technologies that are "fed" by the warehouse, like digital dashboards that track student engagement and provide early warnings about students' potential for success in the classroom.

Across all three periods, the SIS and the resulting student data warehouse are shaped by technologies of racial retrenchment, allowing institutions to track and classify students based on racial categories. D. L. Stewart (2017) refers to this process as the production of docile student bodies, where the system of normalizing judgment that analytical technologies facilitate reinforces the logics of white supremacy. In each period, the SIS and the SDW categorize and classify racially minoritized students, a process that becomes more powerful the further it is removed from human intervention. In the early periods, recordkeeping and documentary technologies are used to limit access. In the final period, when early warning systems become widespread, the historical legacies of racism, sexism, heteronormativity, and cis-normativity are "baked into" the warehouse data that are used to classify a student's "risk" to the institution, framing the data subject as a problem before they've potentially even begun their student experience.

Contemporary Debates on Student Data Systems

Contemporary commentary on the SDW focuses on who has access to student data, how they gain access, and for what purpose. These are important questions that institutions should wrestle with as part of their ethic of care and concern for students. Often, this work focuses on either the behaviors of individuals and their use of data (e.g., Brown, 2020; Taylor, 2020; Whitman, 2020) or on how institutions treat data resources as part of increased datafication efforts (e.g., Brown et al. 2023; Komljenovic, 2020; Smithers, 2023). The SDW often becomes invisible in this analysis, leaving the architecture of datafication likewise invisible.

In this section, I review some of the key contemporary debates about datafication in U.S. higher education. I identify how an explicit focus on what the SDW affords and constrains could help scholars and practitioners identify the potential for harm that comes from datafication initiatives. My research provides insight into one of the core debates regarding datafication: what control individuals should have over their data representations (Brown, 2020; Brown & Klein, 2020).

In a study with faculty using a new dashboard technology, instructors were surprised and frustrated to learn that the technology was collecting data about the assessments they used, attendance by their students, and their choices of instructional artifacts and then reporting it back to their departments (Brown, 2020). Instructors viewed this as a violation of their classroom autonomy, and this resulted in further questioning about other aspects of the technology. Eventually, they decreased (or in many cases ceased) their use of the tool in the classroom.

These instructors had an expectation that departments and colleges had a need to know about their students, but when they were subject to surveillance activities, they opted out to the extent that they could. Regardless, this concern did not generate conversations about technology use in the classroom, as faculty often considered this outside the realm of curricular governance. In their minds, curriculum was content, sequence, and assessment. Technology use was a pedagogical strategy that should be left up to individual instructors. Faculty were not inclined to challenge their departments to figure out how to create student-centered technology systems. Instead, they engaged in resistance in their perceived domain of influence — by building classrooms and courses that defended against the intrusion of data extraction technologies. If they could not control where data went, they would prevent the movement of data at the point of origin.

That technology adoption, implementation, and use were uneven, local, and often independent of conversations about governance and students' rights was perhaps not surprising (Brown & Klein, 2020). In my research on data privacy policies with Dr. Carrie Klein, we observed that institutions rarely update their policies in a way that reflects the speed of technological change. Policy documents generally treat data as a static artifact that is manually updated by people and are silent on the *potential* use of data. Students have little control over their representation in the SDW and generally have no recourse regarding data sharing with third parties. While some institutions might have SDW-specific policies, what we have observed more often are technology-specific policies — for example, a policy for a plagiarism detector that might (albeit rarely) explain where student data are stored and under what conditions.

In a call for further research on the political economy of data assets in *Higher Education*, Janja Komljenovic (2020) argues for scholarship that goes beyond questions about data privacy to consider how data are valued in postsecondary organizations. As institutions work to accrue more data and to convert those data into other forms of value, they will have little incentive to consider the desires of individuals from whom data are extracted. Komljenovic argues that as economies reorganize themselves around rentiership contracts — where individuals must pay regularly to access resources like broadband, streaming services, or other digital platforms — data capture and archiving will become a focal activity of organizations.

In my own research, I have observed how institutions have moved away from externally developed tools — like Turnitin and Proctorio, which harvest student data to build algorithmic technologies that they license back to institutions and students — toward building their own homegrown solutions. Similarly, institutions have renegotiated their data sharing agreements with digital platform technologies, declining to share student data with third-party vendors in order to build their own databases and corpuses for local use. Initiatives like Learning @ Scale at Arizona State University suggest a future where the value of data creates a press on teaching and learning activities to produce more data. The SDW becomes the central organization technology through which this work can occur.

Recent research by Leonard Taylor (2020) illustrates the future that Komljenovic is concerned about. Taylor identifies how data resources become commodities within postsecondary organizations. Without access to data, individuals are unable to access other resources on campus. This competition produces internal data markets where part of an individual's work becomes political labor focused on access to data. The SDW, in this instance, is the technology through which markets are organized and given their power. As such, gatekeepers of the SDW have significant influence over the development of student success programs on campus, determining who gets access to what resources. Understanding who controls the SDW and why, as well as how they engage in decision-making about access to data resources, has significant implications for understanding the organization of higher education institutions.

The SDW can remake the student experience in the same ways that it reorients the work of student success practitioners. Laura Smithers (2023) documents how the pursuit of predictive analytics as part of student success initiatives creates a permanent present through a logic of preemption, reducing activities into measurable and adjustable parameters. Predictive analytics fuel an attachment to a future — either desired or feared — that never arrives. Preemptive action guides practice, allowing individuals, for example, to rationalize decisions in the present. Learning experiences "that lead to futures we could not have predicted" are stolen by preemption made possible through the SDW (Smithers, 2023, p. 119).

In our recent research on curriculum reform, we observed how the SDW holds an outsized influence on the imagination of faculty. Throughout debates about curricular policy and credit transfer, institutional actors on both sides of a debate about credit transfer argued about the data that informed reform proposals. Through "data talk," faculty and administrators argued that data assets existed that could and should be used to support their version of reform. The SDW is imagined to be a capacious archive — an unlimited supply of information that will effectively resolve long-term debates about the sequence and content of the curriculum. Solutions did exist, institutional actors insisted, and they existed in the SDW. The problem was that the wrong data were used, or they were used in the wrong ways.

Throughout the discussion, administrators exercised informatic power, "which entangles strategic and logistic power together through combined systems of incentives and sanctions based upon measurement and analysis which are made possible by computing technologies" (Brown et al., 2023, p. 7). The focus on "data talk" elides core debates about the moral purpose of the curriculum. Rather, time, energy, and thought are given over to questions about relationships to the SDW. How should data assets be used? Who should have access to them? What data should be released? These questions reorient curriculum-making activities around data collection, analysis, and archiving. Curriculum, in this context, can be rationalized and made efficient. As Smithers argues above, the SDW attempts to foreclose futures by a curriculum of pre-emptive action — pathways that are not simply guided but directive.

Understanding the Student Data Warehouse

As institutions move toward increased managerialism and corporate logics of efficiency, there is a critical need for research that conceptualizes what the SDW is, what it does, and how it can be enfolded into collaborative governance activities. The guiding question of this era is a distinction between whether students, faculty, and staff will allow ourselves to be governed by data, or whether we will choose to govern data use. To achieve the latter, we need people-centered models of governance that are collaborative and deliberative, and that prioritize control over data representation. To that end, through a series of guiding questions I offer a conceptual framework that informs research and practice on its configuration and governance.

Contents

First, I argue for a focus on (and transparency regarding) what the SDW contains. Often, the SDW is treated as a black box through which massive data assets flow. But each SDW has a logic of classification and organization that reflects its technological design and the social interactions that it facilitates.

As Ruha Benjamin (2019) notes, the lack of transparency about what digital archives contain allows anti-Black boxes to proliferate. If we are to understand the racial and gendered systems of classification that the SDW affords, we need insight into how information about students and their contexts is encoded. SDWs, for example, reduce complex experiences of racialization and gendered socializations to binaries through the datafication of student experience.

Relationships

Next, we turn our attention to the SDW and its connections. What individuals make the SDW work? And what work does the SDW afford? Identifying who is connected and who is cut off from data resources reveals how informatic power functions. Similarly, what technologies are connected to the SDW? What data do these technologies provide and what data assets do they rely on? When institutions connect new technologies to an SDW, do they contribute or do they extract? What rules and expectations might we need that differ for extraction technologies in contrast to predictive technologies?

Effects

Finally, I argue for work that considers the impacts of the SDW's contents and its relationships. Who is subjected to the effects of the SDW, especially when it is driving extractive or predictive interactions? How far-reaching are the effects of the SDW? What can we learn from exercises of informatic power, especially as they relate to the disciplinary power of prediction?

These questions are offered as a starting point. By situating the historical emergence of the SDW and contemporary debates in higher education related to its function and configuration, we hope to inspire research and practice that allows for people-centered solutions. Too often, in our own work and through the scholarship I detail, we observe that institutions build their technologies outside of governance activities and then use these technologies to unify the means and ends of reform. As institutions move toward models where data have academic and commercial value, it is imperative that institutional actors — especially students — have control over the data extracted from their activities. That the data extracted from student learning are archived from a future where they inform algorithmic models, artificial intelligence, and other institutional imaginaries from which students will never benefit violates institutional ethics of care. We need a full accounting to inform what comes next.

Acknowledgments

This work was supported in part by the Future of Privacy Foundation.

References

Benjamin, R. (2019). *Race after technology: Abolitionist tools for the New Jim Code*. John Wiley & Sons.

Bowman, N. A., Jarratt, L., Polgreen, L. A., Kruckeberg, T., & Segre, A. M. (2019). Early identification of students' social networks: Predicting college retention and graduation via campus dining. *Journal of College Student Development, 60*(5), 617–622. https://doi.org/10.1353/csd.2019.0052

Brown, M. G. (2016). Blended instructional practice: A review of the empirical literature on instructors' adoption and use of online tools in face-to-face teaching. *The Internet and Higher Education, 31*, 1–10. https://doi.org/10.1016/j.iheduc.2016.05.001

Brown, M. (2020). Seeing students at scale: How faculty in large lecture courses act upon learning analytics dashboard data. *Teaching in Higher Education, 25*(4), 384–400. https://doi.org/10.1080/13562517.2019.1698540

Brown, M., & Klein, C. (2020). Whose data? Which rights? Whose power? A policy discourse analysis of student privacy policy documents. *The Journal of Higher Education, 91*(7), 1149–1178. https://doi.org/10.1080/00221546.2020.1770045

Brown, M., Sowl, S. and Steigelder, K. (2023) "May I contribute some data to the discussion?": Negotiating data politics through general education reform. *The Journal of Higher Education, 94*(7), pp. 851–895. https://doi.org/10.1080/00221546.2023.2203629

Cox, B. E., Reason, R. D., Tobolowsky, B. F., Brower, R. L., Patterson, S., Luczyk, S., & Roberts, K. (2017). Lip service or actionable insights? Linking student experiences to institutional assessment and data-driven decision making in higher education. *The Journal of Higher Education, 88*(6), 835–862. https://doi.org/10.1080/00221546.2016.1272320

Komljenovic, J. (2020). The future of value in digitalised higher education: Why data privacy should not be our biggest concern. *Higher Education, 83*(1), 119–135. https://doi.org/10.1007/s10734-020-00639-7

Koopman, C. (2019). *How we became our data: A genealogy of the informational person*. University of Chicago Press.

Krumm, A. E. (2012). *An examination of the diffusion and implementation of learning management systems in higher education* [Doctoral dissertation, University of Michigan]. Deep Blue Documents. https://deepblue.lib.umich.edu/handle/2027.42/96042

Smithers, L. (2023). Predictive analytics and the creation of the permanent present. *Learning, Media and Technology, 48*(1), 109–121.

Stewart, D. L. (2017). Producing "docile bodies": Disciplining citizen-subjects. *International Journal of Qualitative Studies in Education, 30*(10), 1042–1046. https://doi.org/10.1080/09518398.2017.1312598

Taylor, L. D., Jr. (2020). Neoliberal consequence: Data-driven decision making and the subversion of student success efforts. *The Review of Higher Education, 43*(4), 1069–1097. https://doi.org/10.1353/rhe.2020.0031

Williamson, B. (2018). The hidden architecture of higher education: Building a big data infrastructure for the "smarter university." *International Journal of Educational Technology in Higher Education, 15*, Article 12. https://doi.org/10.1186/s41239-018-0094-1

Whitman, M. (2020). "We called that a behavior": The making of institutional data. *Big Data & Society, 7*(1), 2053951720932200.

Part II

Potential Uses to Inform Practice

6

Putting AI into Practice

Applications for Serving Students and Campuses

Brandi Hephner LaBanc, Chrysoula Malogianni,

Zia Ahmed, and Fred H. Tugas

How can campuses build a robust artificial intelligence (AI) ecosystem to better serve students? This chapter, written by a team of campus-based professionals, considers how colleges and universities can use AI to enhance students' experiences, engagement, and success. First, we consider how to develop an effective holistic learning system that weaves together insights from systems that include client relationship manager and learning management systems and from data and metrics related to student engagement and enrollment. Next, we turn to how AI tools can support efforts related to student communication and success. Finally, we highlight key areas that should be taken into account when using AI tools on campus, such as issues related to privacy, accessibility, and continuous improvement. The chapter complements the legal and theoretical analyses in other chapters by demonstrating how these technologies can influence everyday practices on campus.

Elements of an Effective Holistic Learning Ecosystem

Whether constructing systems to support campus-based or online learners, institutions should aim to develop a holistic learning ecosystem that integrates technologies driven by AI support mechanisms (Moghadam et al., 2023). To realize this vision, a robust data-layering system must be constructed and be capable of amalgamating insights from diverse sources (Liu et al., 2017). To that end, this section outlines how campuses might consider designing a holistic approach to engage and support all students more effectively. As covered in this section, to achieve this holistic approach requires attention to client relationship, learning management systems, and student data information on enrollment and engagement, such as metrics related to engagement and time allocation with learning management systems. Coordination of systems, collection of key analytics, and continuous review of outputs will help guide efficiencies and improvements, all of which will result in enhanced student engagement and success.

Client Relationship Manager and Learning Management Systems

Campus-based professionals can use data insights, such as from learning management systems, to creatively challenge and support individual students' journeys on campus. Use of what is referred to as a client relationship manager (CRM) provides an integrated approach for institutions to be able to track and manage data involving interactions with constituencies that include prospective students, enrolled students, and alumni, with the ultimate goal of better serving these individuals. For example, a well-constructed CRM coupled with intentionally designed predictive analytics can enable campuses to recruit, enroll, retain, and engage across the totality of an individual's relationship with an institution, from prospective student, to enrolled student, to alumni. For current students, the CRM can gather inputs about students' preferences and tendencies, and this will help power a personalized and meaningful experience.

Such an integrated data and information approach sets up AI-enabled systems to remind students about relevant opportunities or processes as a way of reinforcing successful behavior and performance. For instance, a student who inquires about financial aid could be nudged to attend a virtual workshop on completing the FASFA; a student who previously self-reported low confidence in math might receive AI-enabled early-action targeted support prompts, such as algebra tutoring resources, or their success coach might receive an alert to reach out to offer guidance.

At the same time, the campus learning management system (LMS) serves as the central hub for course-related activities and interactions and can play a pivotal role in an AI-enabled initiative. The LMS meticulously collects a wealth of data pertaining to student engagement with course materials, including assignment submissions, quiz outcomes, and participation in online discussions. This extensive data collection is crucial for AI systems, which rely on large datasets to train algorithms and make accurate predictions. Data warehousing at this level does create privacy concerns that should be analyzed and adopted with great ethical care. Nonetheless, by analyzing patterns in student engagement and performance, AI can provide personalized recommendations and interventions, identifying students who may need additional support and tailoring resources to their needs. However, for holistic support and AI integration, it is equally essential to delve into the temporal dimension of student interactions within the LMS (Chen et al., 2023). A significant portion of the learning experience in higher education is dedicated to non-learning tasks, from navigating courses to accessing study materials and submitting assignments. Understanding this temporal aspect helps refine the LMS user interface and related support, reducing the administrative burden on students. This, in turn, allows AI systems to more effectively pinpoint areas where students can benefit from automation and personalized assistance, thereby enhancing the overall learning experience.

Student Profiles

Integrating academic histories, goals, and student preferences into comprehensive profiles takes center stage in campus efforts to provide automated, personalized support (Walkington & Bernacki, 2020). These profiles serve as the foundation for tailoring recommendations and services to the unique needs of each student. AI technologies play a crucial role in this process by analyzing vast amounts of data to detect patterns and predict future behaviors. By leveraging AI, institutions can further enrich these profiles, incorporating data and generating inquiries related to enrollment patterns and form completions, such as when students enroll in courses and complete administrative forms, including financial aid applications. AI systems utilize these data to inform predictive models for identifying students who may be at-risk of matriculating, which enables proactive support and interventions for those facing academic obstacles (Smithers, 2023). Likewise, campus-based CRM systems can streamline data to personalize student profiles and generate engagement opportunities as students' interests and needs evolve. These systems ensure timely interventions, providing students with the support they need precisely when they need or request it. Institutions that leverage comprehensive, integrated student profiles gain an edge in delivering a high-quality, personalized, and adaptive student experience. By integrating AI into student success practices, higher education administrators can make more thoughtful inquiries and foster genuine connections with students.

Enrollment Patterns and Engagement Metrics

Examining enrollment patterns and the efficiency of form completion processes can reveal insights into students' initial interactions with the campus learning environment — whether on campus or online (Thompson, 2023). Data on when students enroll in courses, how promptly they complete necessary forms (e.g., registration, financial aid applications), and whether there are any bottlenecks in these processes can inform improvements in the onboarding experience.

In order to personalize and provide timely support, engagement metrics emerge as a pivotal facet of AI-enabled strategy (Almusaed et al., 2023). These metrics encompass variables such as video views, time spent on course materials, and login frequency, all meticulously collected and analyzed. These insights form the foundation for developing instructional materials and delivering personalized recommendations, ensuring that students receive content tailored to their specific needs (Chen et al., 2023). To refine this aspect further, a deeper investigation into the timing of student engagement is warranted. This will guide academic leaders on when to schedule live virtual sessions or release critical course content aligned with students' peak engagement periods. (We explore cocurricular engagement a bit later in the chapter.)

Administrative Tasks and Time Allocation

In addition to academic engagement, understanding the time students allocate to administrative tasks within the digital learning environment is crucial (Liu et al., 2017). These tasks may include navigating the course management system, managing communications with instructors and peers, accessing resources, and submitting assignments. This information is vital for optimizing the user experience and streamlining administrative processes to reduce student workload. And tracking the time students take to complete various tasks — such as registering for courses, accessing resources, or submitting assignments — can also provide insights into workflow efficiencies. For instance, monitoring the disbursement of financial aid and its impact on students' academic progress is essential. Analyzing the timing of financial aid disbursements in relation to students' needs and academic milestones can help institutions better support financially disadvantaged students. These data can also shed light on the effectiveness of financial aid programs in promoting student success (Rahm, 2023).

In synthesis, by expanding data collection efforts to encompass not only what students do but also when they do it and how they do it, we are poised to construct a comprehensive and highly responsive holistic learning ecosystem within our digital campus. This approach ensures that the student experience is deeply personalized and marked by timeliness and proactive support, all contributing to elevated student success and satisfaction within the context of a broader AI-enabled educational vision.

Communication Channels

A nuanced understanding of communication patterns and their temporal dimensions is crucial for the campus-based and online ecosystem (Chen et al., 2023; Moghadam et al., 2023). AI plays a significant role in analyzing data encompassing meeting records and interactions on messaging platforms, providing valuable insights into how students collaborate and communicate, and facilitating improvements in support services and interactions. However, campuses must also consider the timing of these interactions. By leveraging AI algorithms, campuses can identify patterns and critical moments when students are most likely to seek help or engage with instructors and peers, such as just before assignment deadlines or during exam preparation. These AI-driven insights guide the allocation of support resources and timely interventions, enhancing the overall effectiveness of communication and support services.

Surveys and Feedback

Qualitative data derived from course evaluations and student satisfaction surveys hold the key to enhancing student engagement and learning (Thompson, 2023). AI can analyze these qualitative data at scale, uncovering patterns and trends that may not be immediately apparent through manual analysis. This analysis offers invaluable insights into student satisfaction, challenges, and expectations, empowering institutions to fine-tune support mechanisms and address specific pain points. By using AI to assess feedback collected at strategic intervals throughout a course, such as after major assignments or at midterm, institutions can implement timely improvements in response to student concerns, ensuring a more responsive and effective educational environment.

Enhancing Student Engagement and Success

Once the data architecture has been built and synthesized, AI tools allow campuses to innovate with technology while complementing the human experience within the intricacies of the campus environment they are required to navigate. While there remains skepticism about whether AI-enabled technologies will eliminate jobs, it is already evident in many offices that this technology allows higher education professionals to save time on many transactional administrative tasks and reallocate that time to focus on the most important aspects of their work. Stated simply, AI-enabled processes will allow higher education practitioners to further their educational mission and deepen their work related to student success.

Whether working with students on campus or virtually, AI tools should be leveraged to handle transactional work so humans can focus on connections and meaningful engagements that accelerate student success. These tools position staff to be more proactive than ever before. AI technology allows campus leaders to cultivate and nurture connections beginning at the college application stage, through orientation and onboarding engagements, and across the matriculated experience of the learner. This allows campus leaders to align stated goals and motivations with career aspirations to promote academic determination and student involvement.

Simply put, AI will elevate the student experience by seamlessly blending technology and daily human interactions. Today's traditional students — as well as adult students juggling numerous responsibilities — expect rapid accessibility, personalization, and in-the-moment awareness of available resources. To improve effectiveness in these areas, AI-enabled tools, such as chatbots or virtual assistance programs, provide low-complexity, routine information to automate functions that assist in facilitating student support and success. This remainder of this section explores applied opportunities within enrollment management and student services where AI-enabled interventions can create a better campus environment for students.

Chatbots and Virtual Student Support

Chatbots have emerged as a tool to enhance engagement and support, designed to enable automated interactions between students, faculty, staff, and institutions to provide instant responses to inquiries. On a daily basis, most people encounter these types of AI-enabled tools; thus, they should be leveraged to facilitate efficient engagement across campus. A primary advantage of chatbots is their ability to offer personalized support to students. Some examples include

> highlighting available academic programs to a prospective students;
> providing course options and suggested sequencing for current and returning students;
> answering family members' questions as they navigate the financial aid process; and
> providing office hours and after-hours crisis resources for individuals researching counseling services.

Through interactions with a chatbot, the CRM can gather information about a student's specific needs, interests, and enrollment status to provide adequate, real-time support throughout that student's educational journey. It is important to mention that a chatbot or like tool is only useful with reliable and dynamic data to pull from. To this end, websites must be accurately maintained and frequently refreshed to provide high confidence in the AI-enabled tools. When websites are outdated or have broken links the chatbot is likely rendered ineffective.

Another distinct advantage of this type of AI are the operational efficiencies that can result. Chatbots reduce staff workload by addressing routine tasks and inquiries; virtual assistants provide excellent information and support, as they are designed to complement the professional as they address more complex and personalized student interactions. As mentioned earlier, this is advantageous, as staff and faculty can set aside the more bureaucratic elements of their positions and focus on meaningful dialogue and direction.

Also consider that getting a chatbot system set up will likely challenge administrators to demystify their complex processes and procedures to ensure that the technology can communicate effectively and accurately with the end user. This administrative exercise often provides insight into outdated process and burdensome protocols — in other words, barriers to student success. Once designed with simplicity and implemented with comprehensive support information, chatbots can prove transformative as they streamline administrative processes, promote timely student engagement, and reduce the burden on staff, allowing time for developmental engagement.

As mentioned, chatbots can enhance communication from the point of prospect throughout the student experience. For prospective students navigating a university website, an integrated AI-powered chatbot complements the digital experience by providing proactive support while collecting data-driven insights about the interaction to inform future inquiries. For current students, chatbots can provide reminders about upcoming assignment due dates, administrative deadlines like tuition payment and course registration, and invitations to campuswide events.

Since chatbots complement and connect students to human interactions, the technology can encourage students to utilize critical campus resources and aid them in doing so. If a student continues to log in to their LMS but neglects to complete quickly approaching assignments, a chatbot could suggest an academic support resource relevant to the course. The data collected from a chatbot interaction could identify, for example, that a student navigates their LMS or other authenticated sites consistently in the early morning hours and subsequently suggest available stress-reduction or sleep health resources. In cases of immediate crisis, chatbots can be programmed to recognize terms that indicate a student may be in urgent need of support interventions. Of course, chatbots do not replace human interactions and intervention, and the intentional design and implementation of these systems with data privacy and ethical considerations is paramount.

Facilitating Peer Connections

Another significant aspect of student success is the quality of peer engagement and meaningful relationships — in a word, *belongingness*. In addition to enhancing the institutional engagement experience, AI can facilitate engagement among peers so as to contribute to a greater sense of belonging, well-being, and academic success. At various points in a student's engagement journey, feedback can be solicited and behaviors can be tracked to better understand what that student wants from their campus experience. Algorithms can then be employed throughout the journey to match students based on their interests, goals, personal needs, and academic majors.

From the point of application to an institution, students can indicate their high school involvement, academic interests, athletic participation, hobbies, and other special interests and preferences. These data points can help connect the student to like-minded roommates in each of the various residential facilities. In the weeks leading up to their new student orientation, AI tools can suggest specific orientation dates to facilitate connections within small groups based on academic curiosities and user-provided personal interests. If a student values resources related to well-being, once they are on campus the AI-enabled tools can highlight pertinent resources and activities, and even build in a daily reminder to meditate. As the technology provides insight into how a new student engages with content, peer connections, and the residential experience, the predictive algorithms can better personalize information and communication throughout the student journey. To that end, AI can recommend student organizations that align with the student's passions, career aspirations, and social interests. Arguably AI-enabled tools may not always get things right, and there is potential they could limit students' engagement — but more than likely the technology will foster a sense of discovery, exploration, and responsibility in the critical transition period of the first-year student experience.

The ability to enable meaningful relationships extends way beyond the social acclimation of the new first-year student. AI-powered virtual communities and forums can provide dynamic spaces for students within a student organization or academic college to interact, share experiences, and collaborate on projects. For more advanced students, predictive analytic software can facilitate career connections with alumni or relevant companies based on strengths and interests. AI-enabled tools can direct students to key campus resources to augment their courseload or direct them to new job postings that align with their career goals.

AI technology can also be utilized to support mentoring relationships by providing resources for both mentors and mentees. For instance, decision-support technology can be paired with staff or peer mentors to provide comprehensive, targeted, and personalized support for a mentee. The combination allows for the continued engagement of a mentor with adequate knowledge of resources and services while maintaining the critical authenticity and connection that comes from peer-to-peer mentoring interactions. Whether the mentor is a peer within a specific academic discipline or an alumnus who supports students of underrepresented backgrounds in their field, AI can play a crucial role in providing space for community and individual connection based on interests and needs. Although traditional-aged students are highly comfortable with technology, there may be varying levels of comfort with predictive data when used for non-academic purposes. Nonetheless, AI technology can prove beneficial to elevating social connections and social mobility, whether interactions are primarily online or in person.

Dining Services

Thus far we have provided some broad-based examples of the power of AI when it comes to driving student engagement and success. Here we will explore some very specific applications that have transformational impact on daily campus life. In particular, dining services plays a pivotal role in shaping the overall student experience in university campus life, and innovations in food and technology have become prominent factors in enhancing this experience. Indeed, cutting-edge AI-enabled technologies redefine how students access meals and optimize time management while supporting sustainable practices.

Mobile Ordering: A Student-Centric Revolution

Mobile ordering is a significant leap forward in modernizing dining services on university campuses. Mobile applications leverage AI to streamline ordering and receiving meals, putting the power of choice and convenience in the hands of students. The implementation of mobile ordering — allowing students to browse menus, customize orders, and pay seamlessly from their smartphones — significantly enhances accessibility and convenience. Students can order meals from anywhere on campus, minimizing wait times and providing a more efficient way to access food during busy schedules. This seamless integration of technology into their daily routine exemplifies the adaptability and responsiveness of modern campus dining services.

Mobile apps can empower students to manage many variables affecting their time, making the process more streamlined and efficient. For instance, they can readily assess live wait times through the app and make informed decisions about when to place an order. Moreover, an app enables customized order placement tailored to individual preferences, enhancing the user experience. An example is the app's ability to recommend orders from history, allowing users to avoid specifying modifications or dietary preferences each time they place an order. Mobile ordering technology facilitates more seamless and personalized time utilization, promoting efficiency and convenience for busy students.

Mobile ordering systems utilize AI algorithms to analyze individual preferences and ordering patterns. This data-driven approach enables personalized recommendations, suggesting meal options that align with students' dietary needs and previous orders. Students can declare their dietary preferences in the mobile app, which can help make the future ordering process more seamless. For instance, if students consistently order vegan meals, AI algorithms can suggest new vegan options that align with their taste preferences. Through such personalization, students feel a stronger connection with the campus dining services, fostering a positive and engaging experience. This level of personalization enhances the dining experience and encourages nutritionally balanced eating habits among students, promoting overall well-being.

Autonomous Food Delivery: The Future of Dining Services

Notably, most residential college campuses are not optimally designed for regular food delivery using traditional vehicles since individual food delivery programs using conventional cars were rare where these campuses were built. The challenge lies in the need for more convenient parking spaces. Spaces that are available often require lengthy walks to the delivery destination. This inconvenience introduces significant inefficiencies in the delivery process and often leads discouraged students off campus to find food options.

Autonomous food delivery emerges as a solution to the pressing need for swift and punctual meal deliveries, particularly during peak hours when demand is high or when the weather is unpleasant. Indeed, autonomous food delivery represents a futuristic vision becoming a reality on several university campuses. While autonomous food delivery can present challenges to pedestrians or may be damaged on busy roadways, in general, AI-powered robots (rovers) effectively navigate campuses, delivering meals directly to students' desired locations. This innovation transcends traditional delivery methods, offering a blend of efficiency, novelty, security, and sustainability. Integrating AI algorithms, optimized delivery routes, and timing ensures a seamless and efficient process for students to receive their orders promptly. Heightened speed and efficiency significantly enhance the overall dining experience, allowing students to adhere to their schedules while enjoying their meals without compromise.

Moreover, traditional food delivery may raise safety concerns among students regarding the identity and intentions of the person delivering their food. Autonomous delivery rovers offer an alternative solution that alleviates these concerns. These self-operating vehicles can access residence halls more efficiently and provide students with a heightened sense of security, addressing apprehensions related to human interactions during delivery. This amalgamation of technological advancement and enhanced security fosters a conducive environment for streamlined and secure food delivery on college campuses.

Adoption of autonomous vehicles also contributes immensely to sustainable practices. Autonomous rovers have been proven to operate with remarkable energy efficiency, emitting significantly less environmentally harmful gases that conventional vehicles typically demand (Chu, 2024). And integrating advanced AI into these vehicles allows for perpetual enhancement and refinement of their route-planning algorithms. This dynamic AI-enabled capability ensures a continuous search for the most efficient routes, significantly minimizing energy consumption during travel.

In sum, mobile ordering empowers students to tailor their dining experiences, optimizing their schedules and choices through intuitive AI-enabled mobile applications. This innovation enhances accessibility, promotes efficient time management, and cultivates a personalized connection with dining services. Autonomous food delivery, an embodiment of the future, addresses the need for rapid, efficient meal deliveries while aligning with sustainability goals. Integrating AI algorithms optimizes delivery routes, significantly reducing the carbon footprint associated with traditional delivery methods.

Other Critical Considerations

As campus leaders put AI into practice, there are many things to consider. Constructing an effective ecosystem is critical, and consideration for the powerful ways these technologies can enhance student engagement and success is germane to early and rapid adoption. In addition to the elements mentioned previously, it is important to adopt several key strategies to ensure alignment. These are briefly explored below.

Ethical Considerations and Data Privacy

As campuses venture into AI deployment, they must prioritize ethical considerations, including safeguarding data privacy, promoting transparency in algorithmic decision-making, and proactively addressing potential biases inherent in AI models (Chen et al., 2020; Hillman, 2023; Nemorin, 2023). Rigorous security measures and data-privacy protocols must be firmly in place to protect sensitive student data, aligning AI endeavors with ethical principles.

Accessibility, Inclusivity, and Student-Centric Design

Prioritizing accessibility and inclusivity in AI-powered solutions is imperative. This entails the implementation of features such as speech-to-text, text-to-speech, and various assistive technologies to cater to a wide range of student needs, including for students with disabilities. Likewise, a student-centric approach to developing AI-powered tools and services involves students in the design and testing phases to gather their feedback and insights. This approach ensures that AI solutions are user-friendly, align with student preferences, and address their specific needs (Rham, 2023).

Faculty and Staff Empowerment Through Training

To fully harness the potential of AI, it is imperative to offer comprehensive training and professional development opportunities for faculty and staff. Educators must gain a profound understanding of how AI can enhance their teaching efforts and amplify the student experience (Wu et al., 2023). Training initiatives should encompass a spectrum of topics, including AI tool proficiency, ethical guidelines, data security best practices, and considerations surrounding intellectual property and copyright.

Continuous Improvement and Quality Assurance

The journey toward an AI-enabled ecosystem is marked by a commitment to continuous improvement. AI-powered systems should be subject to ongoing evaluation and refinement, guided by user feedback and performance data (Chen et al., 2020; Nemorin, 2023). We need to establish feedback loops to actively engage students and instructors in the process, thereby identifying areas ripe for enhancement. This iterative approach ensures that AI technology remains effective and agile, adapting to the evolving needs of the learning community.

Establishing rigorous data governance practices ensures the accuracy, consistency, and reliability of the data that AI systems rely on. This includes data validation, cleansing, and ensuring data quality standards are consistently met (Thompson, 2023). High-quality data are essential for generating meaningful insights and accurate AI-enabled recommendations.

Research and Evaluation

Sustaining ongoing research and evaluation is crucial to gauge the influence of AI integration on student outcomes, retention rates, and overall satisfaction (Almusaed et al., 2023). Consistently disseminating findings in academic journals and sharing insights within the wider educational community contributes significantly to the collective knowledge base concerning AI in education. In adherence to these strategies, we solidify our commitment to an AI-enabled holistic learning ecosystem that seamlessly aligns with our vision to offer students proactive, personalized support, bridging the virtual classroom with the broader educational experience and propelling us toward a future of educational excellence.

Conclusion

Putting AI into practice in higher education has powerful possibilities — possibilities that further the educational impact and practices of those focused on facilitating student development and success. Nonetheless, it is important for campus leaders to carefully design the infrastructure that will support these tools and related engagement functions — specifically, enrollment and communication. We have shared a few practical examples to begin to highlight the power of AI-complemented practice. This is just a sampling of the myriad ways practice can be amplified with these tools.

Of course, just as has always been the case, higher education leaders should approach this evolution of practice with acute attention to ethics, security, and the appropriate training for staff to maximize impact. Systems and practices should be student-centered, inclusive, and accessible to facilitate wide adoption and engagement. And leaders need to establish a cadence of assessment and continuous improvement as technologies and practice expand. Higher education is on the cusp of technologies that will continue to innovate and disrupt in the near future. As such, putting AI into practice will require a growth mindset, but doing so will take our traditional practices to new heights.

References

Almusaed, A., Almssad, A., Yitmen, I., & Homod, R. Z. (2023). Enhancing student engagement: Harnessing "AIED"'s power in hybrid education — A review analysis. *Education Sciences*, *13*(7), 632. http://dx.doi.org/10.3390/educsci13070632

Chen, C.-T., Chen, C.-M., & Tsai, H.-T. (2023). Using the instant semantic analysis and feedback system for mining effective behavioral patterns to facilitate learning effectiveness of online discussion. *Interactive Learning Environments*. Advance online publication. https://doi.org/10.1080/10494820.2023.2197960

Chen, L., Chen, P., & Lin, Z. (2020). Artificial intelligence in education: A review. *IEEE Access*, *8*, 75264–75278. https://doi.org/10.1109/ACCESS.2020.2988510

Chu, Y. (2024). *The impacts of sidewalk autonomous delivery robots on vehicles travel and emissions: A focus on on-demand delivery*. UCLA Institute of Transportation Studies. https://escholarship.org/uc/item/2r3286pg

Hillman, V. (2023). Bringing in the technological, ethical, educational and social-structural for a new education data governance. *Learning, Media and Technology*, *48*(1), 122–137. https://doi.org/10.1080/17439884.2022.2052313

Liu, D., Bartimote-Aufflick, K., Pardo, A., & Bridgeman, A. J. (2017). Data-driven personalization of student learning support in higher education. In A. Peña-Ayala (Ed.), *Learning analytics: Fundamentals, applications, and trends* (pp. 143–169). Springer. https://doi.org/10.1007/978-3-319-52977-6_5

Moghadam, T., Darejeh, A., Delaramifar, M., & Mashayekh, S. (2023). Toward an artificial intelligence-based decision framework for developing adaptive e-learning systems to impact learners' emotions. *Interactive Learning Environments*. Advance online publication. https://doi.org/10.1080/10494820.2023.2188398

Nemorin, S. (2023). AI hyped? A horizon scan of discourse on artificial intelligence in education (AIED) and development. *Learning, Media and Technology*, *48*(1), 38–51. https://doi.org/10.1080/17439884.2022.2095568

Rahm, L. (2023). Education, automation and AI: A genealogy of alternative futures. *Learning, Media and Technology*, *48*(1), 6–24. https://doi.org/10.1080/17439884.2021.1977948

Smithers, L. (2023). Predictive analytics and the creation of the permanent present. *Learning, Media and Technology*, *48*(1), 1–13. http://dx.doi.org/10.1080/17439884.2022.2036757

Thompson, T. (2023). Returning the data gaze in higher education. *Learning, Media and Technology*, *48*(1), 153–165. https://doi.org/10.1080/17439884.2022.2092130

Walkington, C., & Bernacki, M. (2020). Appraising research on personalized learning: Definitions, theoretical alignment, advancements, and future directions. *Journal of Research on Technology in Education, 52*(3), 235–252. https://doi.org/10.1080/15391523.2020.1747757

Wu, P., Ma, F., & Yu, S. (2023) Using a linked data-based knowledge navigation system to improve teaching effectiveness. *Interactive Learning Environments, 31*(5), 3273–3284. https://doi.org/10.1080/10494820.2021.1925925

7

Predictive Policing in American Schools and Universities

Vanessa Miller

The integration of artificial intelligence (AI) and big data in school and university policing is a growing concern. Often referred to as predictive policing, predictive algorithms and analytics in the regulation of student behavior has raised significant concern amongst scholars, practitioners, families, and community members. This trend raises ethical, legal, and social issues, as it extends the reach of state control and surveillance in educational environments, exacerbating biases and targeting vulnerable populations. The chapter provides an overview of predictive policing in K–12 and higher education and discusses several implications of using surveillance technologies. The discussion underscores the tension between safety, privacy, technological advancements, and the public good of education, cautioning against the adoption of these algorithms and analytics due to their impact and perpetuation of systemic biases.

Big data and artificial intelligence—often in the forms of technologies, algorithms, and predictive analytics—are used to operate many facets of our society. From weather forecasting to retail recommendations, these technologies can improve business operations, optimize marketing strategies, and detect fraud. The criminal-legal system is increasingly relying on data-driven initiatives to guide legal and policy decisions (Rigano, 2019). Predictive algorithms are used by judges to determine whether to hold a defendant in custody before trial (Elyounes, 2020), probation officers to assess a defendant's likelihood of recidivism (Goel et al., 2021), and police officers to allocate resources to patrol locations or surveil specific persons (Cai, 2017). While advocates of predictive analytics in the criminal-legal system purport that algorithms maintain objective mathematical principles, critics argue these algorithms, and the systems they operate within, are not neutral (Ferguson, 2017; Heaven, 2020; Noble, 2018). Automated machine-learning-based algorithms are designed with already existing racially biased data and, when applied, further enforce racially discriminatory practices by judges and police (Ferguson, 2017).

American institutions of education (P–20) also use and rely on algorithms and predictive analytics to help operate important institutional functions, such as admissions, enrollment, instruction, and student success management (Lyon, 2021; Norman, 2023). For example, Starfish Solutions, a widely used student

retention program, tracks and monitors student attendance and grades to predict students who are "at-risk" of failing. Element451, an artificial intelligence marketing service used by college admissions offices, rates the likelihood of success of prospective students based on how they interact with university messaging. Additionally, virtual reality technologies are enhancing classroom instruction by allowing students to become hands-on learners in a variety of disciplines in science education.

Schools and universities are increasingly turning to algorithms and predictive analytics for another critical institutional function—policing. The most salient use of artificial intelligence and big data by school and university police is the incorporation of surveillance technologies that have the ability to ascertain or recognize behavioral patterns, including body-worn cameras, automated license plate scanners, biometric data, and drones (Maass, 2021). School administrators have also turned to and adopted law enforcement surveillance technologies in fulfilment of their duties. A school district in Iowa equipped its principals and assistant principals with body-worn cameras to record interactions between administrators and students as well as between administrators and parents (Ryan, 2015).

In addition to surveillance technologies, the use of predictive algorithms in policing as a viable and legitimate method to surveil and monitor students is emerging. In higher education, the University of Miami Police Department used video analytics to locate and contact students involved in a protest over the university's handling of COVID-19 safety measures (Ceballos, 2020). At the K–12 level, school resource officers (SROs) in Pasco County, Florida, relied on a predictive policing program to identify children who are "destined for a life of crime" (NAACP Legal Defense and Educational Fund, 2021, para. 3). The program calculates an algorithmic risk assessment based on aggregate data from grades and disciplinary histories. The Southern Poverty Law Center, NAACP Legal Defense and Educational Fund, and Southern Legal Counsel sued the Pasco Sherriff's Office because the assessment subjects children to persistent and intrusive surveillance and has a greater impact on Black and Brown students (Southern Poverty Law Center et al., 2022).

While the use of artificial intelligence and big data in law enforcement more generally is developing, its use in school and university policing is garnering attention from researchers and scholars. For example, computer scientists have attempted to model "fair" and "reliable" algorithms to predict crime on campus (Akabari, 2019). Criminologists have researched the impact of body-worn cameras by campus police departments (Gaub, 2022). Journalists are documenting the prevalence of surveillance technologies in campus policing (Maass, 2021). Education researchers are challenging institutional reliance on campus police officers and other carceral practices meant to surveil and monitor students (Johnson & Dizon, 2021; Miller & Russell-Brown, 2023; Suriel et al., 2024).

The movement to incorporate technologies, algorithms, and predictive analytics into school and campus policing will likely dominate how institutions of education surveil, discipline, and police students. Institutions will enhance traditional policing models with video analytics, risk assessments, and data surveillance, further placing students under state control while they are in learning environments. This movement is concerning because school and university police already maintain a substantial and continuous presence in the lives of students and community members, particularly vulnerable populations (Allen & Noguera, 2023; Suriel, et al. 2024). School and university police often have unabridged authority and engage in surveillance and criminalization practices that contradict the public good of education (Fedders, 2021; Miller & Russell-Brown, 2023; Miller, 2024b; Miller, 2024c). Extended models of police presence and surveillance will only exacerbate biases and target vulnerable populations.

With these concerns in mind, this chapter presents a preliminary overview of the use of artificial intelligence and big data in school and campus policing. It provides a synopsis of contemporary iterations and issues of using artificial intelligence and big data in school and campus policing and also discusses legal, ethical, social considerations and implications. This chapter neither suggests nor implies the value of artificial intelligence or big data as entities, but rather highlights their use in policing students in American public schools and universities.

Predictive Policing in Schools and Universities

Predictive policing is a law enforcement model or strategy that incorporates data and algorithms with the intention of anticipating and preventing potential criminal activity (Ferguson, 2017). Generally, predictive policing models analyze crime data, social patterns, and other relevant information to identify trends in order to predict when and where crime is likely to occur (Lau, 2020). Experts and scholars might disagree as to the kinds of data and algorithms that most effectively identify crime trends; however, artificial intelligence and big data facilitate the kinds of data and algorithms generally associated with predictive policing models.

This phenomenon of data-driven policing in educational institutions as a method of surveillance is emerging nationally and globally. For example, the Utah State University Police Department is turning to predictive crime models to map crime "hotspots" to analyze sexual assault and drinking violations on campus (Tanner, 2023). The Michigan State University Security Operations Center maintains a new AI-powered software capable of tracking persons and vehicles (Walters & Scheer, 2024). In the United Kingdom, schools in Bristol use a database that monitors and profiles schoolchildren and uses predictive alerts about those who are at-risk for criminality (Morris, 2023). While not explicitly addressed in this chapter, it is important to also note that institutions surveil and police student access to information, such as access to LGBTQIA+ and race-related content (Laird & Dwyer, 2023).

Despite the growing integration of artificial intelligence and big data across our society, very few research studies have explored its use, application, challenges, or benefits in school and campus policing. This gap in research warrants a space for interdisciplinary scholarship to determine the operation and implications of advanced technologies in varying educational environments, because it not only limits educators' and administrators' understanding of how artificial intelligence and big data impact school safety and student privacy but also impedes development of policies and equity-oriented practices. Likewise, it is imperative that schools and universities are transparent about the kinds of advanced technologies used by their police to implement ethical and effective regulation of technology use. This chapter provides only a brief starting point and highlights contemporary examples of the use of data and algorithms by school and university police as well as the challenges it raises.

Policing and Surveilling K-12

In 2015, police officers arrested a 16-year-old student just days after he started a new high school in Pasco County, Florida (Solon & Farivar, 2021). The student had transferred from another county following an expulsion. Police showed up to his home, searched the house, and claimed to find traces of marijuana in a sandwich bag in his bedroom (Solon & Farivar, 2021; Plaintiff's Complaint for Damages, Declaratory, and Injunctive Relief, 2021, p. 13). As outlined by Solon and Farivar (2021), the student spent 3 weeks in juvenile detention before the judge dismissed the charges due to a lack of measurable marijuana. Following his release, the student was a suspect anytime a crime was reported in the area, leading to officers showing up to the family home at all hours of the day to inquire about him. The student's father was also subjected to police harassment: After refusing officers to conduct warrantless searches in his home, he was cited by police for property code violations, such as overly long grass or missing numbers on his mailbox, and he was arrested five times in 6 months, including for marijuana possession and child neglect (Plaintiff's Complaint for Damages, Declaratory, and Injunctive Relief, 2021, pp. 14–15).

The student was identified by the Pasco Sheriff's Office's (PSO) "intelligence-led policing" (ILP) program as an at-risk youth (Solon & Farivar, 2021). Officers were able to collect and analyze records of former interactions with law enforcement and used his disciplinary and criminal history as a measure to place him "at-risk" of future criminal activity (Bedi & McGrory, 2020). The PSO vehemently contends that its ILP program is an intervention and resource-based approach through which at-risk youth are matched with the resources needed to prevent crime. The program relies on the principles laid out by Jerry Ratcliffe (2016) in *Intelligence-Led Policing*. This book, which is mentioned more than 20 times in the Pasco Sheriff's Office (2020b) manual for identifying at-risk youth, provides a comprehensive overview of the origins and aims of ILP as well as methods of evaluation for ILP models. Of importance, Ratcliffe describes ILP as an approach that "places significant emphasis on data and intelligence analysis as a central component of police strategic thinking" (p. 5).

ILP differs from other policing frameworks, such as the standard model of policing, which is overwhelmingly reactionary. Under the standard model of policing, police respond to an incident and "withdraw to await the next incident that requires attention" (Ratcliffe, 2016, p. 16). This model of "fire brigade" policing is not strategic, with no long-term objectives and "no purpose beyond coping with the here and now" (Ratcliffe, 2016, p. 16). It also differs from community policing, which Ratcliffe argues is a "moving target" that "continually changes with the whims of the public in line with their concerns regarding community safety" (p. 51). Instead, ILP uses data to develop "an objective decision-making framework that [prioritizes] crime hot spots, repeat victims, prolific offenders, and criminal groups" (p. 66). Applying Ratcliffe's principles of ILP to the PSO program, the PSO manual purports law enforcement must be "effective at dealing with crime" (PSO, 2018, p. 6). In particular, the manual emphasizes "[o]ur market is crime and criminals, and we are in the business of crime prevention and reduction" (p. 8). Law enforcement officers are therefore directed to look at "problem people, problem places, and problem groups" (p. 8).

Five years after the arrest of the 16-year-old student, the PSO ILP program made national headlines. On November 19, 2020, the *Tampa Bay Times* published a groundbreaking exposition of the PSO's collection and use of data to identify at-risk youth in local middle and high schools (Bedi & McGrory, 2020). The harrowing report uncovered the PSO's decade-long program to determine criminality and subject students to state control and surveillance (Bedi & McGrory, 2020; Muller, 2023). Leading education and privacy outlets covered the PSO story and published articles covering the legal implications related to FERPA, student data, and school police access to student data (Lieberman, 2020; Reddy, 2020).

The PSO pulled data from three sources to create a list of students they believed were at-risk for engaging in criminal activity: (a) Pasco County Schools; (b) the Florida Department of Children and Families; and (c) the Pasco Sheriff's Office. The data included "educational risk factors, criminological risk factors, and adverse childhood experiences" (PSO, 2018, p. 70) to identify "at-risk youth who are destined to a life of crime" and prevent them "from developing into prolific offenders" (p. 13). Students were categorized as "on-track," "at-risk," or "off-track." Educational risk factors included grades, grade point average, school attendance, and office discipline referrals (p. 70). Criminological risk factors included age of first crime, being a victim of personal crime, having delinquent friends, having a history of running away, being subjected to a custody dispute, and having a gang affiliation (p. 71). Adverse childhood experiences included the frequency of exposure to adverse childhood trauma, such as household member incarceration, physical or emotional abuse, or household substance abuse (p. 72).

The agreement to share data between schools and law enforcement faced intense scrutiny from community members and advocacy groups over concerns of risking children's data and privacy (NAACP Legal Defense and Educational Fund, 2021; Reddy, 2020). A group of civil rights organizations sued the sheriff to disclose the information related to the program because of its intentional design to put children at greater risk of interaction with law enforcement officers (Petition for Writ of Mandamus, 2022).

Approximately 30,000 students in the county's middle and high schools were subject to the PSO ILP program, and over 400 children were identified as at-risk for criminal behavior (Bedi & McGrory, 2020). Access to the list and underlying data is extremely limited (Bedi & McGrory, 2020). Parents are not notified if their child is placed on the list or, if they are on the list, of any factors that placed them in the system (Reddy, 2020). The PSO does not provide a way for parents or guardians to access the data and has asserted that a juvenile intelligence analyst and SROs are the only persons with access to the information (Bedi & McGrory, 2020). The superintendent and school principals of two schools were unaware of the program or list of students identified as at-risk; it is unclear whether the Florida Department of Children and Families was aware that its data were being used for the program (Bedi & McGrory, 2020).

During their investigation, the *Tampa Bay Times* requested clarification from the PSO on the methods and philosophies of their ILP program as applied to the local schools, such as how data were collected and analyzed to determine whether a student would be considered at-risk. In their response, the sheriff's office argued their use of ILP relied on data shared between agencies to inform intervention and resources, such as developing mentorship opportunities between at-risk youth and officers whereby officers can "connect with students to determine if there are resources that would benefit the student" (Pasco Sheriff's Office, 2020a, p. 6). They fervently opposed any categorization of their ILP methods as "predictive." They alleged that they "DO NOT create intelligence reports" on students, but instead "conduct research based on criminal activity while in school" to determine if intervention is needed for at-risk youth (Pasco Sheriff's Office, 2020a, p. 6).

To emphasize the importance of sharing data between school officials and law enforcement officers, the sheriff's office discussed Nikolas Cruz, the mass murderer who perpetrated the school shooting at Marjorie Stoneman Douglas High School in Parkland, Florida, on February 14, 2018. They pointed to Cruz's long history of disciplinary problems, mental health concerns, and medical conditions. The sheriff noted that the information about Cruz was only known in "silos," and that because this critical information was not shared in real-time between school officials and law enforcement officers, there were "missed opportunities to intervene in [his] life" (Pasco Sheriff's Office, 2020a, p. 3). In fact, the sheriff stated there were a "myriad of missed opportunities to intervene with Nikolas Cruz…in previous tragedies in his life that would have led to an intervention which may have prevented [this] tragedy" (Pasco Sheriff's Office, 2020a, p. 4).

Following the publication of the *Tampa Bay Times* article, the PSO responded again, emphasizing their serious concerns over the confusion between ILP and predictive policing and any evidence their system racially profiles or harasses individuals (Pasco Sheriff's Office, 2020a; Schorsh, 2020). This wouldn't be the first defense of the ILP program by the PSO. A month prior to its exposition of the predictive policing program by SROs at the PSO, the *Tampa Bay Times* published a groundbreaking report on the impact of the sheriff's office's predictive policing program on the larger Pasco County community (McGrory & Bedi, 2020). The investigation, "Targeted," earned *Tampa Bay Times* journalists Kathleen McGrory and Neil Bedi the 2021 Pulitzer Prize for Local Reporting.

Policing and Surveilling Higher Education

Campus police officers have existed at American colleges and universities for over 120 years (Bordner & Peterson, 1983; Fisher & Sloan, 2022). The first iteration began in the 1890s, when campus police were primarily regarded as night watchmen. The second wave of campus police officers developed into campus security officers responsible for monitoring student conduct. Starting in the 1980s, the third wave transformed into quasi-militarized forces on campus. While a fourth wave of campus policing is still in development, it is likely to have begun in the 2000s, following the rise of technology, digital spaces, and social justice movements like Black Lives Matter, Me Too, and March for Our Lives.

Despite calls to defund or abolish campus police, governments and institutions have continued to financially support, expand, and increase policing on campus (Miller & Russell-Brown, 2023). A significant point of concern in the growth of campus police is the use of advanced technologies, analytics, algorithm-driven data, and artificial intelligence to surveil and police students, raising questions about student privacy and the over-policing of racially marginalized students (Maass, 2021). However, similar to the K–12 context, there is little research on the use, challenges, or benefits of advanced technologies or algorithm-driven policing in university police departments.

One reason for the lack of research is the difficulty of ascertaining the kinds of technologies, data, or algorithms used by university police. In fact, post-secondary institutions rarely disclose the kinds of technologies used by their officers or departments. Not until journalists or community activists have gone inquiring have examples been known. For example, the data collected in the Atlas of Surveillance project provide a groundbreaking illustration of the kinds of technologies used by university police departments and the private companies the technologies are purchased from. Such technologies include body-worn cameras, drones, automated license plate readers, social media monitoring systems, biometric information, gunshot detection, and video analytics (Maass, 2021).

How the information collected from these technologies is used to identify potential crime is still vastly unknown and likely varies across institution. Furthermore, the state laws that regulate how university police incorporate advanced technologies, AI, big data, or predictive models of policing vary and are inconsistent. In Virginia, the state legislature approved a bill permitting facial recognition technology to be used by municipal and university police departments (Gilligan, 2022). The law lifts a previous ban that prohibited police from using facial recognition technology (Lavoie, 2021). Scholars rightly point to the broad powers state laws confer to university police and racial equity concerns (Duran, 2022; Miller, 2024a).

Indeed, the law does confer broad powers to officers, authorizing the use of facial recognition in any investigation where the officer finds reasonable suspicion. This is concerning because research has documented the realities of racial profiling and the limited legal protections for those who face discrimination (Quattlebaum, 2018). In Maryland, the state legislature similarly passed a law authorizing Johns Hopkins University Police Department (JHPD) – the state's first private campus police force. The law, titled the Community Safety and Strengthening Act, requires that JHPD policies "ensure the adoption and use of appropriate technologies" (Johns Hopkins University & Medicine, 2022, p. 4). The law does not define, nor does it limit, what "appropriate technologies" are or how policies are to reflect their use.

Emerging scholarship in campus policing reveals a significant gap in the examination of predictive policing, or data-driven policing, within university police departments, including use of advanced technologies, AI, or big data. As postsecondary institutions increasingly adopt sophisticated surveillance tools, such as facial recognition software, there emerges an urgent need for researchers to examine their development and impact, particularly when considering biases, privacy violations, and student civil rights. This chapter therefore provides a brief overview of the ways researchers who are interested in examining systems of surveillance and punishment on campus can contribute to equitable and transparent policing models.

Implications and Conclusion

The use of artificial intelligence and big data for school and university policing is developing; however, opposition to its use will likely intensify as concerns over safety and privacy increase. During what will likely become a new era of school and campus policing, with the integration of technologies and algorithms permeating law enforcement practices, education researchers and legal scholars must pay attention to the growing reliance on and authority of school and university police. They should begin to work with and pull from scholarship relating to algorithmic justice, biases in policing, privacy, abolition, and safety. Of particular importance are the legal, social, and ethical implications and considerations of using advanced technologies, algorithms, analytics-driven data, and artificial intelligence in policing—that is, predictive policing.

Legal considerations include three main components: (a) student privacy; (b) student constitutional rights; and (c) police authority. All three components span the P–20 spectrum with varying levels of protection. First, student privacy concerns implicate state and federal regulation and usage of student data. While each state outlines different levels of protection, particularly for students in K–12 and incarcerated students, federal guidelines govern access to educational information. Under state law, for example, California provides students in K–12 some of the most extensive privacy laws protecting personal information and user data under the Student Online Personal Information Protection Act (Student Online Personal Information Protection Act, 2023). Widely considered one of the first modern student privacy laws, SOPIPA focuses on student data privacy and third-party applications, which is crucial in a perpetual online learning and social environment. Under federal law, the Family Educational Rights and Privacy Act (Family Educational Rights and Privacy Act, 1974) and the Children's Online Privacy Protection Act (Children's Online Privacy Protection Act, 1998) govern the use of student data. FERPA regulates access to educational records and information by public entities, such as educational institutions. COPPA requires websites to include privacy statements directed to children under the age of 13.

Despite seemingly extensive legal protections, questions still remain about the information protected under FERPA—specifically, records produced and used by campus law enforcement derived from advanced technologies, algorithm-based analytics, and artificial intelligence. FERPA creates an exception for "records of the law enforcement unit of an educational agency or institution," which includes "records, files, documents, and other materials that are created by a law enforcement unit; created for a law enforcement purpose; and maintained by the law enforcement unit" (Protecting Student Privacy, n.d., para. 1). The extent to which federal law will or should include aggregated data produced from algorithms or analytics is uncertain. For example, whether aggregated university card swipe data, biometric data, automated license plate reader data, or geospatial analytics are protected will likely find its way into the courts.

Second, student constitutional rights implicate the Fourth Amendment. At public institutions, students are protected against unreasonable searches and seizures from police and school officials (New Jersey v. T.L.O., 1985). The courts have discussed the integration of technology in Fourth Amendment jurisprudence; however, its applicability to surveillance technologies, particularly in school settings, is emerging. For example, in *Ogletree v. Cleveland State University* (2022), a district court found the university violated a student's Fourth Amendment rights when it required a scan of the student's bedroom prior to an online examination. As part of the prerecording instructions, the proctoring software used by the university requires students to place their university ID next to their face and conduct a room scan. The university argued the scans were not an unreasonable violation of privacy because they are routine and the technology is in general use. The virtual room scan, however, occurred in the student's bedroom. The court found the student held a reasonable expectation of privacy against government intrusion in his own home, and the scan therefore amounted to a violation of his Fourth Amendment rights. It is uncertain whether other courts will agree with the district court in Ohio or with the university's reading of technology and privacy rights.

Third, school and university police authority are grounded in expansive state statutes, some of which are inclusive of the use of advanced technologies to surveil and monitor students. In K–12, public schools are generally policed by multiple policing units. Many public schools receive law enforcement services from municipal police, SROs, and school safety officers (generally referred to as "school police"; Allen & Noguera, 2023). In many states, school police have general police powers, including the authority to make arrests, conduct searches and seizures, and carry firearms (Education Commission of the States, 2022). In some states, school police also have the same common law and statutory powers, privileges, and immunities as sheriffs and other law enforcement officers. In higher education, public colleges and university are generally policed by campus police departments (Miller & Russell-Brown, 2023).

Similar to school police, university police in almost every state have general police powers and receive the same privileges and immunities as other law enforcement officers (Miller, 2024b; Miller, 2024c). Their authority is also not confined to the physical boundaries of campus, allowing many campus police departments to exercise their authority off campus or within the entire state. Additionally, state laws are increasingly adding language about advanced technologies that may serve to further the purposes of predictive policing. In Virginia, law enforcement agencies may use facial recognition technologies as an investigative tool (Powers, Simon, & Spivack, 2022). The implications for university police departments are still developing. The legal authority of and institutional support for school and university police continues to expand, leaving many to wonder how the law will empower school and university police to incorporate artificial intelligence and big data under the purview of policing.

In addition to legal implications and considerations, there are several ethical and social implications and considerations to using artificial intelligence and big data in policing American public schools and universities that require attention. For example, ethical considerations require practitioners, education leaders, and school and campus safety officials to reflect on the use of algorithm-based data—largely developed from biased processes—to police students. Should school and university police incorporate predictive algorithms and analytics in rendering law enforcement services? Particularly those algorithms and analytics that are created with biases? Who should have authority or control over the data? Should the public be able to comment on or critique their use? Should students and/or their parents and guardians be able to opt out of programs and services that collect and aggregate data on students? Similarly, should students and/or their parents and guardians be able to easily access any criminal or policing records created from the use of artificial intelligence or big data?

Furthermore, ethical considerations relating to the surveillance of community members is paramount. Should school and university police be able to collect and aggregate data for algorithms and analytics from community members who are unaffiliated with their institution? For example, at many public colleges and universities, university police have authority over campus university functions that involve community members, such as athletics events, concerts, public lectures, and medical facilities. In several states, university police also have authority off-campus and routinely interact with and encounter community members. Unlike their municipal counterparts, campus police departments often do not maintain systems for community members to submit feedback regarding policing techniques (Miller & Russell-Brown, 2023). This raises significant concerns over the ethical collection and reliance on data used to predict or determine criminal patterns.

Finally, social considerations similarly require practitioners, education leaders, and school and campus safety officials to reflect on the long-term impacts of using algorithms and analytics to surveil and police students and community members. Overall, the adoption and use of artificial intelligence and big data play a critical role in the way campuses police and surveil students, demanding an urgent need for further research and scholarly attention.

References

Akabari, V. A. (2019). *Smart campus police: A smart application to provide predictive police service to the Sac State community* [Master's thesis, California State University, Sacramento]. Sac State Scholars. https://scholars.csus.edu/esploro/outputs/graduate/Sac-State-Smart-Campus-Police-An/99257889215401671

Allen, T., & Noguera, P. (2023). A web of punishment: Examining Black student interactions with school police in Los Angeles. *Educational Researcher*. Advance online publication. https://doi.org/10.3102/0013189X221095547

Bedi, N., & McGrory, K. (2020, November 19). *Paso's sheriff uses grades and abuse histories to label schoolchildren potential criminals: The kids and their parents don't know*. Tampa Bay Times. https://projects.tampabay.com/projects/2020/investigations/police-pasco-sheriff-targeted/school-data/

Bordner, D. C., & Peterson, D. M. (1983). *Campus policing: The nature of university police work*. University Press of America.

Cai, L. (2017, November 6). *Use of big data can transform police practices*. The Daily Texan. https://thedailytexan.com/2017/11/06/use-of-big-data-can-transform-police-practices/

Ceballos, J. (2020, October 15). *UM used surveillance to track student protesters*. Miami New Times. https://www.miaminewtimes.com/news/university-of-miami-tracked-protesters-with-video-surveillance-11712139

Children's Online Privacy Protection Act, 15 U.S.C. §§ 6501–6505 (1998).

Duran, T. A. (2022). College campus police abolition. *Kansas Journal of Law and Public Policy* 31(2), 327-362.

Education Commission of the States. (2022, October). *School resource officers: 50-state comparison*. https://reports.ecs.org/comparisons/k-12-school-safety-2022-05

Elyounes, D. A. (2020). Bail or jail? Judicial versus algorithmic decision-making in the pretrial system. *Columbia Science and Technology Law Review, 21*(2), 376–446. https://doi.org/10.7916/stlr.v21i2.6838

Family Educational Rights and Privacy Act, 20 U.S.C. § 1232g (1974).

Fedders, B. A. (2021). The end of school policing. *California Law Review, 109*(1), 1443-1506.

Ferguson, A. G. (2017). *The rise of big data policing: Surveillance, race, and the future of law enforcement*. New York University Press.

Fisher, B. S., & Sloan, J. J. (2022). *Campus crime: Legal, social, and policy perspectives*. Charles C. Thomas Publisher, Ltd.

Gaub, J. E. (2022). Assessing the utility of body-worn cameras for collegiate police agencies. *Police Quarterly, 25*(1), 118–148. https://doi.org/10.1177/10986111211037586

Gilligan, D. (2022, April). Virginia's facial recognition technology bill gives local law enforcement too much leeway. *Georgetown Law Technology*

Review. https://georgetownlawtechreview.org/virginias-facial-recognition-technology-bill-gives-local-law-enforcement-too-much-leeway/GLTR-04-2022/

Goel, S., Shroff, R., Skeem, J., & Slobogin, C. (2021). The accuracy, equity, and jurisprudence of criminal risk assessment. In R. Vogl (Ed.), *Research handbook on big data law* (pp. 9–28). Edward Elgar Publishing.

Heaven, W. D. (2020, July 17). Predictive policing algorithms are racist. They need to be dismantled. *MIT Technology Review*. https://www.technologyreview.com/2020/07/17/1005396/predictive-policing-algorithms-racist-dismantled-machine-learning-bias-criminal-justice/

Johns Hopkins University & Medicine. (2022, August 16). *Summary of the Community Safety and Strengthening Act*. https://publicsafety.jhu.edu/assets/uploads/sites/9/2022/08/Updated-JHPD-bill-summary-08.16.2022-FINAL.pdf

Johnson, R. M., & Dizon, J. P. M. (2021). Toward a conceptualization of the college–prison nexus. *Peabody Journal of Education*, *96*(5), 508–526. https://doi.org/10.1080/0161956X.2021.1991692

Laird, E., & Dwyer, M. (2023, September 20). *Off task: EdTech threats to student privacy and equity in the age of AI*. Center for Democracy and Technology. Retrieved from https://cdt.org/insights/report-off-task-edtech-threats-to-student-privacy-and-equity-in-the-age-of-ai/

Lau, T. (2020, April 1). *Predictive Policing Explained*. Brennan Center for Justice. https://www.brennancenter.org/our-work/research-reports/predictive-policing-explained

Lavoie, D. (2021, March 29). *Virginia lawmakers ban police use of facial recognition*. AP News. https://apnews.com/article/technology-legislature-police-law-enforcement-agencies-legislation-033d77787d4e28559f08e5e-31a5cb8f7

Lieberman, M. (2020, November 24). *Using student data to identify future criminals: A privacy debacle*. EdWeek, https://www.edweek.org/technology/using-student-data-to-identify-future-criminals-a-privacy-debacle/2020/11

Lyon, M. L., (2021). *Effect of academic advisor interventions on course completion after an alert raised by faculty* (Publication No. 7385) [Doctoral Dissertation, Northern Illinois University] Graduate Research Theses & Dissertations, https://huskiecommons.lib.niu.edu/allgraduate-thesesdissertations/7385

Maass, D. (2021, March 9). *Scholars under surveillance: How campus police use high tech to spy on students*. Electronic Frontier Foundation. https://www.eff.org/deeplinks/2021/03/scholars-under-surveillance-how-campus-police-use-high-tech-spy-students#videoanalysis

McGrory, K., & Bedi, N. (2020, September 3). *Targeted*. Tampa Bay Times. https://projects.tampabay.com/projects/2020/investigations/police-pasco-sheriff-targeted/intelligence-led-policing/

Miller, V. (2024a). A critical legal analysis of university police authority. In Y. Suriel, G. Watkins, J. P. Dizon & J. Sloan (Eds.), *Cops on campus: Rethinking safety and confronting police violence* (pp. 17-32). University of Washington Press.

Miller, V. (2024b). A national survey and critical analysis of university police statutes. *Buffalo Law Review, 72*(3), 751-808.

Miller, V. (2025c). The role of state laws in the privatization of police on campus. *Harvard Educational Review, 95*(3), 397-422.

Miller, V., & Russell-Brown, K. (2023). Policing the college campus: History, race, and law. *Washington & Lee Journal of Civil Rights and Social Justice, 29*(3), 59–128. https://dx.doi.org/10.2139/ssrn.4227943

Morris, S. (2023, September 21). *Call to shut down Bristol schools' use of app to "monitor" pupils and families.* The Guardian. https://www.theguardian.com/education/2023/sep/21/calls-to-shut-down-bristol-schools-use-of-think-family-education-app-pupils-and-families

Muller, B. (2023). *"They're targeting people": Man claims Pasco deputies engaging in predictive policing.* WFLA News Channel 8. https://www.wfla.com/news/pasco-county/theyre-targeting-people-man-claims-pasco-deputies-engaging-in-predictive-policing/#:~:text=Pasco%20Intelligence%20Led%20Policing%20was,Pasco%20citizens%20on%20that%20basis.

NAACP Legal Defense and Educational Fund. (2021, April 26). New coalition formed to end Pasco County's predictive policing program. https://www.naacpldf.org/press-release/new-coalition-formed-to-end-pasco-countys-predictive-policing-program/

New Jersey v. T.L.O., 469 U.S. 325 (1985).

Noble, S. U. (2018). *Algorithms of oppression: How search engines reinforce racism.* New York University Press.

Norman, L. (2023, June 3). *Here's which Florida universities offer AI courses, how admissions offices are using AI.* TCPalm, https://www.tcpalm.com/story/news/education/2023/11/03/role-artificial-intelligence-education-admissions-offices-florida-colleges-universities-courses/71405142007/

Ogletree v. Cleveland State University, Case 1:21-cv-00500-JPC (2022).

Pasco Sheriff's Office. (2018). *Intelligence-led policing manual.* https://beta.documentcloud.org/documents/20412738-ilp_manual012918

Pasco Sheriff's Office. (2020a, September 23). [Letter from Office of the Sheriff regarding intelligence-led policing.] https://beta.documentcloud.org/documents/20412739-psoresponseatriskyouth

Pasco Sheriff's Office. (2020b, October 1). [Intelligence-Led Policing Manual]. https://www.documentcloud.org/documents/20412738-ilp_manual012918

Petition for Writ of Mandamus. (2022, March 13). *CAIR Florida v. Christopher Nocco,* Filing No. 157331829 (Fla. 6th Cir. Ct.).

Plaintiff's Complaint for Damages, Declaratory, and Injunctive Relief. (2021, March 10). *Dalanea Taylor, Tammy Heilman, Darlene Deegan, and Robert A. Jones III v. Chris Nocco*, No. 8:21-cv-00555 (M.D. Fla.).

Protecting Student Privacy (n.d.), *What is a "law enforcement record"?* Retrieved from https://studentprivacy.ed.gov/faq/what-law-enforcement-unit-record

Powers, A., Simon, K. & Spivack, J. (2022). From ban to approval: What Virginia's facial recognition technology gets wrong, *Richmond Public Interest Law Review, 26*(1), 155-184.

Quattlebaum, M. (2018). Let's get real: Behavioral realism, implicit bias, and the reasonable police officer. *Stanford Journal of Civil Rights and Civil Liberties, 14*(1) 1–48. https://ssrn.com/abstract=2821227

Ratcliff, J. H. (2016). *Intelligence-led policing* (2nd ed.). Routledge.

Reddy, A. (2020, December 18). *The trouble with Pasco County's predictive policing program.* Student Privacy Compass. https://studentprivacycompass.org/pasco/

Rigano, C. (2019). Using artificial intelligence to address criminal justice needs. *National Institute of Justice Journal, 280*, 37–46. https://www.cep-probation.org/wp-content/uploads/2020/11/252038.pdf

Ryan, M. (2015, July 5). *Body worn cameras making their way into Iowa schools.* Des Moines Register. https://www.desmoinesregister.com/story/news/education/2015/07/05/body-cameras-burlington-schools/29746803/

Schorsh, P. (2020, September 11). *Pasco Sheriff's Office pushes back against allegations of harassment, targeting.* Florida Politics. https://floridapolitics.com/archives/366255-pasco-sheriffs-office-pushes-back-against-allegations-of-harassment-targeting/

Solon, O., & Farivar, C. (2021, June 6). *Predictive policing strategies for children face pushback.* NBC News. https://www.nbcnews.com/tech/tech-news/predictive-policing-strategies-children-face-pushback-n1269674

Southern Poverty Law Center, NAACP Legal Defense and Educational Fund, Southern Legal Counsel, & Council on American Relations-Florida. (2022, September 14). Civil rights groups sue for public records linked to Pasco County's predictive policing program [Press release]. https://www.naacpldf.org/press-release/civil-rights-groups-sue-for-public-records-linked-to-pasco-countys-predictive-policing-program/

Student Online Personal Information Protection Act, Cal. Bus. & Prof. Code § 22854 (2023). https://law.justia.com/codes/california/code-bpc/division-8/chapter-22-2/

Suriel, Y., Watkins, G., Dizon, J. P. M., & Sloan, J. J. (2024). *Cops on campus: Rethinking safety and confronting police violence.* University of Washington Press.

Tanner, C. (2023, March 7). *Solving a marijuana mystery at Utah State University with data.* The Salt Lake Tribune. https://www.sltrib.com/news/education/2023/03/07/how-utah-state-university-is-using/

Walters, A., & Scheer, T. (2024, April 4). *After shooting, MSU promised safety. It delivered surveillance.* The State News. https://statenews.com/article/2024/04/after-shooting-msu-promised-safety-it-delivered-surveillance

8

Artificial Communication and Media Realism for College Admissions

Sebastian Munoz-Najar Galvez, Jinsook Lee, AJ Alvero,

Sheridan Stewart, René F. Kizilcec, and Amy Desiderio

On June 29, 2023, the Supreme Court of the United States argued that colleges had "for too long" drawn the wrong conclusions about "the touchstone of an individual's identity" by fixating on the skin color of applicants (*Students for Fair Admissions, Inc. v. President and Fellows of Harvard College*, 2023). The court's argument implies a model of college admissions as a communication system that traffics in (more or less) authentic markers, "touchstones" of identity. In contrast, an alternative model of college admissions, the media realist perspective, emphasizes how applicants and their advocates (parents, teachers, guidance counselors, etc.) coordinate the content of personal essays and recommendations. Rather than a system where applicants traffic in the *touch*stone of their identity, admissions is a system in which stakeholders exchange drafts of, and feedback for, biographical narratives — communications that serve as *stepping* stones providing footing for coming up with a self-presentation. It is a long series of stepping stones to make sense of an application. Beyond the application materials, admissions officials often require more communications to interpret the profile of a student, for example, in deliberation with colleagues at the admissions office or by touching base with the counselor who wrote the letter for a given applicant.

In this chapter we argue that media realism is necessary in the study of artificial intelligence tools for college admissions. *Media realism* is the research disposition to treat recommendation letters and essays as the results of drafts and discussions — which vary across organizations and admission seasons. The media realist concern with artificial intelligence (AI) in college admissions is, Where does the AI tool fit in the writing processes of students and their advocates? When and how do various stakeholders use AI tools in their routine communications?

Admissions stakeholders organize their writing and reading routines in relation to institutional expectations and time constraints. The stakeholders involved in preparing and evaluating applications themselves span multiple generations arranged in numerous organizations — applicants, guidance counselors, teachers, parents, preparatory service providers, admissions offices, seasonal readers, and others. A media realist research design would not favor analysis of any one stakeholder's AI use but instead focus on the circulation and overlapping of AI-assisted writing across outlines, drafts, comments, and other routine communications.

In the past few years, educators have approached AI writing assistance with different concerns. An EDUCAUSE survey of college and university websites in the United States and Canada as of February 1, 2023, showed that 27.5% of institutions already mentioned ChatGPT at least once on their websites, with substantial institutional variation at higher mention counts. Thematically, 43.9% of mentions came from opinion pieces or lecture announcements regarding AI, 34.1% came from reports of experiments with AI tools, and 22.0% came from discussions of grading or other academic policies (Veletsianos et al., 2023).

In late February of 2023, Rick Clark of Georgia Tech's Center for 21st Century Universities argued that school counselors and teachers, given the burden of high student-to-counselor ratios and the inevitable involvement of AI, should be allowed to use contemporary mediums like voice or video for student recommendations. Further, the author claimed, "The truth is that many of these essays are already overly sanitized or professionally tailored or tampered with. I *hope* the Common Application and Coalition application will modernize their platforms and integrate technology that allows us to more directly hear and/or see students, and the adults who support them" (Clark, 2023). On July 27, 2024, Arizona State University Law School announced that future applicants will be allowed to use ChatGPT in their applications, specifically for their personal statements (Coffey, 2023a). A month later, St. John's College, a private liberal arts institution in Annapolis, Maryland, announced a new "discussion-based" application option that students can select over the traditional process (Knox, 2023). Lira and colleagues (2023) at the University of Colorado at Boulder and the University of Pennsylvania proposed in October 2023 an AI to analyze applicant descriptions of their extracurricular and work experiences. The study claims that the technology could identify traits like teamwork and perseverance in a corpus of over 300,000 applications from 2008 to 2009, each with a 150-word essay. It also documented unexpected model behaviors: If a student were to say they donated heroin to the children's shelter, that claim would yield a high score in the "prosocial purpose" category (Coffey, 2023b).

The commentary about large language models (LLMs) and admissions in the sector's specialized press reveals an emergent trend toward media realism: Concerns about writer authenticity intermingle with recommendations for new media (e.g., video recommendations) and new differentiations (e.g., AI detection tools; students-as-authors vs. students-as-editors; Clark, 2023). College admissions experts are already thinking about AI with a process perspective, looking at different types of routine communications. Our goal is to synthetize and formalize some of these conceptual initiatives.

The rest of this chapter is organized as follows: In the next section, we flesh out our conceptual framework to understand how admissions arguments enact differences between students. In the third section, "The Muppet Model Show," we offer an analogy that illustrates the complexities and limitations of involving LLMs in communications within the admissions system. The final section proposes three orienting principles for social research in the age of generative (re)production.

A note on terminology: We will use AI to refer primarily to LLMs used in writing assistance.[1] We will be explicit when discussing other technologies commonly grouped under the label of AI. And we will unpack the term AI in the third section. Current LLMs are autoregressive next-token prediction algorithms embracing the transformer architecture (Bommasani et al., 2021). This means that an LLM predicts tokens (often words and short phrases) consecutively, appending each new predicted token to the original prompt as additional context for the next prediction. For example, given the partial sentence "I enjoy having a cup of [BLANK]," an autoregressive language model would analyze the words preceding the blank space ("I enjoy having a cup of") and predict the next word. It might suggest words that commonly follow this context, such as "coffee," "tea," or "water," based on the patterns it has learned from the training data. The model is trained in a self-supervised fashion on a massive corpus (typically from internet-based sources; see, e.g., Shumailov et al., 2023). Developers can fine-tune a pretrained model with a custom dataset in order to control how the model participates in specific communications systems. For example, LLMs like those used with ChatGPT are fine-tuned with instruction-solution turn-based exchanges. Fine-tuning allows models to act out the role of assistant effectively specifically in communication routines recorded in the model's training data.

Program Strands in the College Admissions System

Letters and essays, in their finished, submitted form, are iterations of a longer series of texts: drafts, copies, and templates compiled, excerpted, and referenced by students, teachers, counselors, admissions coaches, guidebooks, peers, parents, and social media. There is much more communication happening in admissions — much more sharing, collecting, and consulting of various texts — than the communications recorded in the submission of an admissions portfolio.

The information content of communications in the college admissions system consists of locally relevant differentiations between the applicant as agent of their own life course and the applicant as subject of external conditions. For example, in our study of letter writing (Savitz-Romer et al., 2024), we found that counselors routinely checked in with students and other stakeholders about what information they should include in their recommendation letters. Counselors used "brag sheets," a conventional survey instrument that includes open-ended questions, to collect information from students, and sometimes parents, for their recommendation letters. The questions in the brag sheet provide students with a code[2] to report out their school experiences and future plans with locally relevant categories — both for their individuated merits and their biographies and backgrounds. This code, and the distinctions it highlights, are then reinforced in ensuing communications. Counselors have to figure out what elements of student responses to the brag sheet can be adapted to their available letter templates. Or they can determine that a given response requires a follow-up conversation with the student or with a colleague — for example, to check if the student is comfortable with the letter containing a description of an adverse experience or to ask a coach to corroborate the description of an award.

This understanding of admissions as a communications system builds on prior work by Gebre-Medhin and colleagues (2022), who defined the admissions process as a ritual: a "carefully orchestrated and serially repeated collaborative practice . . . distributed across multiple parties, requiring active participation by applicants, high schools, and colleges according to explicitly specified protocols" (p. 2). Further, Gebre-Medhin et al. proposed that, in this ritual, personal essays (and we add letters) are of a particular genre that is "resistant to commensuration": "They are not commensurable in any a priori fashion known to applicants. Even if particular schools might apply metrical assessments to essays behind closed doors, we know of no instance in which such metrics are easily available to organizational outsiders. Because there is no clear, public, or agreed-upon metric for what 'counts' as an excellent or even acceptable essay" (p. 4).

We advance that the narrative portions of a portfolio are not resistant but *formative* of the more standardized evaluation that applies to quantitative elements of the portfolio. The relation between narrative and quantitative elements of the portfolio is similar to the relation between news and advertising in mass media. Sociologist Niklas Luhmann (2000) describes these as distinct but related program strands, referring to media that apply the code of a system. This characterization might be understood as applying additional structural and functional characteristics to a notion of intertextuality. In mass media, we can observe the information/noninformation distinction within different fields of selection. The news produces information by selecting stories based on surprise, conflict, quantification, and norm violation, among other selectors (Moeller, 2006 pp. 141–142). Advertising, with its openly manipulative selectors, serves a fundamental function for the other program strands: "Advertising is the Jesus Christ of the mass media — by its humility and its willing acceptance of being looked down upon, it grants salvation to the other program strands. Okay, we all know this is just a stupid commercial — thus it is not real and not even very entertaining (we have already seen it a hundred times), but if this is so, then the previous news was really real and the following movie will be truly entertaining" (p. 142).

Analogously, essays and letters constitute a program strand that, like other media in the admissions system, apply the code that differentiates between personal merit and social conditions. This program selects for personal flair and narrative exceptions to the standardized, quantified comparisons between students. In their analysis of student responses to an admissions prompt asking for a narrative of a significant challenge, Gebre-Medhin and colleagues (2022) found 14 primary challenges, ranging "from material (economic insecurity) to physical (health/ability) to affective (inter/intra-personal) challenges and including abuse, academics, death, discrimination, and challenges related to sports" (p. 8). The analysis of these challenges yielded further thematic and framing variations of the primary challenges (85 subcategories; p. 8). By capturing specific topics in a narrative program strand, the application studied by these authors creates a legitimate organization of evaluation — documents for stories; documents for quantities. Quantitative and narrative programs will matter differently at specific points of the evaluation. Relatedly, in our interviews with counselors, for example, some mentioned that powerful narratives are only relevant for applicants who are targeting financial aid at selective schools (Savitz-Romer et al., 2024).

As an example of a quantitative program strand, consider Landscape, developed by the College Board and initially introduced as the Environmental Context Dashboard. Landscape aims to simplify and advance the holistic review process in admissions by providing contextual information, such as the "overall" adversity measure and the SAT context measure.[3] This latter feature presents a student's SAT score alongside the interquartile range of scores from other students at the same high school. By the 2020–2021 academic year, Landscape had been adopted by over 180 colleges, universities, and scholarship organizations for making critical admissions decisions (Bastedo et al., 2022). Contextual information in Landscape's framework is a blend of comprehensive, relevant, and standardized data, synthesized from multiple sources to provide an explicit, actionable view of a student's educational and socioeconomic background.

Like essays and letters, Landscape applies a code that distinguishes between merit and social conditions. However, it eschews the common pitfalls of holistic review, a process that is "fraught with mistrust, subjectivity, and special interests" (Bastedo et al., 2018, p. 783). The ways nonacademic factors are used in this process can often be vague or ambiguous. Evaluation of such factors requires that admissions officers extend evaluative criteria beyond measurable academic achievements, such as GPA and standardized test scores (p. 790). Program strands borrow from each other: "Movies deliberately connect to events in world news. An Oscar-winning film like Gladiator pretends to be historical, but in fact alludes to contemporary political conflicts (between democracies and dictatorships). . . . Conversely, news also copies the form of movies. CNN labeled its coverage of 9/11 and the Iraq War with action movie-like headlines (like "America under Attack") and jingles" (Moeller, 2006, pp. 133–134). Essays and letters both borrow from grade transcripts. A student can advance a narrative of personal adversity that explains or contests formally recorded grade variations. Conversely, many counselors draw useful structures from the quantitative program to organize their writing. Brag sheets can, for example, prime students to report their experiences with near-standardized values that match a counselor's templates and writing routines. Such cases of mutual borrowing do not follow from the content of a student's experience alone; instead, they are the result of routine communications.

The relationship between a counselor and their student — contingent on its depth, longevity, and organizational context — can elicit various types of mutual borrowing between narrative and quantitative programs. In conversations and document revisions, a student and their advocates open up the possibility of using a paragraph in the essay or recommendation to explain a dip in academic performance. Understanding these documents as enmeshed in a web of references between texts, and of mutual borrowings between program strands, extends related work on the sociolinguistic nature of writing and text (Alvero, 2023).

In summary, a dense traffic of communications arrives at a form, the portfolio, which couples media from distinct program strands (quantitative and narrative). LLMs will intervene in the admissions communications system, playing the role of writing/review assistants for various texts, including private drafts, emails, and conversations. The intervention of a new-ish class of interlocutor will open up opportunities for new forms of reference and borrowings in more or less established local communication routines. In the next section, we will argue that to keep communications front and center in our empirical program we must challenge the idea that models encode intelligence.

The Muppet Model Show

In this section, we review the striking similarities between LLMs and Muppets, as outlined by computer scientist Jordan Boyd-Graber. Prior to the advent of modern LLMs like generative pre-trained transformers (more popularly known as GPTs), massive models trained on digitized text that share names with popular characters from the Muppets (ELMo and BERT being the two most prominent examples)[4] dominated the natural language processing landscape (Vincent, 2019). Boyd-Graber (2023b) proposed that Muppet models are, like their namesakes, marvels of engineering and craft that can interact with humans in seemingly magical but unreliable ways. Such models can act out valuable scenes of social interaction and can do so in many languages.

Muppet models can be made to play the roles of writing assistants and portfolio readers in a bounded set of scenes. These scenes carry over interaction patterns and sociolinguistic markers from a predominantly English-language repertoire of past performances (i.e., training data). These models can relay suggestions for structure, grammar, and content. They can act out writing assistance conversations that allow stakeholders to effectively communicate an applicant's qualities and aspirations. But the model can also stray from its source scenes, relay false information, or betray the directions for a communication scene — much like Muppets can comically fail to play out a scene from *A Christmas Carol*.[5]

Muppet models will participate in scenes from routine writing and evaluation practice. Counselors, like admissions officers, face a significant challenge handling large volumes of applications, which require significant amounts of resources and time. UCLA, for example, received over 145,000 applications for fewer than 13,000 openings in the 2022 academic year. Beyond GPAs, AP scores, and extracurriculars, the admissions office also had to handle approximately 580,000 essays (as each applicant wrote four essays). Going through each applicant's file is complex and time-consuming (Lee et al., 2023). Similarly, in an interview study with 40 East Coast counselors primarily from public schools, Savitz-Romer et al. (2024) found that counselors wrote an average of 43 letters per year, with 10% writing 100 or more letters each season. Recommendation letters involve laborious writing that comes at the tail end of a laborious data collection process. In short, Muppet models will be brought in on scenes of mass writing and mass evaluation — scenes that move fast and tend to be repetitive. We don't care what Muppets have in their heads (nothing, or someone's hand); we care about how they can act out these demanding scenes with human communication partners who vary in their levels of experience and organizational support.

To observe Muppets and humans acting out relevant admissions scenes, researchers will have to greatly expand their quantitative text analyses beyond collections of finished texts to better encompass the domain of drafts, messages, conversations, and other references. These interstitial, unreported scenes enforce a locally relevant code, but they do so *cumulatively* — in other words, they build toward socially effective merit/condition distinctions from one communication to the next.

Final documents express locally relevant distinctions but occlude the communication process that produced them. Numerous studies have explored potential machine learning applications in predicting admissions outcomes to aid admissions offices in their holistic review process. These include applications of machine learning methods to predict admissions decisions (Lee et al., 2023; Lux et al., 2016) and computational simulations of how different admissions policies (e.g., test-optional and test-blind admissions) may or may not systematically alter the composition of admitted classes (Baker & Bastedo, 2022; Garg et al., 2021; Lee et al., 2024a; Liu & Garg, 2021). Further, a series of studies analyzing admissions essays submitted to the University of California system found that the contents of these essays were strong predictors of many social dimensions of applicants, such as their household income and SAT scores (Alvero et al., 2021), self-presentation strategies (Giebel et al., 2022), and academic pathways (Alvero et al., 2022).

This literature is essential in that it outlines a key empirical puzzle of admissions: that portfolios vary in constructing more or less successful identity-based arguments. To understand the participation of Muppet models in the admissions process, however, it will be necessary to complement these studies with research on the complete communications system, inhabited as it is primarily with unfinished, private texts. This charge, to look at Muppet models in various scenes, especially those discarded after portfolio submission, would not surprise education anthropologists. This discipline has long agreed that, in general, effective categories of students are organizational achievements. In particular, deficit labels capture students in the wash of school routine, not only by assigning labels authoritatively but also through recurring suggestion, euphemism, ellipsis, and/or metonymy (Varenne & McDermott, 1998).

Centrally, to extend Boyd-Graber's metaphor, one can recognize that, in every scene, the team behind the Muppet model (the developers, their employers) and the actors (the community, the user base) need to behave as if the model has spoken on its own, out of some internal forum or intelligence.[6] As Esposito explains (Carefree Wandering, 2022), it is understandable, if a bit narcissistic, that humans, who take for granted the centrality of their own cognitive involvement in communication, would ascribe intelligence to a really big matrix that can be manipulated using linear algebra and arithmetic (see, e.g., XKCD).[7] However, LLMs do not themselves have human cognitive biases; they simply behave as if they do (Abid et al., 2021; Liu et al., 2021; Alvero et al., 2024), given their limited capability to extrapolate from the interaction scenes recorded in their training data using next-token prediction.

Research on Admissions in the Age of Generative Reproduction

We propose that the first policy front for AI regulation in admissions is to consolidate as public knowledge the recognition that LLMs are Muppets and not intelligences. From this, it follows that their empirical evaluation is the purview of the humans who manage communications in the admissions system. The use of "intelligence" as a framing for Muppet models is a form of *transmuted expertise* (Collins & Evans, 2007). This concept refers to the capacity to deploy technical language associated with a specialism to transmute political or personal judgments into technical judgments.

Open AI chief scientist Ilya Sutskever (Patel, 2023) provides a clear example of transmuted expertise, in a discussion about the limits of next-token prediction:

> What is it about people that creates their behaviors? Well they
> have thoughts and their feelings, and they have ideas, and they
> do things in certain ways. All of those could be deduced from
> next-token prediction. And I'd argue that this should make it
> possible, not indefinitely but to a pretty decent degree to say —
> Well, can you guess what you'd do if you took a person with
> this characteristic and that characteristic? Like such a person

> doesn't exist but because you're so good at predicting the next
> token, you should still be able to guess what that person would
> do. (min. 6:45)

When Sutskever conflates prediction and deduction, his expert judgment transmutes model performance into intelligence for a lay audience. This transmutation contributes to imbuing "intelligence" with social currency in extant public discussions of Muppet models.

We propose that AI regulation in admissions needs to reject this type of expertise from the outset in favor of what Collins (2014) calls *local discrimination*. In our case, this would refer to the judgment of counselors, students, and officers about the expert claims of technologists, based on the routine practice of coordinating admissions across specific educational organizations. In particular, we propose that local discrimination grounded in routine writing practices would be a priority source of expertise for AI regulation.

Policy researchers studying algorithmic fairness report that group attributes, such as race (Grossman et al., 2023) and legacy status (Chetty et al., 2023), influence admissions and sometimes result in disparate impact (Lee et al., 2024a). Arthurs and Alvero (2020) found signal of socioeconomic biases in analogical and word similarity tasks with static word embedding models. From the standpoint of transmuted engineering expertise, one might conclude that the task of the social researcher is to uncover the biases built into models. As long as bias continues to creep into these models at different points in their life cycles, determining the weak points will remain an integral part of understanding AI prior to deployment (Lee et al., 2024b). From the standpoint of supporting local discrimination, the task of the social researcher is different:

> The most significant problem, however, is not that algorithms
> reflect the biases of their creators — who, granted, do tend to
> be white men. Rather, algorithmic bias is only one component
> of the problem. Deeper, and more difficult to manage is what is
> often labeled as "data bias," which does not depend on the val-
> ues of the programmers. Instead, it depends on the underlying
> source of the algorithms' efficiency: the access to the big data
> they find on the web, which frequently builds upon the unco-
> ordinated input of billions of participants, sensors, and other
> digital sources. Machines participate in a communication that
> is neither neutral nor egalitarian, and they learn to work corre-
> spondingly in ways that can be biased very differently from the
> preferences of their designers. (Esposito, 2022, p. 109)

The social researcher should reconstruct the admissions-relevant communication scenes that feed the models. As Esposito explains, models consume these scenes as part of their training data. But, in addition, we argue that chatbot interfaces for writing or evaluation assistance as deployed in specific organization contexts also feed distinct communication scenes to models. Thus, we propose three orienting principles for admissions research in the age of generative reproduction: *Study the communications system.* Our priority as social researchers should be to understand how people use LLMs to make things in the communications system of admissions.

Companies are making things with LLMs to participate in the admissions communications system. Khan Academy released guidelines on how to leverage its platform Khanmigo to help applicants navigate getting general information (e.g., deadlines, requirements) and writing admissions essays and personal statements (Khan Academy, n.d.). We propose that the impact of these technologies falls primarily on the *system assembly* of various models: Khan Academy's platform Khamingo is the environment in which College Essay Guy can give advice to draft letters with GPT (see College Essay Guy, n.d.). Put another way, the stakeholders in admissions (e.g., students and their counselors) are looking at each other, trying to discover what is allowed and what is achievable with LLMs. Understanding this process of collective discovery is a high research priority.

The "I" in AI is metaphoric. What we empirically observe in ChatGPT, for example, is a prediction model that uses/allows a compressed, black-boxed representation of internet discourse to be involved in social communication — to, for example, assist in writing letters or essays. There are a couple of compelling sociology-of-science questions regarding the intelligence metaphor: First, how are specific ideas about human intelligence used (at specific moments in time, in specific organizations) as a metaphor and (in a very constrained, expert sense) a model for technology development? Second, how do institutions use the horizon of AGI (artificial general intelligence) or related notions to legitimize specific forms of accountability to the public? Given the fragmented and vulnerable state of global internet governance, to center intelligence without a smirk amounts to obfuscating the fact that large companies are training predictive tech for commercial use on top of the public domain, inclusive of internet discourse.

We must pay close attention and demand concrete, transparent information from tech companies about data sourcing and the human work that went into their models. Higher education is a primary domain where these trends can be observed. For example, a major source of text used for training LLMs comes from digitized academic research. It is also the case that students and researchers alike use LLMs to help with writing and research. When anyone in higher education uses these tools, they become politically and legally implicated in the issues surrounding the public domain.

Watch out for and speak up against enshittification *in writing and evaluation assistance.* The social history of the internet is instructive of how to observe the race toward intelligent systems. It is a race toward economic monopoly. The decline of internet platforms, their enshittification, has three stages: initially providing good service to users; then exploiting users to benefit business customers; and finally exploiting business customers to maximize platform profit, leading to a decline in value and quality (DEFCONConference, 2023). Researchers will have to remain alert to how various platforms foster or restrict interoperability — defined as the ability to plug into incumbent services without their permission. In the context of college admissions, for example, the researcher will want to know if users of the dominant writing assistant platform are able to generate synthetic data (essays or letters) from the proprietary model to train their own models (Gunasekar et al., 2023). There is also the reasonable expectation that the synthetic output reasonably reflects text that humans would actually generate, an expectation that is not yet fully realized in current models (Alvero et al., 2024), including with prompt engineering for specific sociodemographic identities (Lee et al., 2025). This prospect of training public models with curated outputs from proprietary models continues to invite both enthusiasm and concern from various stakeholders of the AI industry (Shumailov et al., 2023); on that regard alone, it merits the researcher's attention.

Researchers will want to be alert to data collection efforts that recover (or intend to recover) representative samples of effective *written* writing instruction and equitable *written* evaluation (e.g., high-quality comments, edits, annotations, revisions, and discussions). What is construed as successful interaction in these data? To what extent do these data represent a multilingual user base hailing from various mass education systems?

Notes

1   From spell check and Microsoft Clippy making corrections and template suggestions, to more sophisticated writing aids like Grammarly and ChatGPT, there is a social history of computer-assisted writing worth reconstructing. However, this enterprise is beyond the scope of this chapter.

2   A code is a set of rules to communicate distinctions in specific media. The media of college admissions are the transcripts, forms, letters, and essays. The admissions portfolio follows a code in the sense that its constituent documents are written and arranged to represent different aspects of (and perspectives on) the applicant. The portfolio seeks to communicate the contrast between the applicant as agent of their own life course and the applicant as subject of external conditions. To accomplish this, the applicant and their advocates must use the right documents to express or frame the right information; e.g., the counselor recommendation letter may be the right place to frame the transcripts — the letter may reference the transcript to accomplish the distinction between the applicant's academic potential and their past grades. More examples of how media codes work in admissions follow.

3   The development and implementation of Landscape elicited significant controversy among experts and in education news coverage. The Environmental Context Dashboard's adversity score faced immediate criticism and was withdrawn in 2019. CEO David Coleman acknowledged that the organization had "perhaps overstepped" and adopted "a humbler position" by abandoning the notion that "a single score is better" (Hartocollis, 2019). Place-based data tools continue to be under scrutiny in the post–affirmative action era, as analysts have questioned whether these may help explain some institutions' ability to maintain stable racial demographics after the Supreme Court's 2023 decision (Talbert, 2024).

4   By 2020, almost every one of the billions of daily Google searches was processed with a BERT model.

5   RIZZO: How do you know what Scrooge is doing? We're down here and he's up there. GONZO: I keep telling you, storytellers are omniscient. I know everything (Henson, 1992).

6   One interesting place where Boyd-Graber's metaphor breaks is the differentiation between behind and in front of the Muppet model.

7   XKCD: A webcomic of romance, sarcasm, math, and language, *Machine learning*, https://xkcd.com/1838/

References

Abid, A., Farooqi, M., & Zou, J. (2021, July). Persistent anti-Muslim bias in large language models. In *Proceedings of the 2021 AAAI/ACM Conference on AI, Ethics, and Society* (pp. 298–306).

Alvero, AJ (2023). Sociolinguistic perspectives on machine learning with text data. In C. Borch & J. P. Pardo-Guerra (Eds.), *The Oxford handbook of the sociology of machine learning* (pp. 79–98). Oxford Handbooks. https://doi.org/10.1093/oxfordhb/9780197653609.013.15

Alvero, AJ, Giebel, S., Gebre-Medhin, B., antonio, a. l., Stevens, M. L., & Domingue, B. W. (2021). Essay content and style are strongly related to household income and SAT scores: Evidence from 60,000 undergraduate applications. *Science Advances*, *7*(42), Article eabi9031. https://doi.org/10.1126/sciadv.abi9031

Alvero, AJ, Lee, J., Regla-Vargas, A., Kizilec, R., Joachims, T., & antonio, a. l. (2024). Large language models, social demography, and hegemony: Comparing authorship in human and synthetic text. *Journal of Big Data, 11*(1), 138. https://doi.org/10.1186/s40537-024-00986-7

Alvero, AJ, Pal, J., & Moussavian, K. M. (2022). Linguistic, cultural, and narrative capital: Computational and human readings of transfer admissions essays. *Journal of Computational Social Science*, *5*(2), 1709–1734. https://doi.org/10.1007/s42001-022-00185-5

Arthurs, N., & Alvero, AJ (2020). Whose truth is the "ground truth"? College admissions essays and bias in word vector evaluation methods. In A. N. Rafferty, J. Whitehill, V. Cavalli-Sforza, & C. Romero (Eds.), *Proceedings of the 13th International Conference on Educational Data Mining* (pp. 342–349). Educational Data Mining.

Baker, D. J., & Bastedo, M. N. (2022). What if we leave it up to chance? Admissions lotteries and equitable access at selective colleges. *Educational Researcher*, *51*(2), 134–145. https://doi.org/10.3102/0013189X211055494

Bastedo, M. N., Bell, D., Howell, J. S., Hsu, J., Hurwitz, M., Perfetto, G., & Welch, M. (2022). Admitting students in context: Field experiments on information dashboards in college admissions. *The Journal of Higher Education*, *93*(3), 327–374. https://doi.org/10.1080/00221546.2021.1971488

Bastedo, M. N., & Bowman, N. A. (2017). Improving admission of low-SES students at selective colleges: Results from an experimental simulation. *Educational Researcher*, *46*(2), 67–77. https://doi.org/10.3102/0013189X17699373

Bastedo, M. N., Bowman, N. A., Glasener, K. M., & Kelly, J. L. (2018). What are we talking about when we talk about holistic review? Selective college admissions and its effects on low-SES students. *The Journal of Higher Education*, *89*(5), 782–805. https://doi.org/10.1080/00221546.2018.1442633

Bommasani, R., Hudson, D. A., Adeli, E., Altman, R., Arora, S., von Arx, S., Bernstein, M. S., Bohg, J., Bosselut, A., Brunskill, E., Brynjolfsson, E., Buch, S., Card, D. Castellon, R., Chatterju, N., Chen, A., Creel, K., Davis, J. Q., Demszky, D., . . . Liang, P. (2021). On the opportunities and risks of foundation models. arXiv (Article 2108.07258). https://doi.org/10.48550/arXiv.2108.07258

Boyd-Graber, J. (2023a, October 2). *Do iid NLP data exist? [Lecture]* [Video]. YouTube. https://www.youtube.com/watch?v=GVRUmpxoRIc

Boyd-Graber, J. (2023b, March 23). *What general term should you use for models like BERT and GPT? [Rant]* [Video]. YouTube. https://www.youtube.com/watch?v=u0DgoRVLTE8https://www.zotero.org/google-docs/?niXcrQ

Carefree Wandering. (2022, July 27). *Why algorithms can't think: "Artificial communication" by Elena Esposito* [Video]. YouTube. https://www.youtube.com/watch?v=L5ptc9WWcJc&t=2118s

Chaka, C. (2023). Detecting AI content in responses generated by ChatGPT, YouChat, and Chatsonic: The case of five AI content detection tools. *Journal of Applied Learning and Teaching, 6*(2). https://doi.org/10.37074/jalt.2023.6.2.12

Cheng, M. M., & Hackett, R. D. (2021). A critical review of algorithms in HRM: Definition, theory, and practice. *Human Resource Management Review, 31*(1), Article 100698. https://doi.org/10.1016/j.hrmr.2019.100698

Chetty, R., Deming, D. J., & Friedman, J. N. (2023). *Diversifying society's leaders? The causal effects of admission to highly selective private colleges* (Working Paper No. 31492). National Bureau of Economic Research. https://opportunityinsights.org/wp-content/uploads/2023/07/CollegeAdmissions_Paper.pdf

Clark, R. (2023, February 22). What's next for university admissions? *Times Higher Education.* https://www.timeshighereducation.com/campus/whats-next-university-admissions

Coffey, L. (2023a, August 4). Law schools split on using ChatGPT in admissions essays. *Inside Higher Ed.* https://www.insidehighered.com/news/tech-innovation/artificial-intelligence/2023/08/04/law-schools-split-using-chatgpt-admissions_

Coffey, L. (2023b, November 9). Study uses AI to review admissions essays. *Inside Higher Ed.* https://www.insidehighered.com/news/quick-takes/2023/11/09/researchers-create-ai-tool- admissions-essays

College Essay Guy. (n.d.). *College Essay Guy @ NACAC 2023.* Retrieved June 2, 2024. https://www.collegeessayguy.com/nacac

Collins, H. (2014). *Are we all scientific experts now?* John Wiley & Sons.

Collins, H., & Evans, R. (2007). *Rethinking expertise.* University of Chicago Press.

DEFCONConference. (2023, September 14). *An audacious plan to halt the Internet's Ensh*ttification — Cory Doctorow* [Video]. YouTube. https://www.youtube.com/watch?v=rimtaSgGz_4

Esposito, E. (2022). *Artificial communication: How algorithms produce social intelligence.* MIT Press.

Garg, N., Li, H., & Monachou, F. (2021, March). Standardized tests and affirmative action: The role of bias and variance. In *FAccT '21: Proceedings of the 2021 ACM Conference on Fairness, Accountability, and Transparency* (pp. 261–261). Association for Computing Machinery. http://dx.doi.org/10.1145/3442188.3445889

Gebre-Medhin, B., Giebel, S., Alvero, AJ, Domingue, B. W., & Stevens, M. L. (2022). Application essays and the ritual production of merit in U.S. selective admissions. *Poetics, 94*, Article 101706. https://doi.org/10.1016/j.poetic.2022.101706

Giebel, S., Alvero, A. J., Gebre-Medhin, B., & Antonio, A. L. (2022). Signaled or suppressed? How gender informs women's undergraduate applications in biology and engineering. *Socius, 8.* https://doi.org/10.1177/23780231221127537

Grossman, J., Tomkins, S., Page, L. C., & Goel, S. (2023). *The disparate impacts of college admissions policies on Asian American applicants* (Working Paper No. 31527). National Bureau of Economic Research. https://www.nber.org/system/files/working_papers/w31527/w31527.pdf

Gunasekar, S., Zhang, Y., Aneja, J., Mendes, C. C. T., Del Giorno, A., Gopi, S., Javaheripi, M., Kauffmann, P., de Rosa, G., Saarikivi, O., Salim, A., Shah, S., Behl, H. S., Wang, X., Bubeck, S., Eldan, R., Kalai, A. T, Lee, Y, T., & Li, Y. (2023). Textbooks are all you need. *arXiv* (Article 2306.11644v2). https://doi.org/10.48550/arXiv.2306.11644

Hartocollis, A. (2019, August 27). SAT "adversity score" is abandoned in wake of criticism. *The New York Times.* https://www.nytimes.com/2019/08/27/us/sat-adversity-score-college-board.html

Henson, B. (Director). (1992). *The Muppet Christmas Carol.* Walt Disney Pictures; Jim Henson Productions.

Khan Academy. (n.d.). *Your AI prompt guide.* https://blog.khanacademy.org/wp-content/uploads/2023/10/Free-guide-How-to-use-an-AI-chatbot-to-help-you-get-into-college-Khan-Academy-1.pdf

Knox, L. (2023, September 5). Are face-to-face admissions practices gaining traction? *Inside Higher Ed.* https://www.insidehighered.com/news/admissions/traditional-age/2023/09/05/are-face-face-admissions-practices-gaining-traction

Lee, H., Kizilcec, R. F., & Joachims, T. (2023). Evaluating a learned admission-prediction model as a replacement for standardized tests in college admissions. In *L@S '23: Proceedings of the Tenth ACM Conference on Learning@ Scale* (pp. 195–203). https://doi.org/10.48550/arXiv.2302.03610

Lee, J., Harvey, E., Zhou, J., Garg, N., Joachims, T., & Kizilcec, R. F. (2024a). Ending affirmative action harms diversity without improving academic merit. In *Proceedings of the 4th ACM Conference on Equity and Access in Algorithms, Mechanisms, and Optimization* (pp. 1–17). https://doi.org/10.1145/3689904.3694706

Lee, J., Hicke, Y., Yu, R., Brooks, C., & Kizilcec, R. F. (2024b). The life cycle of large language models in education: A framework for understanding sources of bias. *British Journal of Educational Technology, 55*(5), 1982–2002. https://doi.org/10.1111/bjet.13505

Lee, J., Alvero, A. J., Joachims, T., & Kizilcec, R. (2025). Poor alignment and steerability of large language models: Evidence from college admission essays. arXiv preprint (arXiv:2503.20062).

Lira, B., Gardner, M., Quirk, A., Stone, C., Rao, A., Ungar, L., Hutt, S., Hickman, L., D'Mello, S. K., & Duckworth, A. L. (2023). Using artificial intelligence to assess personal qualities in college admissions. *Science Advances, 9*(41), Article eadg9405. https://doi.org/10.1126%2Fsciadv.adg9405

Liu, R., Jia, C., Wei, J., Xu, G., Wang, L., & Vosoughi, S. (2021, May). Mitigating political bias in language models through reinforced calibration. In *Proceedings of the AAAI Conference on Artificial Intelligence* (Vol. 35, No. 17, pp. 14857–14866). https://doi.org/10.1609/aaai.v35i17.17744

Liu, Z., & Garg, N. (2021). *Test-optional policies: Overcoming strategic behavior and informational gaps.* Equity and Access in Algorithms, Mechanisms, and Optimization. https://arxiv.org/pdf/2107.08922

Luhmann, N. (2000). *The reality of the mass media.* Stanford University Press.

Lux, T., Pittman, R., Shende, M., & Shende, A. (2016, May). Applications of supervised learning techniques on undergraduate admissions data. In *CF '16: Proceedings of the ACM International Conference on Computing Frontiers* (pp. 412–417). https://doi.org/10.1145/2903150.2911717

McDermott, R. P., & Roth, D. R. (1978). The social organization of behavior: Interactional approaches. *Annual Review of Anthropology, 7*(1), 321–345. http://dx.doi.org/10.1146/annurev.an.07.100178.001541

Moeller, H. G. (2006). Luhmann explained: From souls to systems (Vol. 3). Open Court Publishing.

Naveed, H., Khan, A. U., Qiu, S., Saqib, M., Anwar, S., Usman, M., Akhtar, N., Barnes, N., & Mian, A. (2023). A comprehensive overview of large language models. arXiv (Article 2307.06435). https://doi.org/10.48550/arXiv.2307.06435

Patel, I. (2023, March 27). *Ilya Sutskever (OpenAI chief scientist): Building AGI, alignment, spies, Microsoft, & enlightenment* [Video]. YouTube. https://www.youtube.com/watch?v=YfIo0TQzry8&t=399s

Radhakrishnan, A., Nguyen, K., Chen, A., Chen, C., Denison, C., Hernandez, D., Durmus, E., Hubinger, E., Kernion, J., Lukošiūtė, K., Cheng, N., Joseph, N., Schiefer, N., Rausch, O., McCandlish, S., El Showk, S., Lanham, T., Maxwell, T., Chandrasekaran, V., . . . Perez, E. (2023). Question decomposition improves the faithfulness of model-generated reasoning. arXiv (Article 2307.11768v2). https://doi.org/10.48550/arXiv.2307.11768

Savitz-Romer, M., Nicola, T., Ha, J., DiLorenzo, J., Munoz-Najar Galvez, S., Desiderio, A., & Nicola, M. (2024). *Crafting merit: School Counselors' choices to reference adversity in college recommendation letters*. [Manuscript submitted for publication].

Shumailov, I., Shumaylov, Z., Zhao, Y., Gal, Y., Papernot, N., & Anderson, R. (2023). The curse of recursion: Training on generated data makes models forget. arXiv (Article 2305.17493v3). https://doi.org/10.48550/arXiv.2305.17493

Students for Fair Admissions, Inc. v. President and Fellows of Harvard College, 600 U.S. 181, 20–1199 (2023). https://www.supremecourt.gov/opinions/22pdf/20-1199_hgdj.pdf

Talbert, H. (2024, October 8). Analysis: Could this new admissions tool explain Yale's post-affirmative action racial demographics? *Yale Daily News*. https://yaledailynews.com/blog/2024/10/08/analysis-could-this-new-admissions-tool-explain-yales-post-affirmative-action-racial-demographics/

Varenne, H., & McDermott, R. (1998). Disability as cultural fact. In H. Varenne & R. McDermott (Eds.), *Successful failure: The school America builds*. Westview Press. https://doi.org/10.4324/9780429497056

Veletsianos, G., Kimmons, R., & Bondah, F. E. (2023, March 15). ChatGPT and higher education: Initial prevalence and areas of interest. *EDUCAUSE Review*. https://er.educause.edu/articles/2023/3/chatgpt-and-higher-education-initial-prevalence-a nd-areas-of-interest

Vincent, J. (2019, December 11). Why are so many AI systems named after Muppets? *The Verge*. https://www.theverge.com/2019/12/11/20993407/ai-language-models-muppets-sesame-street-muppetware-elmo-bert-ernie

9

Understanding Challenges Repaying Student Loans

An In-Depth Study Utilizing BERT Models for Emotion Recognition and Issue Classification

Yunhong Yang, Hiba Agha, Bahar Akman,

Dan Kheloussi, and Qiwei He

Student loan debt is the second-largest component of overall consumer debt in the United States (Bruckner & Ryan, 2022). The increasing cost of college and the scarcity of grants and aid have compelled many students to rely on loans to cover their educational expenses (Houle, 2014). Since 2000, state funding for higher education has decreased by 25% (Hiltonsmith, 2013), and the total amount of student loan debt continues to rise. Though this debt significantly assists students to achieve their academic goals and earn college degrees, it can also impose emotional and financial burdens, and the application and repayment process can be quite complex (Hodson et al., 2014). From navigating the various types of loans available, understanding interest rates, and meeting eligibility criteria to managing repayment plans and staying on top of deadlines, students often find themselves overwhelmed. Additionally, the intricacies of deferment, forbearance, and potential loan forgiveness programs add further layers of complexity. This can lead to confusion and stress, making it essential for borrowers to seek guidance and thoroughly educate themselves on their options (Bruckner & Ryan, 2023).

According to a recent report from Pew Charitable Trusts (2019), approximately 43 million Americans have student loans from federal government programs, making it the largest part of the education loan market. However, this system faces significant challenges as many borrowers find it difficult to repay their loans, a situation worsened by the complicated repayment process. Around 20% of borrowers are in default — meaning they have not made a payment in at least 270 days. Additionally, millions of borrowers are behind on their payments, and over one million loans default each year. Repayment challenges can worsen students' loan burdens and negatively affect their credit scores. Although student loan repayment was paused during the COVID-19

pandemic, it resumed in fall 2023, which led to significant disruption in the student loan repayment system and caused hardships for borrowers and resulted in many avoidable loan delinquencies and defaults.

In this chapter, we examine data from the Consumer Financial Protection Bureau (CFPB) Consumer Complaint Database to analyze borrower perceptions of the student loan system using natural language processing (NLP) techniques and a large language model (LLM). Our goal is to show how artificial intelligence (AI) can be used to understand semantic attitudes expressed in textual complaints and automatically classify them into topics.

Analysis of Student Loan Complaints

The CFPB offers a platform for borrowers to lodge complaints about their student loans, covering issues with private lenders, servicers, and collectors of all types of student loans. Borrowers can submit their complaints online or via phone, and the CFPB collaborates with relevant companies to resolve these issues. Borrowers can simply fill out a form online, or input a longer narrative to describe the complaints in detail. The CFPB's Consumer Complaint Database serves as a valuable tool for identifying common problems faced by borrowers. By analyzing these complaints, the CFPB can detect trends and systemic issues within the student loan industry, which helps inform policy decisions and enhance borrower protections.

Bruckner and Ryan (2022) studied borrowers' subjective views on whether traditional or financial technology (i.e., fintech) student loan lenders and servicers provide a better customer experience. Using qualitative research methods to analyze 30,678 complaints filed with the CFPB against 212 student loan companies, their study found that consumers initiated far fewer complaints against fintech lenders compared to traditional lenders. However, the study also revealed that fintech lenders are 28 times more likely than traditional lenders to receive complaints for making confusing or misleading advertisements.

Bruckner and Ryan (2023) categorized the most common student loan complaints and identified patterns of discontent in four primary areas: (1) a mismatch between the ability to repay and repayment options, including issues with forbearance, deferments, the Public Service Loan Forgiveness program, income-driven repayment plans, and loan cancellation options; (2) customer service problems, such as sudden and unexplained changes in payment obligations; (3) inappropriate payment processing, including misapplying payments; and (4) unauthorized loans or outright scams. Building on Bruckner and Ryan's (2023) work, we set out to consider how these challenges might be addressed utilizing adaptive monitoring systems with advanced techniques to fine-tune repayment policies and information.

Text Analysis of Student Loan Complains with LLMs

The unstructured textual data in student loan complaints were ripe for exploration using NLP and LLMs, an advanced AI technique. Previously, Haendler and Heimer (2021) utilized the Flesch Reading Ease score to assess the complexity of student loan complaints submitted to the CFPB. Additionally, they applied the Gunning Fog Index to identify complaints with the lowest readability and highest complexity. These textual metrics served as indicators to explore the relationship between narrative differences across socioeconomic groups before and after President Trump's administration (2017–2021) took control of the CFPB.

Bastani et al. (2019) proposed an intelligent approach using latent Dirichlet allocation (LDA) to analyze consumer complaints filed with the CFPB. The aim was to extract latent topics from the complaint narratives and explore their associated trends over time. The study identified 39 latent topics and clearly visualized the projected trajectory of each topic in future years. For example, complaints related to account management, credit reporting, credit scores, fraud, and rewards and promotions significantly increased over time, while complaints regarding harassment and mortgages dropped dramatically in recent years. These time trends were used to evaluate the effectiveness of CFPB regulations and their impact on fostering a consumer-oriented culture within financial institutions.

BERT (Bidirectional Encoder Representations from Transformers) is a powerful LLM that is advantageous in its bidirectional approach that can be used to provide contextual understanding. BERT offers a robust framework for capturing intricate linguistic nuances. Specifically, BERT enhances our ability to delve into the multifaceted nature of texts. Shin and Kim (2024) utilized the BERT model to analyze over 820,000 complaints collected by the CFPB. Their study confirmed that the use of LLMs enhances a comprehensive set of linguistic features, thereby increasing the persuasiveness of messages to receivers with diverse linguistic preferences (i.e., linguistic feature alignment). Raju et al. (2022) applied BERTopic to the CFPB textual complaint data and found that BERTopic was flexible and provided meaningful and diverse topics compared to LDA. Correa and Correa (2022) conducted a neural text classification on the CFPB dataset, with recurrent bidirectional long short-term memory (Bi-LSTM) and transformer neural networks (DistilBERT and FinBERT), to automatically classify textual complaints into nine predefined product categories. The study resulted in 88.05% accuracy in prediction, which significantly overperformed traditional machine learning on bag-of-words (BoW) representation. The main reason for this impressive finding was that the textual complaint documents were viewed as sequences of characters or words over a given vocabulary, with significant structure imposed by language. However, if a document is represented by n-grams, the structure or dependence between bags of words is neglected (He et al., 2017).

Ongoing Need for Novel Approaches to Understand Student Loan Complaints

Prior work underexamined two areas. First, new research was needed to identify the association between emotion recognition and latent complaint topics, especially to check whether emotions may change when repayment policies change over time. Second, it would be helpful to automatically classify student loan complaints into predefined categories so that CFPB could anticipate borrower needs and help solve issues easily. We organize this chapter around two research questions: First, what is the emotional trajectory of student loan borrowers over time, and is there a discernible shift attributable to repayment policy changes? Second, how does a BERT model perform in automatic prediction of complaint topics?

In the subsequent section, we introduce our use of a BERT model and discuss how to apply it in textual analysis for CFPB student loan complaints. Then, we present results from applying the BERT model in semantic analysis and topic prediction. Finally, we conclude the chapter by discussing potential future applications for supporting student borrowers and understanding emotions through textual data.

Method

CFPB Data on Student Loan Complaints

This study leverages the CFPB Consumer Complaint Database to gather data on student loan complaints. This dataset, freely accessible from the CFPB website,[1] originates from a U.S. government agency focused on protecting consumers in the financial sector. Specifically, we examined student loan complaint narratives that were submitted between March 19, 2015, and March 21, 2024, totaling 41,302 records over 9 years. Due to the BERT model's capacity limitations, the maximum textual input per narrative was set at 512 tokens, truncating any longer narratives to the first 512 tokens. Figure 9.1 illustrates the distribution of complaint narrative lengths, which peak between 500 and 600 tokens, indicating minimal loss of textual information despite the truncation.

Figure 9.1. Distribution of length of
complaint narratives (N = 41,302)

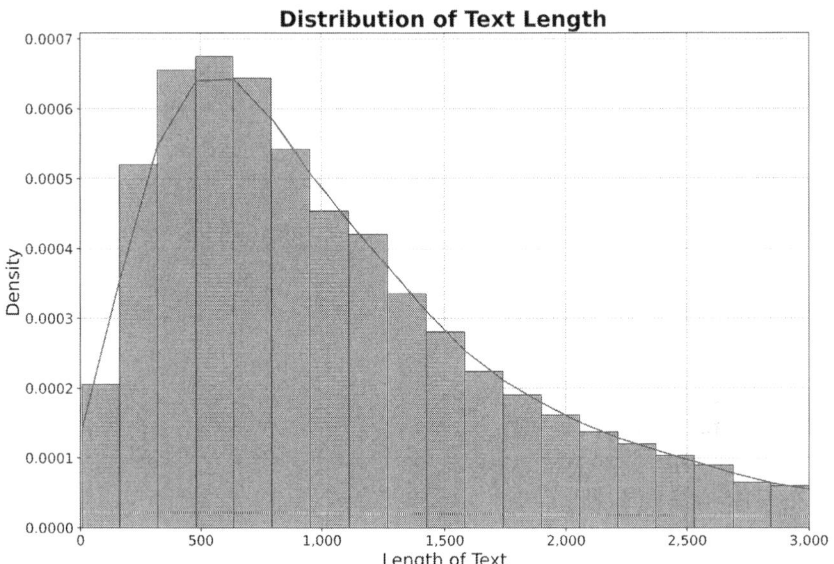

Figure 9.2. The distribution of complaints across years, 2015 to
2024 (N = 41,302). [ALT TEXT STILL NEEDED]

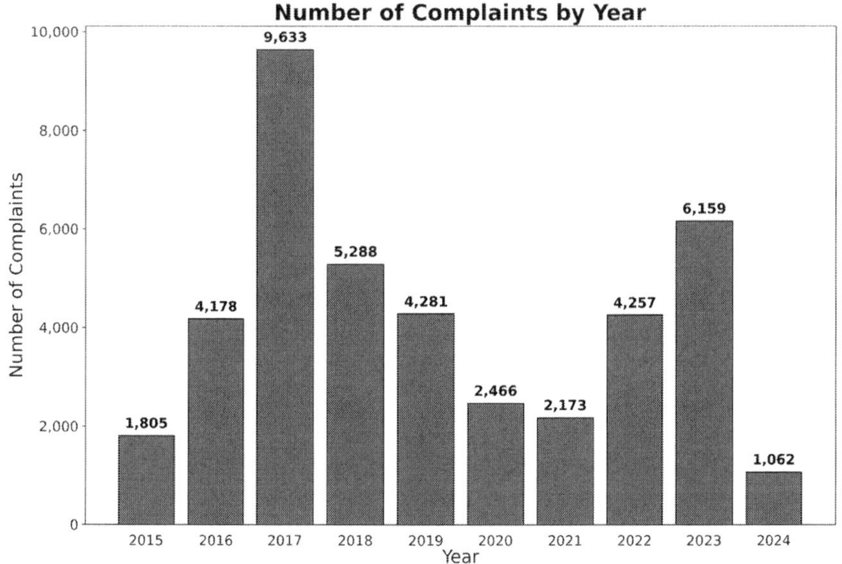

Figure 9.2 displays the distribution of student loan complaints over 9 years. The volume of complaints varies over time, which coincides with student loan policy changes. As seen in figure 9.2, complaints peaked in 2017 and again in 2023. The low volumes of complaints were submitted in 2015, 2020, and 2021. Compared with 2016, the complaints in 2017 increased by 2.3 times within 1 year. During the COVID-19 pandemic period, student loan repayment was postponed, which kept the volume of complaints at their lowest levels during 2020 and 2021. However, when the delayed repayment policy was terminated in 2023, there was a significant increase in the volume of submitted complaints. It is worth noting that nearly 98% of complaints were resolved during the investigation period, and 97% of cases received timely responses.

Preprocessing Narrative Textual Data

To improve the efficiency of training and testing procedures in textual analysis, as well as to increase the ability to generalize to previously unseen data, a preprocessing routine was implemented using the NLTK package in Python (He et al., 2017). This preprocessing step involved screening digital numbers, deducting noninformative "stop-words" (e.g., "I," "to"), common punctuation marks (e.g., "." and ":"), and frequently used abbreviations (e.g., "isn't," "I'm") and "stemming" the rest of the words, Porter's (1980) algorithm, to remove common morphological endings. For example, the terms "complaints," "complaining," and "complaint," though in variant lexical forms, were normalized in an identical stem "complain" by removing the suffixes and linguistic rule-based indicators.

BERT Model

BERT is an innovative method for using extensive amounts of unlabeled text to create models capable of understanding language (Devlin et al., 2018). It is based on Transformer architecture (Vaswani et al., 2017), which replaces traditional sequential text processing with an "attention" mechanism. This mechanism allows BERT to process all words in a sentence simultaneously, leading to a deeper comprehension of language. Central to transformers is the self-attention mechanism, which enables the model to evaluate the significance of each word in relation to every other word in the sentence. This is essential for grasping the contextual meanings of words, allowing the model to interpret multiple meanings based on context.

Tokenization

Tokenization is the first step in BERT, which involves representing sentences with tokens. Figure 9.3 shows an example process of using BERT for text classification tasks. Given a text sequence, a special classification token ([CLS]) is always added as the first token of the text sequence, and a special token ([SEP]) is added to the end of the text sequence. Since the sequence lengths may vary across different sequences, several [PAD] tokens are added to standardize all input lengths.

The input representation for each token is constructed by summing the token embedding, segment embedding, and position embedding. BERT uses WordPiece embeddings (Wu et al., 2019) as token embeddings. The segment embedding is a learned embedding indicating whether the token belongs to sentence A or sentence B. The position embedding is added to preserve the information about the relative or absolute position of the tokens in the sequence. BERT processes input embeddings through several layers of Transformer blocks. Within each block, a multi-head self-attention mechanism is applied first, followed by a feed-forward network.

Pretraining and Fine-Tuning in BERT

During pretraining, BERT learns to utilize the [CLS] token as a comprehensive summary of the entire input sequence. For classification tasks, the final hidden state of this [CLS] token serves as the feature representation for the whole sequence. After pretraining, BERT is fine-tuned for specific classification tasks

Figure 9.3. An example of BERT for text classification Tasks.

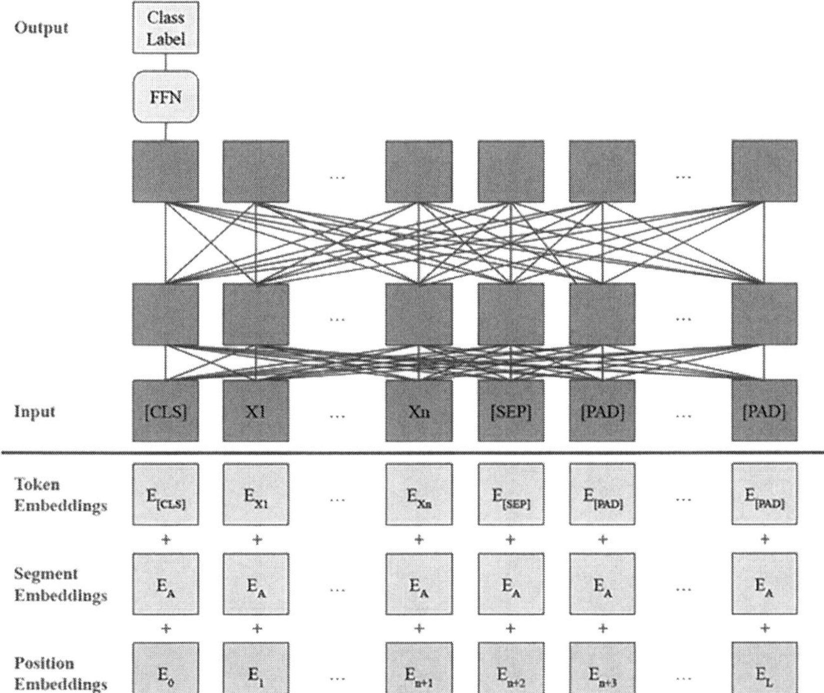

by adding a straightforward classification layer on top of the Transformer's output for the [CLS] token. This layer is trained on a labeled dataset for a particular downstream task, enabling the model to use its pretrained contextual understanding to make precise predictions.

The effectiveness of the [CLS] token in capturing the contextual essence of the entire input sequence makes BERT exceptionally proficient in handling a wide range of classification challenges. BERT simplifies the complexity of text classification by embedding a representation of the whole input text into a single token. This approach enables the model to evaluate the input as a whole, ensuring that the classification decision benefits from a comprehensive understanding of the text's context.

In this study, we utilized the BERT-base-uncased model during the pretraining phase, employing the BERT for Sequence Classification module from the Transformers package in Python (Wolf et al., 2019). This method allows for the configuration of issue labels and the setting of hidden state outputs to True. We selected AdamW as the optimizer, a variant of the Adam stochastic optimization method, which decouples weight decay from the gradient update to improve performance (Loshchilov & Hutter, 2017).

After pretraining, we developed functions to iterate over the training epochs, initiating the fine-tuning process. To evaluate model performance, we used metrics such as accuracy and F1-score, and also examined confusion matrices for deeper insights into the model's predictive capabilities. The fine-tuned model, incorporating the learned parameters, was then saved for potential future applications and analyses. We conducted two textual analyses with BERT in this study. In the first section, we applied a semantic analysis with the BERT-base-uncased emotion model to exhibit the emotional trajectory in students' loan complaints over time, alongside policy changes. In the second section, we tuned both BERT-base-uncased and BERT-base-cased models to automatically classify loan complaints by issue topics.

Semantic Analysis with BERT Emotion Recognition Model

Motivated by the observation in figure 9.2 that complaint volumes fluctuated with changes in loan repayment policies over time, we proceeded to investigate whether the emotional content of complaints also shifted. Understanding semantic variations can provide deeper insights into consumer grievances and predict future trends in complaints when repayment policies change. CFPB and lenders can use that information to anticipate borrowers' needs and assist them with repayment.

In this study, we employed a pretrained emotion recognition model sourced from Hugging Face to discern the polarity of six distinct types of emotions (i.e., angry, joy, surprise, fear, love, sadness) expressed within the text (Wolf et al., 2020). This pretrained BERT-base-uncased-emotion model has been trained on the Twitter Sentiment Analysis dataset, providing a robust foundation for emotion classification (Mann et al., 2023). We divided our data into training, testing, and validation sets with a proportion of 7:1.5:1.5. To improve processing speed and training efficacy, we batched the data prior to initiating the training process.

Classifying Topics of Complaints with BERT

After analyzing complaints for emotions, we then sought to further train the BERT model for automatic classification of complaint topics. Both BERT-base-uncased and BERT-base-cased models were fine-tuned in this research. In the Transformers architecture, each output element is intricately linked to every input element, with the weights between them dynamically calculated based on their relationships (Devlin et al., 2018).

The BERT model consists of two main stages: pretraining and fine-tuning. During the pretraining phase, the model is trained on a large corpus of unlabeled data through various pretraining tasks. This phase aims to provide the model with a comprehensive understanding of the language, capturing contextual nuances and word relationships. The fine-tuning phase then initializes the BERT model with parameters obtained from the pretraining phase. In this stage, all model parameters are fine-tuned using labeled data specific to downstream tasks. Each downstream task has its own fine-tuned models, although they all share the same initialization from the pretrained parameters (Devlin et al., 2018).

This sequential process of pretraining followed by fine-tuning allows the BERT model to generalize its language understanding from the pretraining phase to the specifics of downstream tasks. This method has been shown to improve the model's performance across various NLP tasks, such as analyzing Twitter posts (Müller et al., 2023), medical case labeling (Wu et al., 2021), and law document downstream (Limsopatham, 2021), just name a few, making it a powerful tool for applications such as classification.

Results

Emotion Recognition of Student Loan Complaint Narratives

Figure 9.4 illustrates the distribution of complaint narratives across six emotion labels, as predicted by a pretrained BERT model. Approximately 50% of the complaint narratives predominantly expressed "anger," while around 25% conveyed "joy," likely reflecting posts made after loan repayment issues were resolved. The emotion tag "love" was the least frequently expressed among the narratives.

Figure 9.4. The frequency of student loan complaints by six emotional categories.

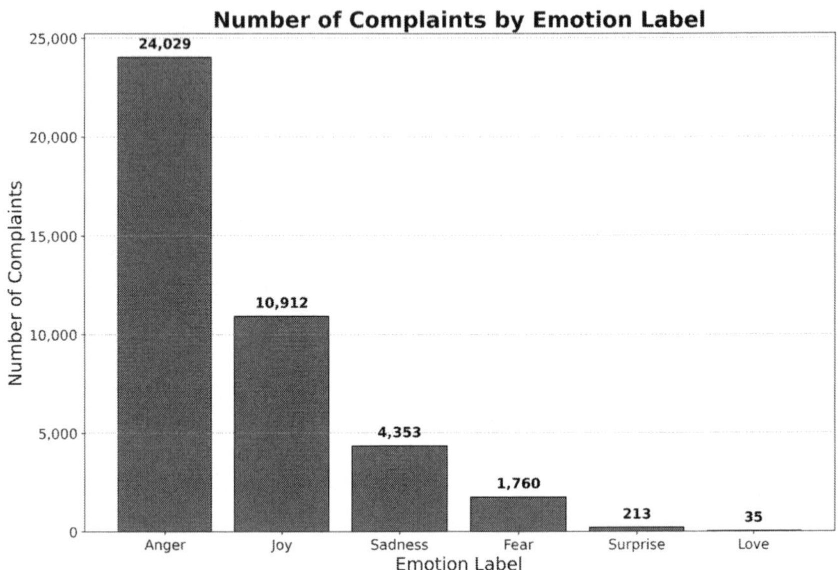

We extracted data from two peak periods identified in figure 9.5 — June 2016 to December 2017 and January 2023 to March 2024, — to examine the trajectory of emotional changes over time. As shown in figure 9.5, the first peak time (panel a) did not exhibit significant emotional changes, while the second peak time (panel b) displayed notable shifts, including a sharp increase in "anger" and a significant decrease in "joy" from February 2024 to March 2024. This substantial change could be attributed to the freezing of student loans in March 2020 due to the COVID-19 pandemic, which were reopened in 2024, potentially leading to concentrated issues and confusion during that period.

Classifying Complaint Narratives by Topics

The CFPB student loan complaint narratives were initially categorized into 14 groups (see table 9.1). However, the distribution of narratives across these categories was imbalanced. The category "dealing with your lender or servicer" accounted for the largest proportion at approximately 52%, while "issue with income share agreement" represented the smallest proportion at around 0.02%.

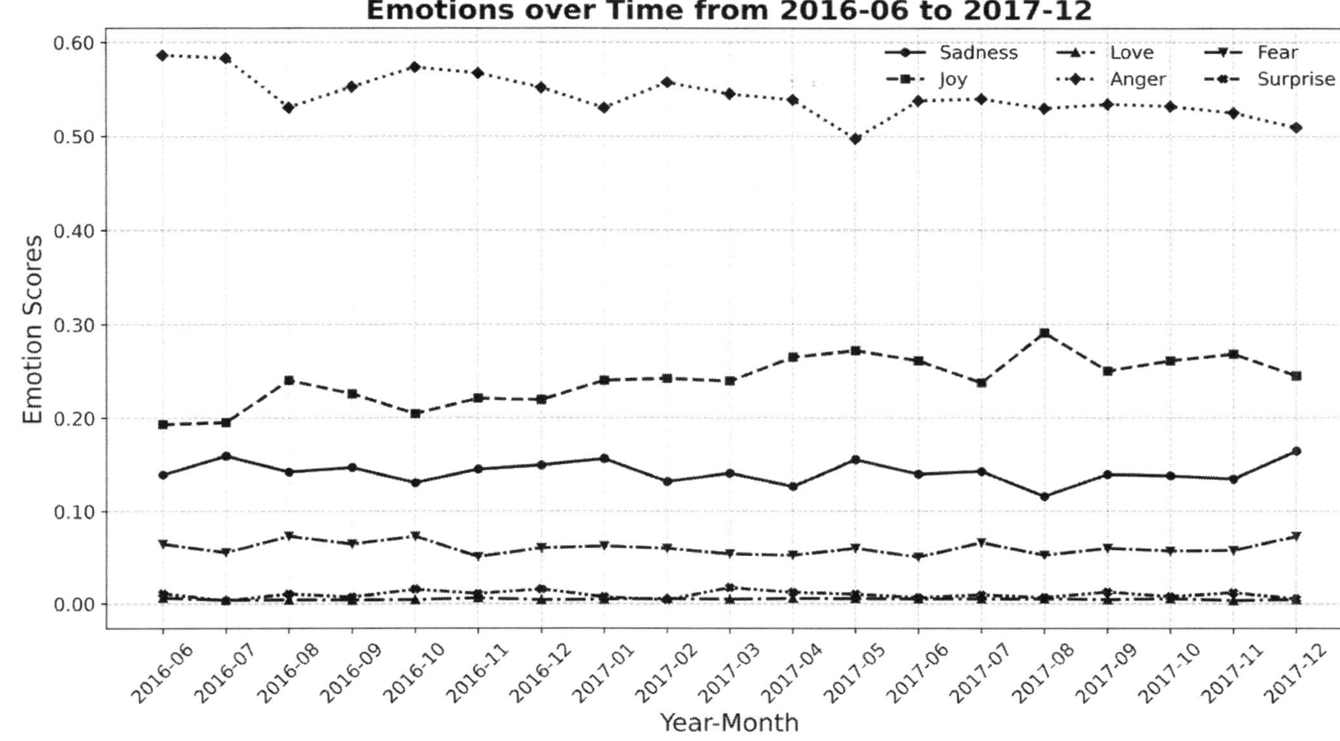

Figure 9.5a. Emotion trajectory during the peak time of student loan complaints.

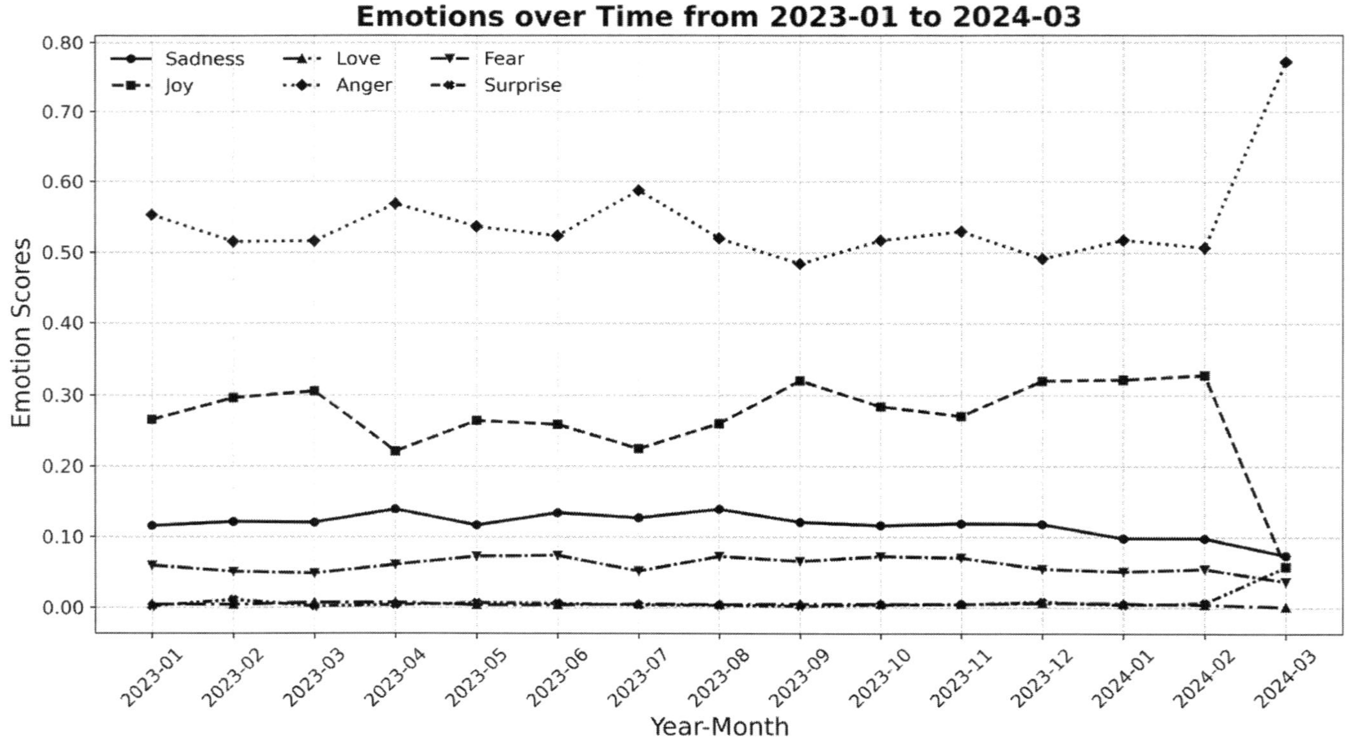

Figure 9.5b. Emotion trajectory during the peak time of student loan complaints.

Table 9.1. Primary Categories of Student Loan Complaints in the Consumer Financial Protection Bureau Database, March 19, 2015, to March 21, 2024

Issue Type	Count	Percentage
Dealing with your lender or servicer	21,490	52.03%
Dealing with my lender or servicer	7,904	19.14%
Struggling to repay your loan	5,825	14.10%
Can't repay my loan	3,057	7.40%
Incorrect information on your report	1,252	3.03%
Getting a loan	786	1.90%
Problem with a credit reporting company's investigation into an existing problem	644	1.56%
Improper use of your report	179	0.43%
Credit monitoring or identity theft protection services	78	0.19%
Problem with a company's investigation into an existing problem	32	0.08%
Problem with fraud alerts or security freezes	19	0.05%
Unable to get your credit report or credit score	18	0.05%
Issue where my lender is my school	10	0.02%
Issue with income share agreement	8	0.02%
Total	41,302	100%

Note: (N = 41,302)

To facilitate easier interpretation of the classification results, we consolidated the 14 categories into four main groups (see table 9.2): "dealing with lender or servicer" (64.35%), "incorrect information on report" (3.75%), "issues on repaying loan" (26.50%), and "others" (5.31%). It is important to note that the category "dealing with my lender or servicer" was removed from the original CFPB dataset in April 2017 and therefore was not included in our study. This resulted in a total of 33,398 complaint narratives being analyzed in the topic classification study.

Table 9.2. Sample with Four Grouping Categories in the Classification Study

Issue Type	Count	Percentage
Dealing with lender or servicer	21,490	64.35%
Incorrect information on report	1,252	3.75%
Issues on repaying loan	8,882	26.50%
Others	1,774	5.31%
Total	33,398	100%

We configured both the uncased and cased BERT models with identical parameters: 6 training epochs, a batch size of 8, and a learning rate of 2×10^{-5}. Figures 9.6 and 9.7 display the confusion matrices for the uncased and cased BERT models, respectively. Both models performed best in predicting the "issues on repaying loan" and "dealing with lender or servicer" categories, while the "incorrect information on report" category had the lowest prediction rate.

Figure 9.6. Confusion matrices for uncased BERT models.

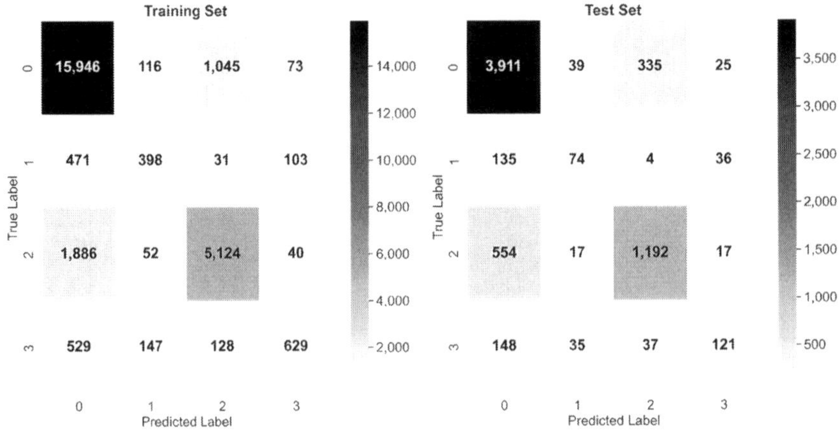

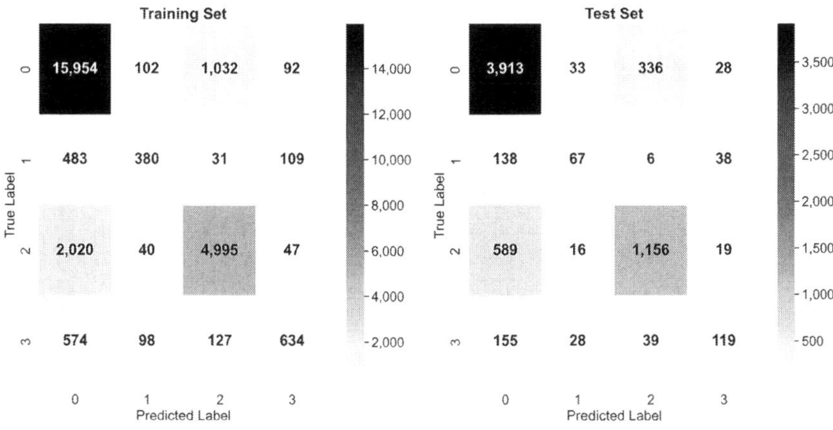

Figure 9.7. Confusion matrices for cased BERT models.

Table 9.3 presents the performance metrics, accuracy and F-1 score, for the different BERT models. On the test set, the BERT-base-uncased model showed a slightly better prediction rate (0.793) compared to the BERT-base-cased model (0.787). Although the F-1 scores were satisfactory, the accuracy was moderately acceptable for either model. This could be due to the low prediction rate in the "incorrect information on report" category, where the complaint narratives might be too diverse.

Table 9.3. Performance Metrics for BERT Uncased and
Cased Models

Model Type	Accuracy	F1-Score
BERT-base-uncased (training)	0.827	0.666
BERT-base-uncased (test)	0.793	0.595
BERT-base-cased (training)	0.822	0.662
BERT-base-cased (test)	0.787	0.584

Discussion

This chapter proposes a novel approach for examining student loan complaint narratives from the CFPB dataset using the BERT model. It highlights the significance of collecting complaint data and demonstrates the BERT model's effectiveness in predicting emotional tags and classifying topics. This approach could potentially be adapted to understand students' challenges and help anticipate and resolve complaints in other types of higher education settings.

The findings from this study offer meaningful insights for a broad range of stakeholders in higher education — including, but not limited to, students, faculty, administrators, and researchers — extending beyond the scope of the CFPB and lenders. For students, understanding the current landscape of loan applications may directly inform financial decision-making related to course selection and career planning. Observed trends in semantic shifts shed light on the evolving impact of loan-related discourse on enrollment decisions, providing valuable input for administrative planning around admissions and informing institutional and governmental policy development to support students' educational pathways. Additionally, the analysis of textual complaints yields dynamic evidence that enhances researchers' understanding of the relationship between public feedback and the evolution of loan systems. In the present context of policy uncertainty, these insights highlight the historical significance and potential of public complaints to inform future policy directions.

The first part of our study shows that emotions embedded in student loan complaints can be analyzed to provide insights for institutions to devise responsive and adaptable strategies. Additionally, our work highlights how policy shifts influenced borrower sentiments. Future research could expand on these findings by exploring more comprehensive data collection methods and conducting a nuanced analysis of emotional signals within longer contextual frameworks. This would ultimately enhance the depth and accuracy of emotion recognition in this context. For example, the high proportion of "joy" expressions in complaints could be an interesting topic for further exploration. Given that the BERT model can only handle 512 tokens, we had to truncate all narratives longer than this limit to the first 512 tokens, which might pose an issue for incomplete data capture. The second part of our project emphasizes the importance of balancing labels before training. The findings of this study highlight the practical utility of the fine-tuned BERT model in detecting and addressing topics discussed on social media, thereby streamlining early-stage textual data analysis for nonprofit organizations or institutes.

It is also noted that several unresolved issues still remain regarding the mechanisms of pretrained LLMs and prompt-based classification. Mao et al. (2022) study prompt-based sentiment analysis and emotion detection, revealing that using fine-grained emotion taxonomies as label-words is more efficient than coarse-grained ones in affective computing tasks. The review explores the multifaceted utility of pretrained LLMs in text analytics and their biases in fine-grained classification tasks. Another concern is the susceptibility of

LLMs to inherent biases present in the training data. Correa and Correa (2022) emphasize the need for proactive measures to mitigate and rectify these biases to ensure fair and unbiased analysis.

Finally, this study acknowledges several limitations. First, the word limit imposed by BERT restricts analysis to texts under 512 words. Future research could explore summarization techniques or alternative models like ChunkBERT, which allows fine-tuning of pretrained models for longer texts (Jaiswal & Milios, 2023). Second, an existing challenge in BERT is its significant running time due to its extensive parameters, making frequent updates costly. Optimizing the structure of the BERT model in future studies could better meet the growing demands of textual analysis. In addition, since the dataset of complaints was primarily analyzed based on textual properties, the representativeness of demographic variables may not have been a central focus of this study. This could introduce potential biases, as groups differentiated by age, region, race, or socioeconomic status may exhibit distinct and nuanced linguistic patterns. Such variations warrant careful consideration in future research. Despite these limitations, results from this study greatly enhance our comprehension of the emotional experiences of student loan borrowers and their connection to policy changes. These insights can offer additional information to monitor the impact of policy changes and assist in making timely adjustments.

Notes

1   The CFPB Consumer Complaint Database records the eligible complaints sent to companies and are only published after the company responds, confirming a commercial relationship or after 15 days, whichever comes first. The database generally updates daily. See details in https://www.consumerfinance.gov/data-research/consumer-complaints/.

References

Bastani, K., Namavari, H., & Shaffer, J. (2019). Latent Dirichlet allocation (LDA) for topic modeling of the CFPB consumer complaints. *Expert Systems with Applications*, *127*, 256–271. https://doi.org/10.1016/j.eswa.2019.03.001

Bruckner, M., & Ryan, C. (2022). The magic of fintech? insights for regulatory agenda from analyzing student loan complaints filed with the CFPB. *Dickinson Law Review*, *127*(1), 49–100. https://laweconcenter.org/wp-content/uploads/2023/04/SSRN-id4101295.pdf

Bruckner, M. A., & Ryan, C. (2023). Student loans and financial distress: A qualitative analysis of the most common student loan complaints. *Loyola Consumer Law Review*, *35*, 203. https://laweconcenter.org/wp-content/uploads/2023/09/SSRN-id4486035.pdf

Correa, N., & Correa, A. (2022). Neural text classification for digital transformation in the financial regulatory domain. *2022 IEEE ANDESCON*, pp. 1–6. https://doi.org/10.1109/ANDESCON56260.2022.9989638

Devlin, J., Chang, M. W., Lee, K., & Toutanova, K. (2018). Bert: Pre-training of deep bidirectional transformers for language understanding. arXiv preprint (arXiv:1810.04805).

Haendler, C., & Heimer, R. (2021). *The financial restitution gap in consumer finance: Insights from complaints filed with the CFPB*. https://dx.doi.org/10.2139/ssrn.3766485

He, Q., Veldkamp, B. P., Glas, C. A., & de Vries, T. (2017). Automated assessment of patients' self-narratives for posttraumatic stress disorder screening using natural language processing and text mining. *Assessment*, *24*(2), 157–172. https://doi.org/10.1177/1073191115602551

Hiltonsmith, R. (2013). *New York's great cost shift: How higher education cuts undermine the state's future middle class*. Demos. https://vtechworks.lib.vt.edu/server/api/core/bitstreams/b15f3b2a-eed5-488a-a817-ac207eee313f/content

Hodson, R., Dwyer, R. E., & Neilson, L. A. (2014). Credit card blues: The middle class and the hidden costs of easy credit. *The Sociological Quarterly*, *55*(2), 315–340. https://doi.org/10.1111/tsq.12059

Houle, J. N. (2014). Disparities in debt: Parents' socioeconomic resources and young adult student loan debt. *Sociology of Education, 87*(1), 53–69. https://doi.org/10.1177/0038040713512213

Jaiswal, A., & Milios, E. (2023). Breaking the token barrier: Chunking and convolution for efficient long text classification with BERT. arXiv preprint (arXiv:2310.20558).

Limsopatham, N. (2021, November). Effectively leveraging BERT for legal document classification. In *Proceedings of the Natural Legal Language Processing Workshop 2021* (pp. 210–216). https://aclanthology.org/2021.nllp-1.22

Loshchilov, I., & Hutter, F. (2017). Decoupled weight decay regularization. arXiv preprint (arXiv:1711.05101).

Mann, S., Arora, J., Bhatia, M., Sharma, R., & Taragi, R. (2023). Twitter sentiment analysis using enhanced BERT. In A. J. Kulkarni, S. Mirjalili, & S. Kumar Udgata (Eds.), *Intelligent systems and applications: Select proceedings of ICISA 2022* (pp. 263–271). Springer Nature Singapore.

Mao, R., Liu, Q., He, K., Li, W., & Cambria, E. (2022). The biases of pre-trained language models: An empirical study on prompt-based sentiment analysis and emotion detection. *IEEE Transactions on Affective Computing, 14*(3), 1743–1753. https://doi.org/10.1109/TAFFC.2022.3204972

Müller, M., Salathé, M., & Kummervold, P. E. (2023). COVID-Twitter-BERT: A natural language processing model to analyse COVID-19 content on twitter. *Frontiers in Artificial Intelligence, 6.* https://doi.org/10.3389/frai.2023.1023281

Porter, M. F. (1980). An algorithm for suffix stripping. *Program, 14*(3), 130–137. https://doi.org/10.1108/00330330610681286

Raju, S. V., Bolla, B. K., Nayak, D. K., & Kh, J. (2022, April). Topic modelling on consumer financial protection bureau data: An approach using BERT based embeddings. In *2022 IEEE 7th International conference for Convergence in Technology (I2CT)* (pp. 1–6). IEEE. https://doi.org/10.1109/I2CT54291.2022.9824873

Shin, M., & Kim, J. (2024). Large language models can enhance persuasion through linguistic feature alignment. https://www.researchgate.net/profile/Minkyu-Shin-2/publication/378920355_Large_Language_Models_Can_Enhance_Persuasion_Through_Linguistic_Feature_Alignment/links/6603b4ae5c41c3139dae3a95/Large-Language-Models-Can-Enhance-Persuasion-Through-Linguistic-Feat

Pew Charitable Trusts. (2019). Student loan system presents repayment challenges. https://www.pewtrusts.org/-/media/assets/2019/11/psbs_report.pdf

Vaswani, A. (2017). Attention is all you need. *Advances in Neural Information Processing Systems.* https://user.phil.hhu.de/~cwurm/wp-content/uploads/2020/01/7181-attention-is-all-you-need.pdf

Wolf, T., Debut, L., Sanh, V., Chaumond, J., Delangue, C., Moi, A., Cistac, P., Rault, T., Louf, R., Funtowicz, M., Davison, J., Shleifer, S., von Platen, P., Ma, C., Jernite, Y., Plu, J., Xu, C., Le Scao, T., Gugger, S., Drame, M.,

Lhoest, Q., & Rush, A. M. (2019). *Huggingface's transformers: State-of-the-art natural language processing.* https://arxiv.org/pdf/1910.03771

Wolf, T., Debut, L., Sanh, V., Chaumond, J., Delangue, C., Moi, A., Cistac, P., Rault, T., Louf, R., Funtowicz, M., Davison, J., Shleifer, S., von Platen, P., Ma, C., Jernite, Y., Plu, J., Xu, C., Le Scao, T., Gugger, S., Drame, M., Lhoest, Q., & Rush, A. M. (2020). Huggingface's transformers: State-of-the-art natural language processing. *Proceedings of the 2020 EMNLP (Systems Demonstrations)* (pp. 38–45). https://aclanthology.org/2020.emnlp-demos.6.pdf

Wu, Y., Wang, S., Song, G., & Huang, Q. (2019, October). Learning fragment self-attention embeddings for image-text matching. In *Proceedings of the 27th ACM international conference on multimedia* (pp. 2088–2096). https://doi.org/10.1145/3343031.3350940

Wu, Y., Liu, Z., Wu, L., Chen, M., & Tong, W. (2021). BERT-based natural language processing of drug labeling documents: a case study for classifying drug-induced liver injury risk. *Frontiers in Artificial Intelligence, 4.* https://doi.org/10.3389/frai.2021.729834

10

Promising Applications for Promoting Disaster Resilience on College Campuses

Seyedeh Mobina Noorani, Changjie Chen, Kaleb E. Smith,

Frank Fernandez, and Karla Saldaña Ochoa

College and university campuses face increasingly severe threats from hurricanes, tropical storms, and floods. Global climate change has made natural disasters increasingly common and severe. In the U.S., the 2023 hurricane season ranked fourth for most-named tropical storms since 1950, including seven hurricanes. Sea temperatures were the warmest on record (National Oceanic and Atmospheric Administration, 2023). A single storm, Hurricane Idalia, caused 17 campuses in Florida and four campuses in Georgia to close for 1 day or more (Donadel, 2023). Compared to previous years, higher education institutions were relatively fortunate in 2023. In a catastrophic year like 2005, more than two dozen colleges and universities reported around $1.4 billion in damage (nearly $2.26 billion in 2024 dollars[1]) from Hurricane Katrina and Hurricane Rita (Mangan, 2005).

When college campuses sustain significant damage, it often takes years for them to recover. The University of Southern Mississippi suffered approximately $200 million in damage from Hurricane Katrina in 2005 and took until 2013 to rebuild its Gulf Park campus. William Carey University (WCU) lost its entire Gulfport campus, which consisted of 16 buildings. Approximately 4 years after the storm, WCU relocated what was the Gulfport campus to a new facility. At Pearl River Community College (PRCC) wind gusts peaked at 179 miles per hour, causing approximately $45 million worth of damage — the most to any community college in Mississippi. PRCC completed final repairs in fall 2014, 8 years after the hurricane hit, and was working through Federal Emergency Management Agency (FEMA) claims a decade after the hurricane (Ciurczak, 2015).

As sea levels rise and storms intensify, coastal areas face increased threats to buildings and human lives. Many higher education institutions are located in cities and states that are routinely at risk during hurricane season. Rising sea levels threaten coastal universities in at least 19 states along the Pacific Coast, the Gulf of Mexico, and the Atlantic Coast — including Alaska and Hawaii

(Myers & Lusk, 2017). For instance, the city of Charleston in South Carolina experienced flooding 75 times during 2023. By around midcentury, Charleston is projected to record flood events on 180 days out of a calendar year. Those floods will put eight campuses (The American College of the Building Arts, The Citadel, College of Charleston, Charleston School of Law, Medical University of South Carolina, Charleston Southern University, Roper Hospital School of Practical Nursing, and Trident Technical College) and their students at tremendous peril (Crawford, 2023; Kim, 2024). Meanwhile, near Norfolk, Virginia, the sea level is projected to rise between 1.4 and 3.9 feet by 2050, which would significantly increase the flood risk to Old Dominion University's nearly $1 billion campus and nearly 17,000 students (Myers & Lusk, 2017). Campus leaders and state policymakers need to focus on promoting disaster resilience to reduce damage from natural disasters (Ellard, 2019).

This chapter considers how higher education leaders can use artificial intelligence (AI) as a tool, among broader efforts, to support disaster resilience. National and global agencies have called for integrating AI and big data into emergency management planning and disaster resilience efforts. The United Nations,[2] the U.S. Chamber of Commerce,[3] and the World Economic Forum[4] have all taken steps toward using AI to promote disaster resilience. However, there is limited attention on how AI can help colleges and universities protect their buildings and students. In the sections that follow, we briefly discuss research on how AI can be used to reduce risks to campuses and provide preliminary findings from our own work training an AI algorithm to map and identify vulnerabilities in the built environment on and around campuses.

Literature Review

Despite the increasing risk of global climate change (Intergovernmental Panel on Climate Change, 2013), most higher education research focuses on campus sustainability or efforts to reduce carbon footprints (e.g., Alexander, 2014; Button, 2009; Cleaves et al., 2009; Helferty & Clarke, 2009; Kautto et al., 2018). A body of work focuses on how national, state, and municipal agencies can adapt to increasing threats from climate change, but relatively little work focuses on disaster resilience in higher education (Owen et al., 2013).

The limited research on disaster resilience in higher education tends to focus on the experiences and actions of people during and after a crisis. For instance, Gill et al. (2006) used survey data to identify the differential impacts of Hurricane Katrina on students with different minoritized identities at Mississippi State University. Other studies have used qualitative data (Johnson & Rainey, 2007) and longitudinal administrative data (Sacerdote, 2012) to examine attrition among students at Louisiana institutions who survived Hurricane Katrina. More recently, scholars sought to examine how students benefit from campus support services after a major natural disaster (Carales & Lopez, 2021).

Few studies have empirically examined how campuses can prepare to exercise disaster resilience. One study examined how university leaders learned from navigating a prior natural disaster to make better decisions and improve their response to a more recent hurricane (e.g., Fernandez et al., 2021). While leaders do consider aspects of the built environment during a crisis — for instance, in deciding whether to evacuate a residence hall — they are weighing many risks and factors, including canceling classes, coordinating with city emergency response personnel, and, of course, the safety of students, staff, and faculty. Individuals can evacuate the campus, but buildings are immobile. Therefore, leaders need tools to help them identify and address vulnerabilities in the roads and structures that are part of the campus, as well as the surrounding infrastructure that makes it possible to evacuate or access the campus before and after a flood.

Apart from educational research literature, scholars have identified AI as holding unique promise for improving disaster resilience and emergency management systems. With increasing risks from climate change, researchers have identified AI as facilitating a broader shift in approach from mitigation and recovery to preparing for and preventing disaster-related damage (Cao, 2023). In their study of how spatial models can be used to optimize the movement and allocation of resources for post-disaster, Patrascu and Mostafavi (2024) showed that AI should incorporate multiple types of data, including physical infrastructure, topographical, population, and hazard (e.g., flood maps) data.

Apart from whether AI *can* support disaster resilience, some scholars have sought to lay out approaches to *how* AI should support disaster resilience. For instance, Ghaffarian et al. (2023) argued that one potential downside to using AI is that because of its "black box" nature, it can be an opaque process for interpreting output or classifications. Similarly, Zolkafli et al. (2024) called for pairing the use of AI with concepts of "community empowerment" to ensure that efforts prioritize protecting the most vulnerable members of a community. These principles align with long-standing traditions of shared governance in higher education (e.g., Hutchens & Fernandez, 2023).

Methodology

The project was executed in three stages: First, a database of campus-built environmental data was created using aerial imagery (including satellite images, flood maps, density maps, and digital elevation models) and human-scale data from street view images to capture both macro- and micro-level flood risks. Second, a user-friendly web interface was developed to integrate and display these data, allowing users to view critical infrastructure and potential flood zones at both macro and micro levels. Third, a 2-day workshop was conducted with participants aged 19 to 40, including university students and faculty, to gather feedback on flood risk perceptions through surveys and focus group discussions. The data collected were analyzed to identify common themes and specific risk factors, providing insights into participants' perceptions of security and the factors influencing them.

Creating a Database of Campus-Built Environmental Data

We collected Google Street View (GSV) maps, flood maps, density maps, and digital elevation models (DEMs), which are representations of the bare earth or topographic surface of the Earth excluding trees and buildings. We used Google API and ArcGIS to gather corresponding street views and aerial imagery. To extract the campus geolocation as data for our project, we used Open Street Map (OSM) API to extract the road network of each campus located within the area of a square with 2.5 km sides. We created a grid of 12.5 meters to determine the geocoordinates based on the roads' axial. We only selected campuses with 80% or more street view images of their facilities to ensure we had almost a complete set of images for identifying potential campus vulnerabilities. We collected 675,486 images from 30 universities in Gulf Coast states, including 96,498 satellite images, 192,996 street view images, 96,498 flood maps, 96,498 density maps, and 96,498 DEM maps. On average, each campus had 3,721 geocoordinates.

The flood data consists of the Special Flood Hazard Areas (SFHA) from the Flood Insurance Rate Map (FIRM) provided by FEMA, featuring a cell size of 10 meters (FEMA, 2023). WorldPop's annual estimates (top-down unconstrained) of population density for the year 2020 were used, with a source cell size of 100 meters (WorldPop, 2018). Both of these datasets are made available by Esri as Image Servers and were retrieved for all points using the ArcGIS REST API. DEM data for each site was retrieved from the 3D Elevation Products (3DEP) by the U.S. Geological Survey, offering a 1-meter resolution (U.S. Geological Survey, 2023). We clipped these three data layers using a square with sides of 25 meters at each coordinate to ensure consistency in spatial analysis.

Web Interface Development

The web interface is designed to be user-friendly and visually informative, employing an intuitive layout that facilitates easy navigation between different views and data layers. High-resolution images, clear icons, and interactive maps effectively display information. The web interface for our project integrates two primary inputs to provide a comprehensive understanding of flood risk perception among students. First, the interface displays remote sensing imagery, which includes satellite images, flood maps, density maps, and DEMs sourced from governmental and commercial providers. This input offers a macro-level view of the campus and surrounding areas, highlighting potential flood zones and vulnerable regions. GSV images provide a micro-level or human-level perspective, capturing detailed visuals of streets, buildings, and natural elements like trees and water bodies. These street-level images are essential for understanding the immediate environment and specific risk factors perceived by students.

Second, the web interface included a survey to capture how campus stakeholders (e.g., students and faculty) perceive the risk of flooding and identify specific concerns regarding campus safety during flood events. The survey included questions about students' awareness of local flood risks, personal experiences with flooding, perceived vulnerabilities on campus, and suggestions for improving flood preparedness. The responses were collected and stored in a database then linked with geographic coordinates to pinpoint the exact locations of concern raised by students.

Overall, the web interface was a pilot tool designed to capture and visualize student perceptions of flood risk on campus. Integrating survey data with remote sensing imagery provides a detailed and comprehensive view of macro- and micro-level flood risks. Its user-friendly design and advanced data integration capabilities made it a platform for understanding and addressing concerns about campus vulnerabilities and solely relying on AI as a "black box" (Ghaffarian et al., 2023). Although our study primarily focused on capturing perceived flood risks, the web interface was designed to support future comparison between perceived and actual risks. Integrating FEMA flood maps, population density layers, and DEMs alongside user-submitted perceptions allows researchers to analyze where subjective concerns align — or diverge — from environmental risk data. Recognizing that perceived risk does not always correlate with actual physical vulnerability, future work will incorporate this comparison to guide disaster preparedness strategies more robustly. Therefore, the web interface allowed us to pair geographic data with human observations about risks to improve campus safety and preparedness.

Designing the Web-Based Interface to Collect Data from Campus Stakeholders

The web interface organizes the collected dataset using an unsupervised clustering algorithm —self-organizing map (SOM) — to reduce the number of examples shown to participants by selecting the most representative ones. A SOM is an unsupervised machine learning technique used to produce a low-dimensional representation of a higher-dimensional dataset while preserving the topological structure of the data. We experimented with various clustering algorithms, such as k-means, but ultimately chose SOM for its ability to not only group similar data points but also provide an intuitive, grid-based visual representation. We use pretrained convolutional neural network (CNN) models, including InceptionV3, DenseNet169, EfficientNetB5, EfficientNetB7, VGG16, VGG19, and ResNet50, for feature extraction from street view images. Each model extracts meaningful features with high dimensionality based on its architecture. These feature vectors are then fed into the SOM, which organizes the images into clusters based on their similarity. Unlike k-means, which partitions data into clusters without a spatial structure, SOM creates a structured 2D grid, making it ideal for visualization. This approach helps create a grid (figure 10.1) that highlights the most representative campus environments, allowing us to efficiently organize similar campus facilities based on built environment imagery.

Figure 10.1. Self-organizing maps for Google Street View
images.

The interface shows a trained SOM that visualizes the street view images closest to the best matching unit (BMU) per cell. Clicking on an image takes the user to another window where the image enlarges, and all other information from the site is shown. The website displays a street view image side by side with the same image with objects automatically identified by an algorithm called Inception-ResNet-v2. This neural network combines Inception[5] and ResNet[6] architectures to achieve high object detection accuracy. To adapt to the literature review on flood risk in urban environments, we filter the categories from the objects included in the Inception-ResNet-v2 algorithm to fit into one of the following categories, which have been previously validated by other studies using GSV (Blanco-Vogt & Schanze, 2014; Dülks et al., 2023; Mollaei et al., 2021). These categories include:

- Sill height: window
- Building typology: building, office building, skyscraper, house, tower
- Street: road, sidewalk, street
- Structure attached to adjacent building: porch, stairs, door, window, door handle
- Vehicles and related: land vehicle, truck, bus, car, van, train
- Electricity pole: electricity, electric network, cable, power cables, power grid
- Fence
- Outdoor decor
- Signage: traffic sign, stop sign, billboard
- Streetlight

The second window of the web interface is shown in figure 10.2. The second window includes additional street view images from surrounding places. With this information, students were asked to answer the following questions:

- "Does this image look like it is on a college or university campus?"
- "Which objects might be at risk during a hurricane?"
- "Are there any additional objects not detected that might be at risk during a hurricane?"
- "If you walk in this place, do you feel safe?"

Responses were recorded based on geolocation, and all similar locations were clustered within that cell.

Workshop and Data Analysis

The workshop was conducted over 2 days with a diverse group of participants aged 19 to 40. Participants included university students and faculty members from different disciplines. Participants interacted with the web interface during the workshop, providing feedback on their perceptions of flood risks. We used surveys and focus group discussions to gather qualitative data on their concerns and suggestions. After collecting more than 205 inputs through the web interface, we analyzed survey answers to understand campus stakeholders' primary concern with the built environment in the potential case of a flooding event. These data were triangulated to inform built environment practices to prevent damage during hurricanes and floods. We employed qualitative analysis techniques to understand the participants' perceptions and the factors contributing to their sense of security or insecurity.

Throughout the workshop, students provided unique insights into risk perception during a flooding event. This project leveraged mixed methods approaches, integrating qualitative insights with quantitative data analysis, which was vital in identifying and understanding the nuances of flood risk

Figure 10.2. Labeling interface per cell of the self-organizing map.

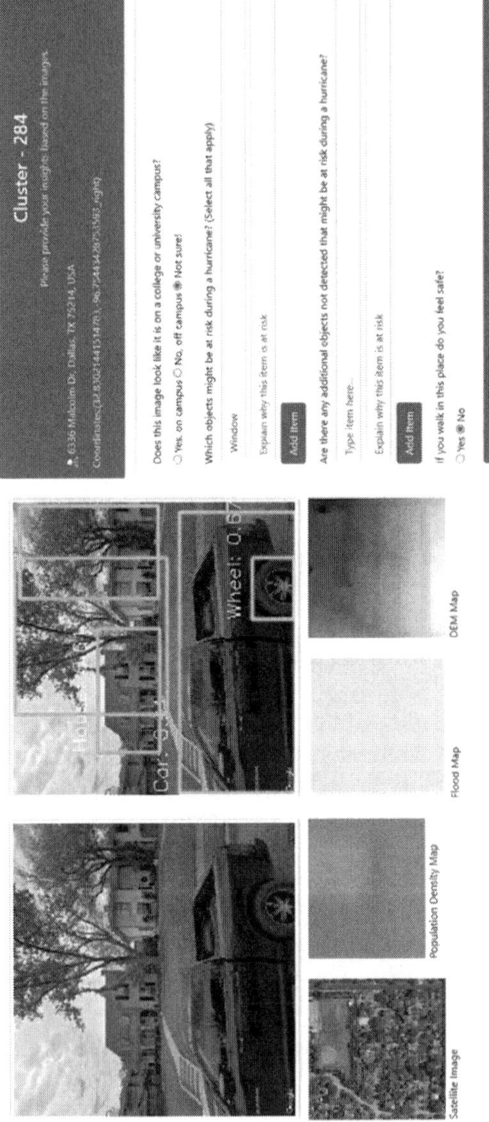

from human perceptions. Attendees held diverse areas of expertise (e.g., data science, geographic information systems, and urban planning), which helped facilitate a robust analysis framework that combined technological tools with human-centric data. This interdisciplinary approach allowed for the capture of students' perceptions to analyze their concerns, which provided a clear understanding of campus vulnerabilities and can help develop practical insights for improving disaster preparedness and response at university campuses from a student perspective.

Ethical Considerations and Participatory Design Approach

This project followed an ethical participatory AI design approach in which university students and faculty were both study subjects and knowledge co-creators. The web interface allowed participants to annotate images, express subjective judgments about risk and safety, and provide written feedback on elements that might have been missed by automated object detection. Including multiple image types (e.g., GSV, satellite, DEM, flood maps) enhanced transparency and encouraged critical reflection. Ethical measures included informed consent, anonymized data collection, and the option to opt out, ensuring equitable and respectful engagement throughout the research process.

Results

Results show that, based on street view images, most students felt they would be unsafe walking in certain areas. Attendees mentioned that some street view images did not resemble typical campuses, which may be due to seeing campuses and campus-adjacent neighborhoods from other cities and states than their own university (figure 10.3).

The text analysis, which included word clouds and heatmaps, provided valuable insights into the common concerns and themes within the dataset (figure 10.4). The word clouds and frequency analysis highlighted the most frequently mentioned terms used to describe images of campuses and their surrounding areas. Items such as "tree," "building," "vehicle," and "power cable" were identified as significant subjects of concern. Similarly, the analysis of user descriptions showed frequent terms like "fall," "wind," "damage," and "flood," suggesting significant concerns about flooding risks and their impact on vehicles and residential properties. The frequent mention of trees as potential hazards during windy conditions points to a specific area of concern that could be prioritized in urban planning and campus safety measures.

The heatmap revealed clusters of high-frequency keywords associated with specific items, providing clear indications of common hazards and concerns related to objects such as cars, buildings, and power cables (figure 10.5).

Figure 10.3. Campus stakeholders' perceptions of safety during flooding and their perceptions of whether street view images resemble a campus.

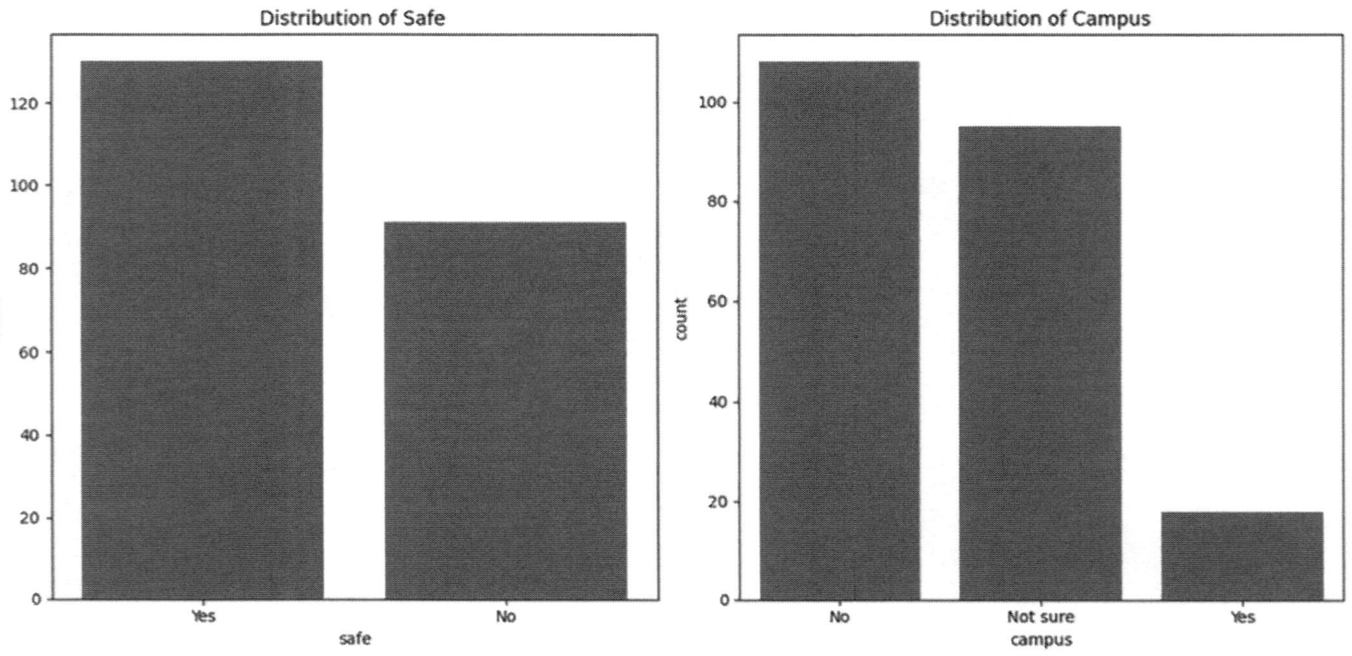

Figure 10.4a-b. Descriptions of campus and campus-adjacent images and perceptions of vulnerabilities.

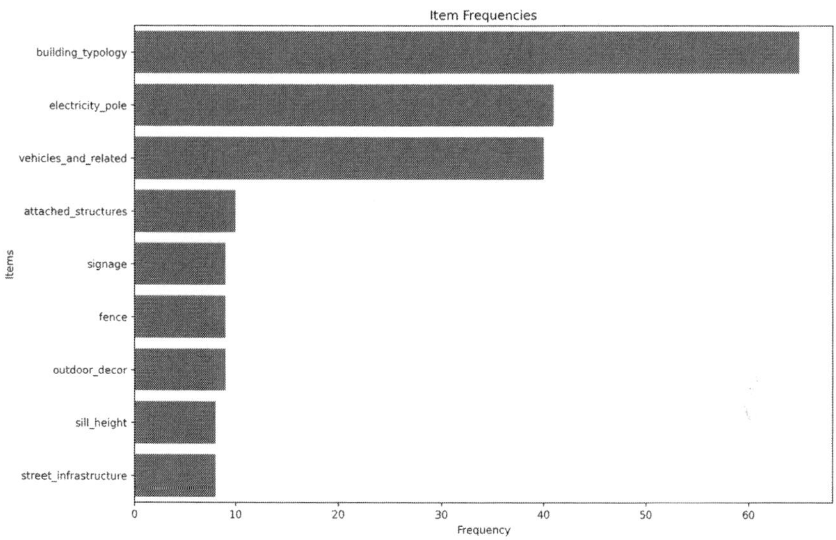

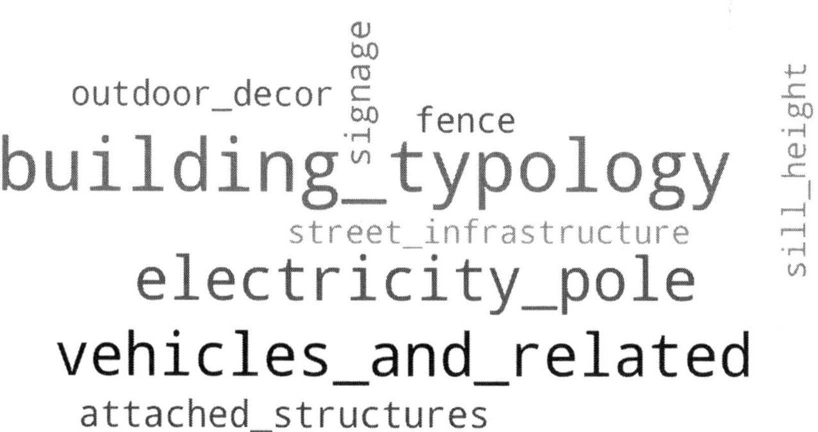

Figure 10.4c-d. Descriptions of campus and campus-adjacent images and perceptions of vulnerabilities.

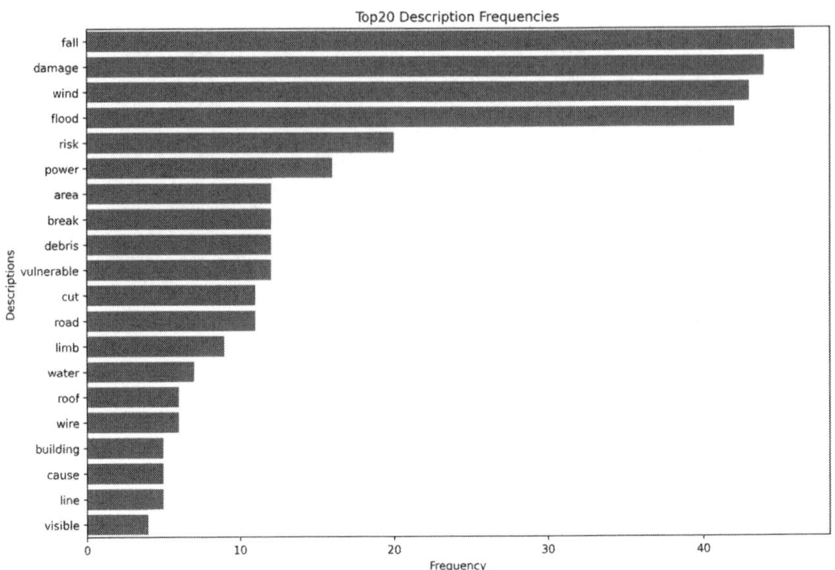

• *Buildings* are commonly associated with terms like "damage" and "flood," indicating concerns about structural integrity.
• *Vehicles* are often linked to "damage" and "risk," suggesting worries about vehicle safety.
• *Electricity pole* frequently appears with "fall" and "power," highlighting the risks associated with power infrastructure during adverse conditions.

These insights emphasize the need for effective flood risk management strategies to protect critical assets from potential flood damage. For buildings, ensuring structural integrity against floods is crucial. For electricity poles, preventive measures against falling and power-related incidents are vital. Meanwhile, vehicles require protective measures against potential damage in risky conditions. This detailed analysis helps identify priority areas for risk assessment and mitigation efforts. Additionally, if these data are associated with places that have been labeled as not safe, planning experts could identify objects at risk and propose strategies to prepare campuses before a disaster occurs.

Additional Perceptions of Campus Safety

Our data analysis offered additional insights into areas of campus and campus-adjacent neighborhoods that community members perceived as safe or unsafe, providing a resource for urban planners, safety officials, and community leaders. Figure 10.6 contrasts locations perceived as safe (displayed on the right) and those perceived as unsafe (on the left). Large parking lots, large-footprint buildings, and the presence of large trees frequently characterize unsafe areas. Conversely, safe areas are typically densely populated and have different characteristics. The primary differences between areas perceived as safe and those perceived as unsafe are their physical and environmental characteristics.

Characteristics of Safe Places:

• Typically, these are densely populated areas.
• Key features include more buildings (46 instances) and vehicles (26 instances), which indicate human presence and activity.
• Additional elements such as electricity poles (17 instances), carports (8 instances), roads (7 instances), fences (6 instances), and windows (6 instances) contribute to the perception of safety.

Characteristics of Not Safe Places:

• They are often characterized by large parking lots and large-footprint buildings with large trees, which can create isolated and less

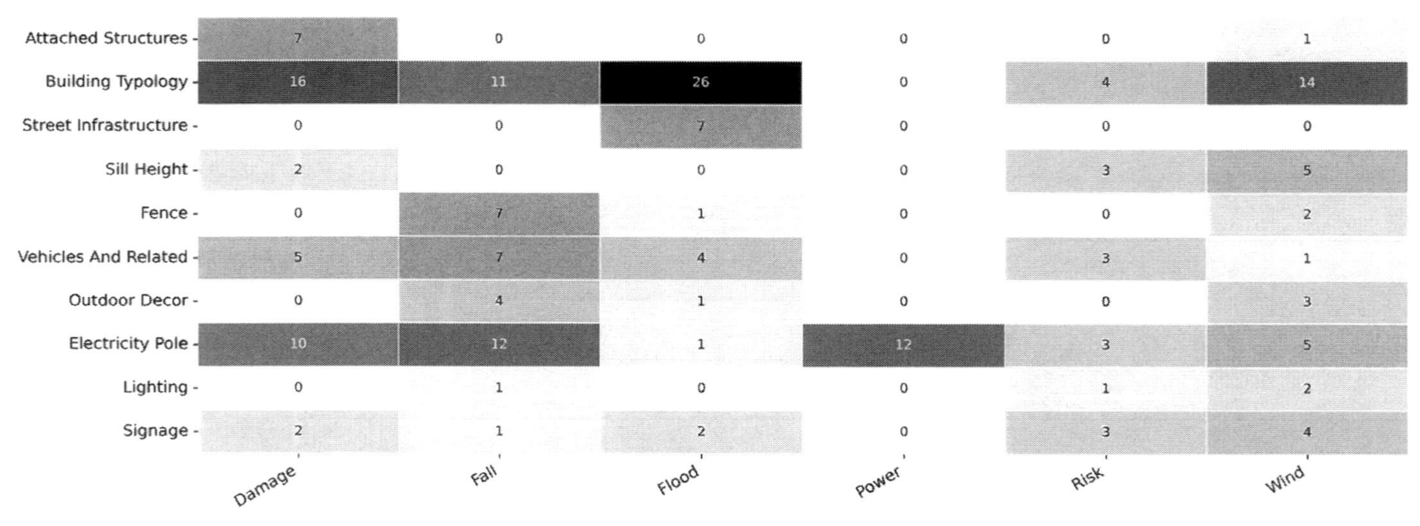

Figure 10.5. Heatmap of most frequent items and descriptors words.

visible areas.

•Predominant features include electricity poles (21 instances), buildings (19 instances), and vehicles (14 instances), which in this context might contribute to a sense of abandonment or lack of human activity.

In essence, the perception of safety is significantly influenced by the density of human activity and the type of structures present. Safe places tend to have more human presence and active use, whereas unsafe places are marked by larger, more isolated structures that can lead to feelings of insecurity. These findings underscore the importance of specific urban features in influencing the perception of safety. Identifying these attributes can guide urban planners in designing safer communities by minimizing features associated with unsafe perceptions and promoting those linked to safety.

Discussion and Conclusion

This project aimed to use AI to identify vulnerabilities in the built environment and to pilot an approach that integrates human perceptions of risks on and around college and university campuses. To undertake this project, we collected data in two primary categories: aerial imagery (including satellite images, flood, density maps, and DEMs) and human-scale data (GSV images). Subsequently, we created a web-based interface curated to display specific information on campus infrastructure to capture student perceptions of the risk of flooding. During a 2-day session in spring 2024, we conducted a workshop with university stakeholders aged 19 to 40 to collect an initial dataset to understand perceptions of risk and the objects or built environment factors contributing to such perceptions. In conclusion, the most frequently mentioned concerns included risks associated with trees falling due to wind and flood damage onto houses and cars, highlighting the need for targeted interventions to mitigate these risks. Additionally, students often felt unsafe on campus and in surrounding neighborhoods based on views of street-level images, emphasizing the importance of enhancing campus infrastructure and safety measures to improve overall security and preparedness.

Around the country, universities are beginning to develop centers or institutes to support the use of AI for disaster resilience planning and emergency management. For instance, the University of Southern California's Center for AI in Society hosts a project titled "AI for Disaster Planning and Response."[7] At Texas A&M University, the Zachry Department of Civil and Environmental Engineering hosts a research team that is using AI to better understand how to prepare and recover from natural disasters like floods and hurricanes.[8] Even the University of Illinois, which is not on a coastline, supports the Critical Infrastructure Resilience Institute that holds the designation of a U.S. Department of Homeland Security Center of Excellence. The Illinois institute

Figure 10.6. Areas perceived as safe and unsafe based on satellite view images, derived from student surveys and risk analysis.

recently developed an online resource titled "Leveraging AI for Disaster-Resilient Infrastructure Mitigation Planning."[9] This chapter offers an example of how campus leaders and faculty can work together to collect data and learn from campus stakeholders about their perceptions of safety and risk to take data-informed approaches to improving campus resilience.

In conclusion, our analysis highlights the need for a nuanced approach to urban design, where the presence and arrangement of specific elements can significantly impact the perceived safety of an area. Although this pilot work focused on risks associated with hurricanes and flooding, preliminary findings suggest that AI approaches can be used to assess and improve campus safety and accessibility more generally. Our interface allows for meaningful juxtaposition of user-perception data with objective flood hazard layers, enabling future research to visualize and analyze mismatches between where students feel unsafe and where flood risks are highest. Such comparisons could help planners prioritize interventions in both high-risk and high-concern areas. These approaches will be needed to address the increasing dangers that campuses will face from natural disasters throughout the 21st century.

Notes

1   US Inflation Calculator, *Inflation calculator*, https://www.usinflationcalculator.com/.
2   ITU, *Global initiative on resilience to natural hazards through AI solutions*, https://www.itu.int/en/ITU-T/extcoop/ai4resilience/Pages/default.aspx.
3   U.S. Chamber of Commerce Foundation, *The benefits and risks of using AI to build resilient communities*, https://www.uschamberfoundation.org/disasters/the-benefits-and-risks-of-using-ai-to-build-resilient-communities.
4   World Economic Forum, *Natural disasters are increasing in frequency and ferocity. Here's how AI can come to the rescue*, January 14, 2020, https://www.weforum.org/agenda/2020/01/natural-disasters-resilience-relief-artificial-intelligence-ai-mckinsey/.
5   Inception is a CNN for assisting in image analysis and object detection. It used a lot of tricks to push performance, both in terms of speed and accuracy.
6   ResNet, or Residual Network, is a deep learning model and CNN architecture that is used for computer vision applications.
7   USC Center for AI in Society, *AI for disaster planning and response*, https://www.cais.usc.edu/projects/ai-for-disaster-planning-and-response/.
8   Justin Again, *AI for all phases of disaster management*, Texas A&M University Engineering, July 17, 2024, https://engineering.tamu.edu/news/2024/07/ai-for-all-phases-of-disaster-management.html#:~:text=.
9   University of Illinois Urbana-Champaign, *Leveraging AI for disaster-resilient infrastructure mitigation planning*, https://ciri.illinois.edu/events/leveraging-AI-webinar.

References

Alexander, S. E. (2014). Campus climate action plan legacies and implementation dynamics: An integrated assessment method should be used that simultaneously considers quantitative and qualitative, direct and indirect, outcomes. *Planning for Higher Education Journal, 42*(3), 42–57. https://link.gale.com/apps/doc/A382150074/AONE?u=anon~ab1f1036&sid=googleScholar&xid=59ba7cfd

Button, C. E. (2009). Towards carbon neutrality and environmental sustainability at CCSU. *International Journal of Sustainability in Higher Education, 10*(3), 279–286. https://doi.org/10.1108/14676370910972585

Blanco-Vogt, A., & Schanze, J. (2014). Assessment of the physical flood susceptibility of buildings on a large scale–conceptual and methodological frameworks. *Natural Hazards and Earth System Sciences, 14*(8), 2105–2117. https://doi.org/10.5194/nhess-14-2105-2014

Cao, L. (2023). AI and data science for smart emergency, crisis and disaster resilience. *International Journal of Data Science and Analytics, 15*(3), 231–246. https://doi.org/10.1007/s41060-023-00393-w

Carales, V. D., & Lopez, R. M. (2021). Navigating college after a disaster: Understanding the impact and institutional support for community college students after Hurricane Harvey. *Community College Journal of Research and Practice, 46*(3), 145–160. https://doi.org/10.1080/10668926.2021.18 81656

Ciurczak, E. (2015, August 24). Katrina: A long road to recovery for colleges. *Hattiesburg American.* https://www.clarionledger.com/story/news/2015/08/24/katrina-long-road-recovery-colleges/32283093/

Cleaves, S. M., Pasinella, B., Andrews, J., & Wake, C. (2009). Climate action planning at the University of New Hampshire. *International Journal of Sustainability in Higher Education, 10*(3), 250–265. https://doi.org/10.1108/14676370910972567

Crawford, S. (2023). *Charleston: Race, water, and the coming storm.* Pegasus.

Donadel, A. (2023, August 29). At least 21 colleges and universities announce campus closures following Hurricane Idalia. *University Business.* https://universitybusiness.com/at-least-21-colleges-and-universities-announce-campus-closures-following-hurricane-idalia/

Dülks, J., Fekete, A., Karutz, H., Kaufmann, J., & Posingies, C. (2023). Identification of methodologies to quantify education system resilience — A scoping review. *International Journal of Disaster Risk Reduction, 97.* https://doi.org/10.1016/j.ijdrr.2023.103967

Ellard, P. (2019, May 3). Don't think your campus needs to prepare for climate change? Here's why you're wrong. *The Chronicle of Higher Education.* https://www.chronicle.com/interactives/20190505-Ellard

Federal Emergency Management Agency. (2023). *Guidance for flood risk analysis and mapping: Flood insurance rate map (FIRM) database technical reference.* https://www.fema.gov/sites/default/files/documents/fema_rm-firm-database-technical-reference-nov-2023.pdf

Fernandez, F., Coulson, H. L., & Zou, Y. (2021). Leading in the eye of a storm: How one team of administrators exercised disaster resilience. *Higher Education, 83*(4), 929–944. https://doi.org/10.1007/s10734-021-00716-5

Ghaffarian, S., Taghikhah, F. R., & Maier, H. R. (2023). Explainable artificial intelligence in disaster risk management: Achievements and prospective futures. *International Journal of Disaster Risk Reduction, 98.* https://doi.org/10.1016/j.ijdrr.2023.104123

Gill, D. A., Ladd, A. E., Cross, G. W., Fee, V., Edwards, J. F., Marszalek, J., Edwards, A. K., McSeveney, D. R., & Wells-Parker, B. (2006). Impacts of Hurricane Katrina on Mississippi State University students. In Natural Hazard Center (Ed.), *Learning from catastrophe: Quick response research in the wake of Hurricane Katrina* (pp. 373–402). Institute of Behavioral Science, University of Colorado at Boulder.

Helferty, A., & Clarke, A. (2009). Student-led campus climate change initiatives in Canada. *International Journal of Sustainability in Higher Education, 10*(3), 287–300. https://doi.org/10.1108/14676370910972594

Hutchens, N. H., & Fernandez, F. (2023). Academic freedom as a professional, constitutional, and human right: Contemporary challenges and directions for research. In L. W. Perna (Ed.), *Higher education: Handbook of theory and research* (Vol. 38, pp. 1–54). Springer.

Intergovernmental Panel on Climate Change (2013). *Climate change 2013: The physical science basis: Summary for policymakers.* https://www.ipcc.ch/site/assets/uploads/2018/03/WG1AR5_SummaryVolume_FINAL.pdf

Johnson, G. S., & Rainey, S. A. (2007). Hurricane Katrina impact on three historically black colleges and universities (HBCUs): Voices from displaced students. *Race, Gender & Class, 14*(1–2), 100–119. https://www.jstor.org/stable/41675199

Kautto, N., Trundle, A., & McEvoy, D. (2018). Climate adaptation planning in the higher education sector. *International Journal of Sustainability in Higher Education, 19*(7), 1259–1278. https://doi.org/10.1108/IJSHE-02-2018-0028

Kim, J. (2024, May 28). Higher ed and "Charleston: Race, Water, and the Coming Storm": Climate change and the eight most interesting colleges and universities in the U.S. *Inside Higher Ed.* https://www.insidehighered.com/opinion/blogs/learning-innovation/2024/05/28/higher-ed-and-charleston-race-water-and-coming-storm

Mangan, K. S. (2005, November 15). Colleges say hurricanes dealt them $1.4-billion in physical damage. *The Chronicle of Higher Education.* https://www.chronicle.com/article/Colleges-Say-Hurricanes-Dealt/119904

Mollaei, A., Ibrahim, N., & Habib, K. (2021). Estimating the construction material stocks in two Canadian cities: A case study of Kitchener and Waterloo. *Journal of Cleaner Production, 280*(2). https://doi.org/10.1016/j.jclepro.2020.124501

Myers, B., & Lusk, E. (2017, December 6). Rising threat. *The Chronicle of Higher Education.* https://www.chronicle.com/article/rising-waters-threatened-campuses/

National Oceanic and Atmospheric Administration. (2023, November 28). *2023 Atlantic hurricane season ranks 4th for most-named storms in a year: NOAA advances modeling and observation capabilities during the season.* https://www.noaa.gov/news-release/2023-atlantic-hurricane-season-ranks-4th-for-most-named-storms-in-year

Owen, R., Fisher, E., & McKenzie, K. (2013). Beyond reduction: Climate change adaptation planning for universities and colleges. *International Journal of Sustainability in Higher Education, 14*(2), 146–159. https://doi.org/10.1108/14676371311312860

Patrascu, F. I., & Mostafavi, A. (2024). Spatial model for predictive recovery monitoring based on hazard, built environment, and population features and their spillover effects. *Environment and Planning B: Urban Analytics and City Science, 51*(1), 39–56. https://doi.org/10.1177/23998083231167433

Sacerdote, B. (2012). When the saints go marching out: Long-term outcomes for student evacuees from Hurricanes Katrina and Rita. *American Economic Journal: Applied Economics*, 4(1), 109–35. https://doi.org/10.1257/app.4.1.109

U.S. Geological Survey. (2023). *1 meter digital elevation models (DEMs): USGS national map 3DEP downloadable data collection.* https://www.usgs.gov/3d-elevation-program

WorldPop. (2018). Global high resolution population denominators project: Funded by the Bill and Melinda Gates Foundation (OPP1134076). https://doi.org/10.5258/SOTON/WP00645

Zolkafli, A., Mansor, N. S., Omar, M., Ahmad, M., Ibrahim, H., & Yasin, A. (2024). AI for smart disaster resilience among communities. In S. A. Abdul Karim (Ed.), *Intelligent systems modeling and simulation III: Artificial intelligent, machine learning, intelligent functions and cyber security* (pp. 369–395). Springer. https://doi.org/10.1007/978-3-031-67317-7_22

11

Connecting Theory, Ethics, and Practice

Future Directions for AI and Big Data in Higher Education

Rachel Dean Divaker

This volume provides a comprehensive overview of how emerging technologies, specifically artificial intelligence (AI) and the use of big data, are reshaping the field of higher education. It explores potential applications and implications of AI technologies in higher education while highlighting legal, moral, and ethical ramifications associated with their use. To conclude this volume, I reflect on lessons learned and insights gained from contributors. I also offer recommendations for a wide range of higher education stakeholders, including administrators, faculty, student affairs professionals, students, policymakers, and industry partners, to consider moving forward.

AI is fundamentally changing the landscape of higher education. From student recruitment and admissions to teaching, learning, and administrative processes with managing facilities and processing student loan appeals, AI technologies offer novel opportunities for increasing efficiency and innovation; they also raise threats to academic integrity, equity, bias, and information security (Gill et al., 2022; Gleason, 2022; Selwyn, 2022). Thus, integrating emerging technologies in higher education brings both opportunities and unique challenges for researchers and practitioners. The rise of AI in higher education is not confined to the U.S., but rather, we are seeing its legal, ethical, and policy implications on a global scale. As we look ahead, it remains to be seen how educational leaders and members will navigate uncertainties surrounding the future of AI in higher education. I summarize five takeaways from this volume for higher education leaders and members to consider as they make unavoidable decisions about how to navigate the use of AI in higher education.

Align AI Implementation with Institutional Mission and Values

As AI becomes increasingly integrated within all areas of society, higher education leaders must consider how these tools will fit into the greater mission and values of their institutions. Campus leaders should strive to be *mission-centered* even as they use AI to be *market-smart* (Zemsky et al., 2005). Improving efficiency in education is not about changing what we aim to do to reduce costs — it should be about experimenting with practice and using cost-effectiveness analysis to find more inexpensive and streamlined ways to preserve or expand the good things we're already doing (Levin & Belfield, 2017).

Higher education leaders may consider the following questions to guide responsible use of AI technologies:

- What measures can we take to ensure that AI use upholds campus values, as well as meets legal standards, for security, inclusion, fairness, and safety?
- How can we prevent reinforcing existing biases or marginalizing vulnerable groups?
- How can AI safely improve the experiences of all campus stakeholders (e.g., students, administrators, faculty, and staff personnel)?

AI and big data analytics hold potential to significantly influence the field of higher education. However, as discussed in part I of this volume, educational leaders must carefully consider their social, ethical, and legal implications. Some considerations apply to all institutions. For instance, how will colleges and universities protect sensitive student data? At campuses that use selective admissions practices, how will admissions offices and financial aid offices ensure that their decisions do not perpetuate biases? Prior research has suggested that campuses try to improve graduation metrics by declining to admit applicants who are seen as less likely to complete (e.g., Umbricht et al., 2017). If institutions are committed to broadening college access, particularly for rural or low-income students, they should be cautious about using AI to improve institutional performance at the cost of moving away from their missions. For campuses that serve specific minoritized populations, such as Hispanic-Serving Institutions, leaders should explore opportunities to use AI to satisfy calls for increasing "servingness" and go beyond merely enrolling large percentages of racially minoritized students (e.g., Garcia et al., 2019).

Once there is an established understanding of how AI fits into the institution's broader mission, educational leaders can take steps to prevent potential harm and capitalize on opportunities afforded by AI technologies. For example, as discussed by Noorani, Chen, Smith, Fernandez, and Ochoa in chapter 10 of this volume, AI can support campus disaster resilience by identifying environmental threats to campus safety. Educational leaders have a responsibility to proactively protect the campus community from foreseeable harm. Just as institutions are expected to do with regard to physical threats, they should uphold a *duty of care* (Witting, 2005) to protect student privacy from potential risks. It is critical for the institution to prioritize its primary stakeholder group, students, by aligning the use of AI with principles reflected in the broader mission of the institution.

Upon Careful Consideration of Institutional Values, Develop, and Implement a Governance Plan

After institutional leaders have carefully considered how AI aligns with institutional ethics and standards, they must define the boundaries of AI usage by establishing a governance plan to continuously ensure fairness, transparency, and accountability (Cambria et al., 2023; Chan, 2023; Slimi, 2021). This will require active collaboration across various academic disciplines and stakeholder groups to ensure a comprehensive plan (Dahlin, 2021). This plan must cover the appropriate use and implementation of AI in key areas of concern, such as data privacy and security, bias and fairness, and accessibility and equity. AI models should be continually evaluated and retrained on representative data that reflects real-world conditions and populations to prevent inaccurate and biased outputs (Chan, 2023, Dahlin, 2021; Tozzi, 2024). Public trust in higher education is already at an all-time low (e.g., Blake, 2023), and campuses should proactively avoid any malfeasance from internal or external actors that could further erode confidence in higher education institutions to serve the public good.

Within the campus community, campus leaders should communicate about how AI is being used across campus departments to establish and maintain trust with students, faculty, and other employees (Cambria et al., 2023). To maintain transparency with campus stakeholders, institutions should share how information is collected, used, and stored along with measures to address threats. To maintain accountability, institutions should consider establishing an ethics committee to oversee AI data-driven decisions to ensure they meet governance criteria (Theodorou & Dignum, 2020). Transparency and accountability measures must be reviewed, evaluated, and updated regularly to ensure the responsible use of AI technologies. In short, the governance plan should be widely known.

Monitor Emerging Trends in AI and Higher Education and Recognize Opportunities and Limitations

There is no doubt about the potential of AI tools to increase productivity and streamline time-intensive processes (Slimi, 2021). Higher education is notoriously labor-intensive. It is one of the few sectors of the economy that has not used new technology or substituted inputs to achieve greater efficiency. Instead, higher education is singled out as having become less productive over time when measured by class size or dollars spent per instructor (Triplett & Bosworth, 2004). This cost problem led researchers to conclude that the United States is incapable of improving higher education attainment unless colleges and universities commit to "permanent restructuring of costs and greater attention to productivity" (Desrochers et al., 2010, p. 42).

AI holds potential to disrupt higher education's dependence on faculty and staff to complete repetitive manual tasks and instead allow institutional personnel to focus on more meaningful tasks and interactions with students. AI tools like chatbots can improve efficiency by providing immediate responses and reducing wait times (Aftabi et al., 2024; Crompton & Burke, 2023). Additionally, AI can optimize tasks like grading so faculty can spend more time researching and supporting students (Popenici et al., 2024).

Advances in AI technology can also improve the long-held and controversial holistic review process of college admissions applications (Alvero et al., 2020; Bastedo et al., 2018). According to Alvero et al. (2020), applicant demographic characteristics, such as gender and income levels, can be inferred from a biased and unfair review of application essays. By employing natural language processing to extract key information from applications, admissions officers can make more equitable decisions when reviewing applications. Further, using machine learning predictive analytics in the review process can support campus diversity initiatives by reviewing applications beyond commonly-used review metrics like GPA and test scores (Barnard, 2022).

AI-powered learning models are transforming how educational content is delivered to students. Adaptive learning systems tailor course material and teaching methods to meet student learning needs and preferences (Aftabi et al., 2024; Somasundaram et al., 2021). If a student struggles to grasp the material, the AI-powered system can detect learning patterns, predict learning behaviors, and adjust lesson plans (Crompton & Burke, 2023). Immediate feedback from students improves the effectiveness of these learning systems and contributes to student learning outcomes and engagement levels (Kolluru et al., 2018; Slimi, 2021).

These are a few of the benefits that AI offers higher education. However, campus leaders and members must remain on guard against the potential threats caused by its use. It is a fair and necessary question to ask when and where AI should be used in higher education. The answer to this question depends on the careful consideration of several factors to determine its use. Will AI enhance decision-making and accuracy, or will it compromise ethical boundaries? Are appropriate safeguards in place with sufficient human oversight? Are there existing concerns or risks related to its use in higher education, and what insights do scholars and experts have? Prior studies have raised serious concerns about the accuracy of predictive models in assessing college success for students from underrepresented backgrounds and the potential for these models to perpetuate social injustices through algorithmic biases (Anderson et al., 2019; Gándara et al., 2024; Gill et al., 2022; Lee & Kizilcec, 2020; Yu et al., 2020; Yu et al., 2021). For instance, if predictive algorithms are used to make college admissions decisions, users must be aware that models could deny access to some student groups based on demographic and background factors (Gándara et al., 2024).

While these models can significantly streamline admissions processes, higher education leaders and members must understand the potential harms of using these tools. Additionally, collecting vast amounts of student data raises privacy and consent concerns (Zhang & Aslan, 2021). Students should be informed how their personal information is collected and used. Data breaches or privacy violations could expose sensitive student information (e.g., academic or financial records), leading to serious legal consequences. Further, many faculty members raise concerns about academic dishonesty due to the ability of students to use large language models (e.g., ChatGPT) to generate work that is not their own or to cheat during exams (Neumann et al., 2023). Researchers have already warned that many students do not show statistically significant learning in college (Arum & Roksa, 2011). Other work shows that what were once considered "high-impact practices" have only modest or nonsignificant — or even negative correlations — with student outcomes (e.g., Katsumoto & Bowman, 2023). Just as high-impact practices were once looked upon as having potential to transform student learning, we should recognize that heavy reliance on technology to complete assignments and take tests and quizzes could fail to improve student learning (at best) and have long-term, adverse effects on students' learning and critical thinking skills (at worst). Educational leaders must remain aware of emerging opportunities and potential risks.

Promote Collaborative Empirical Research to Propel Innovation in the Field of Higher Education

One way campus leaders can watch for promising and potentially perilous new avenues related to the use of AI is to collaborate in research-to-practice partnerships with data scientists. Many research-intensive universities employ faculty with appropriate training and have invested in costly computing resources. When campuses do not have their own capacity to undertake such projects, they can collaborate with academic, industry, or other researchers to explore opportunities to develop and apply algorithms to improve efficiency.

AI technologies and data collection methods hold the potential to significantly accelerate both applied and basic research across disciplines. The ability of AI to mimic human-like intelligence and behavior through machine learning, natural language processing, and deep learning (Kopalle et al., 2022) places human-machine interaction (HMI) at the forefront of research in this area. HMI, powered by computer vision, machine learning, natural language processing, speech recognition, and robotics, involves a two-way interaction between humans and machines (Gill et al., 2022). Within HMI, humans assist machines with interpreting outputs, while machines enhance human cognitive capabilities (Huang et al., 2019).

As AI technology evolves, some scholars predict a shift in machines performing analytical tasks to engaging in more interpersonal and empathetic interactions. Huang et al. (2019) describe this advancement as the emergence of the *feeling economy*, where AI moves from performing simple thinking tasks to complex feeling tasks. For instance, in chapter 9 of this volume, Yang, Agha, Akman, Kheloussi, and He show one potential advance toward using AI to identify emotions. This raises questions about whether machines will eventually use contextual data to respond to human feelings and emotions.

On the contrary, other scholars (Mitchell, 2021; Selwyn, 2022) argue that there is a widespread misunderstanding about the nature of AI. They counsel the importance of having realistic expectations about its capabilities. Mitchell (2021) argues that AI lacks independent intelligence, common sense, and the ability to exhibit human emotions. Widespread misconceptions about the complexity of replicating human intelligence and applying common sense to real-world scenarios are critical to this argument. Edwards and Cheok (2018) explain that machines are limited in their ability to mimic human personality, social interaction, and emotional affect. Although intelligent machines have made considerable progress since the Turing test in the 1950s, an assessment of a computer's ability to mimic human behaviors, replicating human cognitive abilities is not a current reality (Turing, 1950, 2009). Although the adoption and implementation of AI and big data in higher education are still in the early stages, higher education is uniquely positioned to facilitate collaboration across disciplines such as engineering, social sciences, data science, computer science, and the humanities to evaluate how AI will meaningfully progress (Dahlin, 2021; Luan et al., 2020; Mitchell, 2021; Theodorou & Dignum, 2020).

See the Implementation of AI in Higher Education as a Continually Evolving Process

When campuses and their members commit to integrating AI into existing practice, they are embarking on a long-term process, not making a one-time choice, such as choosing a vendor. While it may seem like AI is a new phenomenon and leaders must choose whether to adopt it or not, this technology has been evolving for decades and shows no signs of slowing. Since Alan Turing introduced the concept of "thinking machines" in 1950, AI research has made significant strides across many fields (Zhang & Aslan, 2021). Looking ahead, we should pause to consider the long-term effects, both intended and unintended, of the widespread adoption of AI in higher education.

Innovation is inevitable, but it is essential to examine its processes and outcomes with a critical lens. Innovation requires creativity, experimentation with new ideas, and a willingness to rethink established practices. However, this does not guarantee success on the first attempt or that the disruptive process is seamless and for all. Humans have historically been reluctant to adopt breakthrough technologies that transform everyday life (Juhász et al., 2024). Technology has been both the primary source of economic progress and a source of anxiety about impacts on society (Mokyr et al., 2015). Predictions about technological progress, such as fear about machines replacing labor and contributing to higher unemployment or technology dehumanizing work, were ultimately unfounded (Mokyr et al., 2015). For example, Johannes Gutenberg's printing press invention in the 15th century enabled mass dissemination of knowledge through the distribution of printed materials. This groundbreaking invention faced significant skepticism as people feared rapid job displacement. However, the printing press ultimately created new jobs and opportunities to develop skills in publishing, illustrating, printing, and proofreading and contributed to the development of new printing technologies (Eisenstein, 2005).

Yet history also shows how emerging technologies can have harmful effects on society. For example, consider Fredrick Winslow Taylor's (1911) approach to increasing productivity particularly in factory settings, known as *mechanical Taylorism* or *scientific management*. In the early 20th century, Taylor introduced a scientific approach to managing labor that reduced worker autonomy by breaking down complex jobs into simple, standardized tasks. This method aimed to maximize efficiency and productivity but resulted in dehumanizing the workplace by breaking down tasks into small and mundane steps that could be completed as quickly as possible (Brown et al., 2011). In the 21st century, many scholars argue that we are now experiencing a similar era referred to as *digital Taylorism*, caused by the rise of digital tools in the workplace (Brown et al., 2011; Konuk et al., 2023; Lee et al., 2024; Noponen et al., 2024; Park & Ryoo, 2023). Such tools can be used to manage employee output by tracking their performance and productivity. Amazon's fulfillment centers are an example of digital Taylorism where employees received handheld scanners that provided instruction on how to break down tasks and recorded their performance. While these tools successfully increased worker productivity, they also reduced worker autonomy through constant surveillance and pressure to work without taking breaks (Lee et al., 2024).

As with any emerging technology, AI should not replace human intelligence but rather complement it. Higher education institutions should implement measures to address concerns and ensure that AI enhances human learning, decision-making, and processes. In the ongoing process of implementing, evaluating, and improving the use of AI, we recommend that higher education leaders actively listen to the concerns of institutional stakeholders. Selwyn (2022) points out that decision-making involving AI is typically made by the privileged select, often excluding the voices and concerns of marginalized groups. To ensure a meaningful and representative discussion around the future of AI in higher education, higher education leaders must seek greater diversity in conversations and provide practical guidelines on the ethical use of AI technologies in higher education (Theodorou & Dignum, 2020; Zhang & Aslan, 2021).

Conclusion

Throughout this volume, we have discussed opportunities and challenges AI presents in higher education. The chapters in this volume explored legal and ethical considerations and practical applications of AI in institutional practices and academic research. Our goal in this volume was to extend the conversation and propose recommendations for higher education leaders to consider moving forward.

On behalf of the editors of this volume, I encourage higher education leaders to consider how AI practices fit into their institutional missions and develop governance plans that reflect institutional ethics. It is critical for educators to stay informed about the possibilities and pitfalls of AI technologies and engage in collaborative empirical research that addresses ethical concerns. We recommend that they build and maintain trust with campus stakeholders through communication built on transparency and authenticity by openly discussing the use of AI in higher education and listening to the concerns of all stakeholder groups. Finally, as forward-thinking leaders, we hope that campus members will keep an open mind to advancing AI innovation to refine and enhance existing practices in the field.

References

Aftabi, E., Shirazi, B. N., Safavi, A. A., Salimi, G., & Aftabi, H. (2024). A framework for customized course design and personalized learning with AI. In *2024 11th International and the 17th National Conference on E-Learning and E-Teaching* (pp. 1–6). https://doi.org/10.1109/ICeLeT62507.2024.10493063

Alvero, A. J., Arthurs, N., Antonio, A. L., Domingue, B. W., Gebre-Medhin, B., Giebel, S., & Stevens, M. L. (2020). AI and holistic review: Informing human reading in college admissions. In *Proceedings of the AAAI/ACM Conference on AI, Ethics, and Society* (pp. 200–206). https://doi.org/10.1145/3375627.3375871

Anderson, H., Boodhwani, A., & Baker, R. S. (2019). Assessing the fairness of graduation predictions. In C. F. Lynch, A. Merceron, M. Desmarais, & R. Nkambou (Eds.), *Proceedings of the 12th International Conference on Educational Data Mining* (pp. 488–491). UQAM. https://www.upenn.edu/learninganalytics/ryanbaker/EDM2019_paper56.pdf

Arum, R., & Roksa, J. (2011). *Academically adrift: Limited learning on college campuses*. University of Chicago Press.

Barnard, B. (2022, December 21). The real A.I. in college admission. *Forbes*. https://www.forbes.com/sites/brennanbarnard/2022/12/21/the-real-ai-in-college-admission/

Bastedo, M. N., Bowman, N. A., Glasener, K. M., & Kelly, J. L. (2018). What are we talking about when we talk about holistic review? Selective college admissions and its effects on low-SES students. *The Journal of Higher Education, 89*(5), 782–805. https://doi.org/10.1080/00221546.2018.1442633

Blake, J. (2023, July 11). American confidence in higher ed hits historic low. *Inside Higher Ed*. https://www.inside-highered.com/news/business/financial-health/2023/07/11/american-confidence-higher-ed-hits-historic-low

Brown, P., Lauder, H., & Ashton, D. (2011). Digital Taylorism. In *The global auction: The broken promises of education, jobs, and incomes* (pp. 65–82). Oxford University Press. https://doi.org/10.1093/acprof:oso/9780199731688.003.0016

Cambria, E., Mao, R., Chen, M., Wang, Z., & Ho, S.B. (2023). Seven pillars for the future of artificial intelligence. *IEEE Intelligent Systems, 38*(6), 62–69. https://doi.org/10.1109/MIS.2023.3329745

Chan, C. K. Y. (2023). A comprehensive AI policy education framework for university teaching and learning. *International Journal of Educational Technology in Higher Education, 20*(38), 1–25. https://doi.org/10.1186/s41239-023-00408-3

Crompton, H., & Burke, D. (2023). Artificial intelligence in higher education: The state of the field. *International Journal of Educational*

Technology in Higher Education, 20(22), 1–22. https://doi.org/10.1186/s41239-023-00392-8

Dahlin, E. (2021). Mind the gap! On the future of AI research. *Humanities and Social Sciences Communications, 8*(1), 1–4. https://doi.org/10.1057/s41599-021-00750-9

Desrochers, D. M., Lenihan, C. M., & Wellman, J. V. (2010). *Trends in college spending: 1998–2008.* Delta Cost Project. https://files.eric.ed.gov/fulltext/ED539421.pdf

Edwards, B. I., & Cheok, A. D. (2018). Why not robot teachers: Artificial intelligence for addressing teacher shortage. *Applied Artificial Intelligence, 32*(4), 345–360. https://doi.org/10.1080/08839514.2018.1464286

Eisenstein, E. L. (2005). *The printing revolution in early modern Europe.* Cambridge University Press.

Gándara, D., Anahideh, H., Ison, M. P., & Picchiarini, L. (2024). Inside the black box: Detecting and mitigating algorithmic bias across racialized groups in college student-success prediction. *AERA Open, 10*, 1–17. https://doi.org/10.1177/23328584241258741

Garcia, G. A., Núñez, A. M., & Sansone, V. A. (2019). Toward a multidimensional conceptual framework for understanding "servingness" in Hispanic-serving institutions: A synthesis of the research. *Review of Educational Research, 89*(5), 745–784. https://doi.org/10.3102/0034654319864591

Gill, S. S., Xu, M., Ottaviani, C., Patros, P., Bahsoon, R., Shaghaghi, A., Golec, M., Stankovski, V., Wu, H., Abraham, A., Singh, M., Mehta, H., Ghosh, S. K., Baker, T., Parlikad, A. K., Lutfiyya, H., Kanhere, S. S., Sakellariou, R., Dustdar, S., Rana, O., Brandic, I., & Uhlig, S. (2022). AI for next generation computing: Emerging trends and future directions. *Internet of Things, 19*, 1–34. https://doi.org/10.1016/j.iot.2022.100514

Gleason, N. (2022, December 9). *ChatGPT and the rise of AI writers: How should higher education respond?* The Times Higher Education. https://www.timeshighereducation.com/campus/chatgpt-and-rise-ai-writers-how-should-higher-education-respond

Huang, M. H., Rust, R., & Maksimovic, V. (2019). The feeling economy: Managing in the next generation of artificial intelligence (AI). *California Management Review, 61*(4), 43–65. https://doi.org/10.1177/0008125619863436

Juhász, R., Squicciarini, M. P., & Voigtländer, N. (2024). Technology adoption and productivity growth: Evidence from industrialization in France. *Journal of Political Economy, 132*(10). https://doi.org/10.1086/730205

Katsumoto, S., & Bowman, N. A. (2023). The link between high-impact practices and college success among international students in the US. *Journal of Diversity in Higher Education, 16*(6), 734–744. https://doi.org/10.1037/dhe0000364

Kolluru, V., Mungara, S., & Chintakunta, A. N. (2018). Adaptive learning systems: Harnessing AI for customized educational experiences.

International Journal of Computational Science and Information Technology, *6*(3), 13–26. https://doi.org/10.5121/ijcsity.2018.6302

Konuk, H., Ataman, G., & Kambur, E. (2023). The effect of digitalized workplace on employees' psychological well-being: Digital Taylorism approach. *Technology in Society*, *74*, 1–17. https://doi.org/10.1016/j.techsoc.2023.102302

Kopalle, P. K., Gangwar, M., Kaplan, A., Ramachandran, D., Reinartz, W., & Rindfleisch, A. (2022). Examining artificial intelligence (AI) technologies in marketing via a global lens: Current trends and future research opportunities. *International Journal of Research in Marketing*, *39*(2), 522–540. https://doi.org/10.1016/j.ijresmar.2021.11.002

Lee, H., & Kizilcec, R. F. (2020). Evaluation of fairness tradeoffs in predicting student success. *FATED (Fairness, Accountability, and Transparency in Educational Data) Workshop at EDM 2020*. https://arxiv.org/abs/2007.00088

Lee, T. L., Tapia, M., Aranzaes, C. L., Sapre, S. R., Shimek, S., Pinto, S., & Bustamante, A. R. (2024). The militarization of employment relations: Racialized surveillance and worker control in Amazon fulfillment centers. *Work and Occupations*, 1–38. https://doi.org/10.1177/07308884241292733

Levin, H. M., & Belfield, C. R. (2017). Cost-effectiveness and educational efficiency. In G. Johnes, J. Johnes, T. Agasisti, & L. López-Torres (Eds.), *Handbook of contemporary education economics* (pp. 338–356). Edward Elgar Publishing.

Luan, H., Geczy, P., Lai, H., Gobert, J., Yang, S. J. H., Ogata, H., Baltes, J., Guerra, R., Li, P., & Tsai, C. C. (2020). Challenges and future directions of big data and artificial intelligence in education. *Frontiers in Psychology*, *11*, 1–11. https://doi.org/10.3389/fpsyg.2020.580820

Mitchell, M. (2021). Why AI is harder than we think. In *Proceedings of the Genetic and Evolutionary Computation Conference (GECCO '21)*. New York: Association for Computing Machinery, 1–12. https://doi.org/10.1145/3449639.3465421

Mokyr, J., Vickers, C., & Ziebarth, N. L. (2015). The history of technological anxiety and the future of economic growth: Is this time different? *Journal of Economic Perspectives*, *29*(3), 31–50. https://doi.org/10.1257/jep.29.3.31

Neumann, M., Rauschenberger, M., & Schön, E.-M. (2023). "We need to talk about ChatGPT": The future of AI and higher education. In *2023 IEEE/ACM 5th International Workshop on Software Engineering Education for the Next Generation (SEENG)* (pp. 29–32). https://doi.org/10.1109/SEENG59157.2023.00010

Noponen, N., Feshchenko, P., Auvinen, T., Luoma-aho, V., & Abrahamsson, P. (2024). Taylorism on steroids or enabling autonomy? A systematic review of algorithmic management. *Management review quarterly*, *74*(3), 1695–1721. https://doi.org/10.1007/s11301-023-00345-5

Park, S., & Ryoo, S. (2023). How does algorithm control affect platform workers' responses? Algorithm as a digital Taylorism. *Journal of Theoretical and Applied Electronic Commerce Research, 18*(1), 273–288. https://doi.org/10.3390/jtaer18010015

Popenici, S., Catalano, H., Mestic, G., & Ani-Rus, A. (2023). A systematic review of the artificial intelligence implications in shaping the future of higher education. *Educatia 21 Journal, 26*(11), 102–107. https://doi.org/10.24193/ed21.2023.26.11

Selwyn, N. (2022). The future of AI and education: Some cautionary notes. *European Journal of Education, 57*(4), 620–631. https://doi.org/10.1111/ejed.12532

Slimi, Z. (2021). The impact of AI implementation in higher education on educational process future: A systematic review. *Research Square*, 1–10. https://doi.org/10.21203/rs.3.rs-1081043/v1

Somasundaram, M., Junaid, K. A. M., & Mangadu, S. (2019). Artificial intelligence (AI) enabled intelligent quality management system (IQMS) for personalized learning path. *Procedia Computer Science, 172*, 438–442. https://doi.org/10.1016/j.procs.2020.05.096

Taylor, F. W. (1911). *The principles of scientific management*. NuVision Publications.

Theodorou, A., & Dignum, V. (2020). Towards ethical and socio-legal governance in AI. *Nature Machine Intelligence, 2*(1), 10–12. https://doi.org/10.1038/s42256-019-0136-y

Tozzi, C. (2024, September 4). *AI model optimization: How to do it and why it matters*. TechTarget. https://www.techtarget.com/searchenterpriseai/tip/AI-model-optimization-How-to-do-it-and-why-it-matters

Triplett, J. E., & Bosworth, B. P. (2004). *Productivity in the US services sector: New sources of economic growth*. Brookings Institution Press.

Turing, A. M. (1950). Computing machinery and intelligence. *Mind, 59*(236), 433–460.

Turing, A. M. (2009). *Computing machinery and intelligence* (pp. 23–65). Springer.

Umbricht, M., Fernandez, F., & Ortagus, J. C. (2017). An examination of the (un)intended consequences of performance funding in higher education. *Educational Policy, 31*(5), 643–673. https://doi.org/10.1177/0895904815614398

Witting, C. (2005). Duty of care: An analytical approach. *Oxford Journal of Legal Studies, 25*(1), 33–63. https://doi.org/10.1093/ojls/gqi003

Yu, R., Lee, H., & Kizilcec, R. F. (2021, June). Should college dropout prediction models include protected attributes? [Conference session]. In *Proceedings of the Eighth ACM Conference on Learning@ Scale* (pp. 91–100). Virtual. https://doi.org/10.1145/3430895.3460135

Yu, R., Li, Q., Fischer, C., Doroudi, S., & Xu, D. (2020). Towards accurate and fair prediction of college success: Evaluating different sources of student data. In A. N. Rafferty, J. Whitehill, V. Cavalli-Sforza, & C. Romero

(Eds.), *Proceedings of the 13th International Conference on Educational Data Mining (EDM 2020)* (pp. 292–301). International Educational Data Mining Society.

Zemsky, R., Wegner, G., & Massey, W. (2005). *Remaking the American university: Market-smart and mission-centered.* Rutgers University Press.

Zhang, K., & Aslan, A. B. (2021). AI technologies for education: Recent research & future directions. *Computers and Education: Artificial Intelligence, 2*, 1–11. https://doi.org/10.1016/j.caeai.2021.100025

Contributors

Dr. Bahar Akman Imboden is a dedicated researcher and thought leader, committed to advancing social justice through innovative solutions that promote social, economic, and racial equity. With a PhD in political science and over 15 years of experience, she specializes in program evaluation, policy analysis, and community-engaged research. As managing director of the Hildreth Institute, Dr. Akman Imboden leads initiatives centered on equity, inclusion, and affordability in higher education. Her impactful work has shaped key policy debates on financial aid reform and student loan protections, driving progress toward a more just and inclusive society.

Hiba Agha is a research professional with a focus on social justice and addressing systemic socioeconomic challenges. She advocates for breaking down barriers that disempower communities rather than placing the burden on individuals to navigate these issues. Hiba aims to create more inclusive, equitable, and just systems. She holds a BA in Middle Eastern studies from the American University in Cairo and an MA in political science from McGill University, with expertise in managing programs, research departments, and capacity-building initiatives. She is committed to community-engaged research, believing that affected communities are best equipped to find solutions to their own challenges.

Dr. Zia Ahmed is associate vice president for the residential experience at The Ohio State University, an area that encompasses dining services, housing and residence education, off-campus and commuter student engagement, facilities, sponsorship, planning, project, and space management. Dr. Ahmed earned a bachelor's degree, a Master of Business Administration degree from the University of Akron, and a Doctor of Education degree from Ohio State University. Dr. Ahmed has nearly 30 years of experience working in higher education. Utilizing his Lean Certification and Six Sigma training and through the creative use of technology, Dr. Ahmed continually seeks to implement process improvement tools and strategies in a large and complex organization.

AJ Alvero is an assistant research professor at the Cornell University Center for Data Science for Enterprise and Society with affiliations in the departments of information science, computer science, and sociology. His past work described social patterning in a large corpus of college admissions essays using machine learning and natural language processing techniques. Prior to entering academia, A. J. was a high school English teacher in Miami, Florida.

Michael Brown is an associate professor in the Center for the Study of Higher and Postsecondary Education in the Marsal Family School of Education at the University of Michigan, Ann Arbor. Michael's research explores the role of social and technological systems in students' learning and persistence. His current projects explore the influence of undergraduate students' social and academic networks that create or constrain opportunities for engagement in learning interactions, students' time spent in classrooms, and their ability to form relationships in learning communities.

Melissa M. Carleton is a partner and co-chair of the higher education team at Bricker Graydon LLP. She works with colleges and universities across the country on legal issues, including the intersection of student privacy and public records law. Her academic interests include FERPA, Title IX, and mental health/disability rights.

Changjie Chen is an assistant scientist in the Florida Institute for Built Environment Resilience (FIBER) at the University of Florida. His research centers on developing planning support systems that promotes resilient and sustainable urban environments. As an urban researcher, Dr. Chen studies cities' spatial framework and functional dynamics through integrated analysis of land use and transport systems. Connecting geospatial models with 3D graphics, deep learning, and cloud-based web technologies, he is advancing the development of urban digital twins, providing a powerful platform for analyzing current conditions and visualizing as well as predicting future urban landscapes.

Rachel Dean Divaker is a PhD candidate at the University of Florida, specializing in higher education administration and policy. Her research focuses on improving academic performance and persistence outcomes in STEM higher education. She employs generative agent-based modeling and multi-objective optimization methods to examine the impacts of targeted interventions in gateway STEM courses to advance equity and access for underrepresented student populations. With a background as a higher education practitioner, she has extensive experience in admissions and academic advising, working to support undergraduate students in achieving their academic, professional, and personal goals.

Amy Desiderio is a PhD student in the Educational Policy and Program Evaluation program at Harvard University. Her research focuses primarily on the measurement of narrative student assessments, including the role that AI can serve in such assessments.

Frank Fernandez is associate professor of Educational Leadership and Policy Analysis at University of Wisconsin, Madison. He writes about educational equity, leadership, and policy. He coauthored *Transformational University Leadership: A Case Study for 21st Century Leaders and Aspirational Research Universities, Leadership Talks: Candid Conversations with Academic Leaders*, and *The Contested Campus: Aligning Professional Values, Social Justice, and Free Speech* (NASPA). He earned a PhD from The Pennsylvania State

University, a master's degree from Stanford University, a bachelor's degree from University of San Diego, and associate's degrees from Imperial Valley College.

Dr. Qiwei He is associate professor in the Data Science and Analytics Program, and founder and director of the AI-Measurement and Data Science Lab at Georgetown University. Her expertise focuses on advancing methodologies in machine learning, sequence mining, text mining, psychometric modeling, and artificial intelligence on new data sources such as multimodal process data and textual data collected in digital-based assessments in education, psychology, psychiatry, and public health. Dr. He was appointed as OECD Thomas J. Alexander Fellow and has been serving on the Psychometrics and Educational Evaluation Panel for UNESCO Institute for Statistics, Policy Linking Panel for USAID, and Expert Group for OECD PISA-Vocational Education and Training.

Dr. Brandi Hephner LaBanc serves the students and staff of Old Dominion University as vice president for student enrollment, engagement, and services, and associate professor in the higher education program. Before joining ODU, she previously served as the vice chancellor for student affairs and professor of higher education at the University of Mississippi and the University of Massachusetts Amherst. Her research has focused on preparation of student affairs professionals and transition issues for graduate students, and she has published work related to campus crisis management, concealed carry legislation's impact on higher education, and the intersectionality of free speech and campus values.

Neal H. Hutchens, JD, PhD, is professor of higher education at the University of Kentucky. His research focuses on the intersections of higher education law, policy, and practice. He received the 2015 William A. Kaplin Award from the Center for Excellence in Higher Education Law and Policy at Stetson University. He is a coauthor of *The Law of Higher Education: Essentials for Legal and Administrative Practice*. He earned a doctorate in higher education from University of Maryland, College Park, and a juris doctorate from University of Alabama School of Law.

Dan Kheloussi is an energy industry analyst at the Federal Energy Regulatory Commission. Daniel is also a chapter leader for the Washington, DC, chapter of the nonprofit organization DataKind. Daniel holds a Bachelor of Engineering degree in engineering physics from the University of Pittsburgh and a Master of Science degree in applied economics from Johns Hopkins University.

René F. Kizilcec is an associate professor in the Bowers College of Computing and Information Science at Cornell University, where he directs the Cornell Future of Learning Lab. Kizilcec studies behavioral, psychological, and computational aspects of technology in education to inform practices and policies that promote learning, equity, and academic and career success. Kizilcec holds a PhD in communication and an MSc in statistics from Stanford University.

Jeffrey Knight is an attorney specializing in education law, privacy and data protection, and intellectual property, with a particular focus on the intersection of technology and law. He navigates the complexities of emerging technologies in educational and business environments, providing clients with strategic guidance on compliance with privacy and data security regulations, including FERPA, COPPA, GLBA, and myriad international, federal, and state data privacy laws. In addition, Jeff advises clients on the legal implications and compliance requirements associated with AI and GenAI technologies, ensuring that organizations can innovate responsibly while adhering to evolving regulatory standards.

Jinsook Lee is a PhD student in information science at Cornell University. Her research focuses on high-stakes decision-making processes, machine learning, and algorithmic bias in education. Currently, she is studying college admissions with two main areas of focus: (1) evaluating and designing fair machine learning algorithms for the admissions process and (2) analyzing lexical variations between essays written by large language models (LLMs) and those written by humans.

Dr. Chrysoula Malogianni is the associate vice president for digital innovation at Old Dominion University, where she spearheads digital transformation initiatives, including online program development, educational technology solutions, high-performance computing, and AI integration in education. Her work focuses on transforming digital learning and the overall digital experience for faculty, students, and staff, leveraging innovative technologies to create more engaging, accessible, and effective educational environments. Dr. Malogianni is committed to fostering strong partnerships between higher education institutions and technology vendors to drive impactful change in the educational landscape.

Vanessa Miller is an assistant professor of law at Florida International University (FIU) College of Law. Her research focuses on the policing of American schools and universities. Her work has appeared in the *Harvard Educational Review* and *Educational Researcher*, among other law reviews.

Sebastian Munoz-Najar Galvez is the Bluhm Family Assistant Professor of Data Science and Education at the Harvard Graduate School of Education. Sebastian received a doctoral degree in sociology of education from the Graduate School of Education at Stanford University. He is a sociologist of science who uses computational linguistics and network analysis to study the formation of research agendas. He has recently turned toward the study of adolescent experience, college admissions, and technologies of belonging. Sebastian's work has been published in the *American Sociological Review*, *Proceedings of the National Academy of Science*, and *American Educational Research Journal*.

Seyedeh Mobina Noorani is a PhD student at the University of Florida, where she focuses on artificial intelligence research. She holds a master's degree in computer engineering–artificial intelligence. Her research interests include machine learning, computer vision, and image processing. Currently, her work focuses on developing models and techniques to tackle real-world challenges, such as object detection from aerial imagery and Streetview for disaster response and environmental analysis.

Karla Saldaña Ochoa is a tenure-track assistant professor in the School of Architecture at the University of Florida and a faculty affiliate at the AI2 Center, the Center of Latin American Studies, and FIBER. Karla is the director of SHARE Lab, a research group focused on developing projects that leverage the interaction between artificial intelligence and human intelligence applied to boost creativity in architectural design and create tools to analyze Big Data of Urban Phenomena. She collaborates on international projects in Germany, Italy, Switzerland, Mexico, and Ecuador. Karla is an Ecuadorian architect and coder with a Master of Advanced Studies in landscape architecture and a PhD in technology in architecture from ETH Zurich. Her PhD researched the integration of artificial and human intelligence for an accurate and agile response to natural disasters, leveraging a multimodal fusion approach for ML inference.

Kaleb E. Smith, PhD, is an AI and deep learning expert currently serving as a senior data scientist at NVIDIA. He is the higher education and research lead for NVIDIA AI Technology Center (NVAITC) for all of North and Latin America. He also serves as the site lead for the first NVAITC at the University of Florida. Dr. Smith's educational journey is rooted in Florida Institute of Technology, where he earned his BS in aerospace engineering (2011), MS in computer engineering (2016), and PhD focused on AI/deep learning (2020). His professional experience includes leading an AI prototype lab for a U.S. Department of Defense/intelligence community contractor, working as a machine learning/AI subject matter expert at MITRE, and holding various research and internship positions in AI and machine learning. At NVIDIA, which he joined in 2020, Dr. Smith supports higher education research, collaborates with top researchers on AI and deep learning projects, and has worked on training large language models. His focus areas include AI applications in remote sensing, clinical/neuroscience research, architectural design, and smart city planning. Dr. Smith describes his current role at NVIDIA as his "dream job," allowing him to continue AI/deep learning research alongside leading researchers in various fields.

Laura Smithers is an assistant professor of higher education leadership at the University of Nevada, Reno. Laura's research focuses on the possible futures created and foreclosed by assessment regimes in higher education, incorporating sustained interests in critical and queer theories as well as pop culture. With Heidi Fischer and Faith Watrous, she is coauthor of *Impact/Impasse: Revaluing University Classroom Life* (2024). You can read more about her work at laura-smithers.net.

Sheridan Stewart is a senior research analyst at the Harvard Graduate School of Education and a doctoral candidate in the Department of Sociology at Stanford University. He uses natural language processing and survey experiments to answer questions about the relationships among beliefs, dispositions, institutions, and behavior in domains such as work, higher education, and medicine. Sheridan's research has appeared in journals including *Big Data & Society*, *Group Processes & Intergroup Relations*, *Social Science & Medicine*, and *Journal of Environmental Psychology*.

Jeffrey C. Sun, JD, PhD, is a distinguished university professor and associate dean for research and innovation at the University of Louisville. He is also counsel at Manley Burke. His research and practice areas focus on higher education law and professional/career education policies and practice. Dr. Sun has served as project director and principal investigator for over $27 million in externally funded grants that center around the intersection of law, policy, and workforce development in the postsecondary context.

Fred H. Tugas, EdD, is the chief of staff for student enrollment, engagement, and services at Old Dominion University in Norfolk, Virginia. With over a decade of leadership in higher education, his research agenda focuses on student engagement, leadership and professional development, and the impact of belonging and retention initiatives on diverse student populations in higher education.

Yunhong Yang is a data scientist with a master's degree in data science and analytics from Georgetown University and a bachelor's degree in mathematics from Boston University. She has extensive experience working with large datasets, including financial, student loan, and criminal case data, and applies machine learning, statistical modeling, and time series analysis to solve complex problems. Yunhong is skilled in data visualization and is passionate about leveraging data to drive impactful insights, particularly in the field of finance.

Index